# NATURAL SCIENCES IN AMERICA

# THE MAMMALS OF THE ADIRONDACK REGION,

## NORTHEASTERN NEW YORK

BY

## CLINTON HART MERRIAM

### ARNO PRESS
A New York Times Company
New York, N. Y. • 1974

Reprint Edition 1974 by Arno Press Inc.

Reprinted from a copy in The American Museum
  of Natural History Library

NATURAL SCIENCES IN AMERICA
ISBN for complete set: 0-405-05700-8
See last pages of this volume for titles.

Manufactured in the United States of America

————◆————

**Library of Congress Cataloging in Publication Data**

Merriam, Clinton Hart, 1855-1942.
    The mammals of the Adirondack region, northeastern
New York.

    (Natural sciences in America)
    Reprint of the 1884 ed. published by Press of
L. S. Foster, New York.
    1. Mammals--New York (State) 2. Mammals--Adiron-
dack Mountains. 3. Adirondack Mountains. I. Title.
II. Series.
QL719.N7M57  1974    599'.09747'5           73-17832
ISBN 0-405-05750-4

# THE MAMMALS OF THE ADIRONDACK REGION,

## NORTHEASTERN NEW YORK.

WITH AN INTRODUCTORY CHAPTER TREATING OF THE LOCATION AND
BOUNDARIES OF THE REGION. ITS GEOLOGICAL HISTORY,
TOPOGRAPHY, CLIMATE, GENERAL FEATURES,
BOTANY, AND FAUNAL POSITION.

BY

## CLINTON HART MERRIAM, M. D.

*Published by the Author, September, 1884.*

(Reprinted from Vols. I & II, Transactions Linnæan Society, New York.)

NEW YORK:
PRESS OF L. S. FOSTER, 35 PINE STREET.
MDCCCLXXXIV.

# PREFACE.

This book is a verbatim reprint of the first and second instalments of my work upon "The Vertebrates of the Adirondack Region, Northeastern New York," which was published in Vols. I and II of the Transactions of the Linnæan Society of New York. Pages 9–107 (comprising the first instalment) appeared in Vol. I, separate, issued in October, 1882. The paging is unchanged. Pages 108–312 (comprising the second instalment and concluding the mammalia) appeared in Vol. II, which was issued in August, 1884. The paging has here been altered to conform to that of the first instalment, of which it is a direct continuation.

Most of the biographies were written during or previous to the year 1882, and were read at different times before the Linnæan Society of New York. Pages 107–240 received supplemental matter at the time of going to press, the additional material having been acquired after the biographies had been read before the Society. Pages 240–312 were not so augmented, excepting in the article on the Muskrat, for the reason that this portion of the work had already exceeded its intended limits.

Since the first instalment was issued much additional matter pertaining to the species there treated has been gathered; and even while the second instalment has been passing through the press many facts of importance have come into the author's possession.

It will be observed that the second chapter opens with the statement: "In the following pages forty-two species of mammals are enumerated," while as a matter of fact forty-six are given as at present inhabiting the region. This discrepancy is due to the long interval (nearly two years) between the publication of the first and second instalments—the presence of the additional species having been ascertained during this period.

On page 25, after mentioning some of the birds characteristic of the Canadian Fauna, I ventured to predict that the Hudsonian Tit (*Parus Hudsonicus*) would also be found nesting in the Adirondacks. Since the above was published I have found this species breeding in a large balsam and tamarack swamp between Big Moose Lake and Lake Terror, and, more sparingly, in a few other localities.

This work consists, in the first place, of a general account of the prominent features of the region ; and secondly, of a popular narrative of the habits of the animals found within its confines. It is in no sense a technical treatise, and technical matter will but rarely be found in its pages.

In conclusion, it is proper to say that although I have been able to correct some statements of others, and have added to the general fund of knowledge many previously unrecorded facts respecting the habits of mammals ; still, I am deeply conscious that the most complete biography herein contained can be regarded only as a very imperfect contribution to the life history of the species of which it treats.

Locust Grove, New York,
*September* 3, 1884.

C. HART MERRIAM.

# CONTENTS.

# CHAPTER II.

# MAMMALIA.

# CHAPTER I.

# GENERAL INTRODUCTION.

## 1.—LOCATION AND BOUNDARIES.

IN general terms the Adirondack Wilderness may be said to embrace that portion of New York State lying to the north of the Mohawk Valley, and included between Lake Champlain on the east and the valley of the Black River on the west. These limits, however, include much territory not properly belonging to the region under consideration, for its boundaries are more or less irregular, and in many places fall short of the limits above defined. The Adirondacks proper, or the area to which the subject-matter of this paper is restricted, can be stated, with sufficient exactness, to lie between parallels 43° 15′ and 44° 45′ north latitude, hence measuring about an hundred and twenty miles (193,121 metres) in a north and south direction.

The transverse diameter of the region is approximately of equal extent. A large area on its western border is well known by the name of " Brown's Tract," and the whole territory is frequently spoken of as the " North Woods." It covers more or less extensive portions of twelve counties, namely : St. Lawrence, Franklin, Clinton, Lewis, Herkimer, Hamilton, Essex, Warren, Oneida, Fulton, Saratoga, and Washington.

## 2.—GEOLOGICAL HISTORY.

From a geological stand-point, the Adirondacks are interesting as constituting one of the few islands that rose above the level of

2

the mighty Continental sea, previous to Paleozoic time. Its stern Archæan shores were washed by the waves of countless ages before the undermost strata of the Lower Silurian were deposited upon them, entombing and preserving many of the Trilobites, Brachiopods, and other curious inhabitants of that vast ocean. This Lower Silurian zone marked the shore line, so to speak, of the ancient island, and consists of Potsdam sandstone and the lime rocks of the Trenton period. Though broken and interrupted, enough of it still remains to afford us tantalizing glimpses of the life of the time, torn pages of fragmentary chapters that constitute but a half-told story to excite our imagination and regret.

The old Archæan centre, which we call the Adirondacks, is made up mainly of gneiss, and includes areas of syenite, hypersthenite, granite, iron ore, and other metamorphic rocks. The soil, therefore, except that resulting from decomposed vegetation, is largely silicious sand.

### 3.--TOPOGRAPHY.

The topography of the region is diversified, and in some respects peculiar. The mountains and short ranges of high hills have no regular trend, and conform to no definite axis. They are in no sense a chain of mountains, and have no backbone at all; but, on the contrary, consist of more or less irregular groups, isolated peaks, short ranges, and "hog-backs," scattered over the entire area—the highest to the eastward. They slope in all possible directions, according to the position and courses of the valleys and river beds adjacent. Like the grand old Lawrentian Hills of Canada, and other Archæan mountains, they are bold and rugged, with well-defined and often much broken outlines. Nearly thirty peaks exceed four thousand feet (1,219.20 metres) in height, several are about five thousand (1,524 metres), and one, Mt. Marcy, attains an altitude of five thousand three hundred and forty-four feet (1,628.-851 metres).*

The entire region is studded with hundreds of beautiful lakes of various sizes and depths, and two of them are upwards of four thousand feet above tide level. The altitude of the western border of this area is nowhere less than one thousand feet (304.80 metres), and in most places is considerably more than this. From the valley of the Black River the slope is gradual, and the flattened summits of the first range of foot-hills form a terrace of great extent. The dense forests that formerly covered this terrace have mostly been destroyed, and it is now a sandy, barren region, overrun with blackberries and other rank undergrowth. Beyond, to the eastward, lie the ranges of low hills and irregularly distributed mountains, with their many lakes and rivers, that indicate the confines of the Adirondacks.

On the eastward the case is very different. Lake Champlain is not an hundred feet † (30.48 metres) above tide-level, and Lake George is but three hundred and forty-three feet (104.546 metres). From the head (south end) of Lake George to Glen's Falls, a distance of but nine miles (14,484 metres), there is a fall of sixty-one feet (18.69 metres). Glen's Falls, it will be remembered, is directly on the Hudson, just east of Luzerne. Hence it is clear that one can travel from New York city to Montreal on the St. Lawrence River, and by a very direct road, too, without passing over any elevation greater than the shore of Lake George. The route would be : up the Hudson to Glen's Falls thence overland nine miles to Fort William Henry on Lake George, or down the valley to Whitehall, and thence, skirting the Adirondacks, down Lake Champlain and its outlet, the river Richelieu, to Sorel on the St. Lawrence, at the head of Lake St. Peter—about forty miles below Montreal. This is, indeed, the exact pathway traversed, but little more than two

---

* Report of Adirondack Survey, Verplanck Colvin, Superintendent, 1880.
† Exactly 99 feet.

centuries ago, by the fierce war parties of the merciless Iroquois, as they journeyed with a fleet of birch-bark canoes, from their wig- wams on the Mohawk, to harass and imperil the three exposed col- onies of New France—Montreal, Three Rivers, and Quebec— already crippled and disheartened by early struggles with the Hu- rons and Algonquins.   It is well to bear these facts in mind, lest, by forgetting that modern civilization has overcome so many bar- riers and established so many channels of communication between different regions, we lose sight of the great natural avenues that were known so well to the aborigines, and to our forefathers.   This narrow valley, penetrating the primeval forests of the north, and walled in by the Adirondacks on the west, and the Green Mountains of Vermont on the east, exerts a powerful influence over the life of adjoining lands, carrying southern forms into the heart of a great northern wilderness.   Along the opposite border of the Adiron- dacks we have seen that the mountains and foot-hills slope gradually to the westward till they disappear in the valley of the Black River. Here, on the contrary, lofty rugged mountains rise. some from the very water's edge, and many of the highest peaks of the entire region lie within a few miles from the shores of Lakes George and Champlain.   Among these mountains breed such northern birds as the Hermit and Olive-backed Thrushes, the Red-bellied Nuthatch, the Winter Wren, the Yellow-rumped, Blackburnian, Black and Yellow, Mourning, and Canada Fly-catching Warblers, both Cross- bills, the White-throated Sparrow, the Raven. the Canada Jay, both Three toed Woodpeckers, and the Spruce Grouse ; while in the valley below may be found the Wood Thrush, Brown Thrasher, House Wren, Large-billed Water Thrush, Field Sparrow, Chewink, Mourning Dove  and other species supposed to pertain to the Alle- ghanian Fauna, through much more characteristic of the Carolinian. Nowhere, except in the Catskills, do representatives from the Cana- dian and Carolinian Faunæ so  nearly meet as upon the mountain sides bordering the southwestern part of Lake George.

## 4.—CLIMATE.

The climate of the Adirondack Wilderness varies greatly with the season. Snow covers the ground from some time in November till the middle or latter part of April, and in mid-winter averages over four feet in depth on the level. During this period the mercury often falls below —25° Fahr. (—32° C.), and more than once it has been frozen (—40° F. and C.) In summer the days are warm and the nights cool. Owing to the altitude of the region its mean annual temperature falls considerably below that of the surrounding country. Guyot says : " On an average an increase of three hundred and thirty feet of altitude diminishes the temperature one degree Fahrenheit; hence the rate of diminution is about three degrees to every thousand feet." Therefore the temperature at the summit of Mt. Marcy should average sixteen degrees Fahrenheit below that of tide-level in the same latitude. Mr. Verplanck Colvin found, from observations made at three sets of localities, in 1876, that the mean decrease in temperature per each thousand feet increase in altitude, in this region was 2.93° Fahr. in August, 4.11° F. in September, and 4.52° F. in November.* On this basis the mean temperature of that portion of the Adirondacks having an altitude of four thousand feet (1,219.20 metres) would average below that of New York city during the same time, 11.72° F. in August, 16.44° F. in September, and 18.08° F. in November, if in the same latitude.

There are probably few places on this continent that are subject to greater or more sudden changes of temperature than this area. Variations of forty, fifty, and sixty degrees Fahrenheit, during the twenty-four hours, are by no means uncommon; and I have seen the mercury fall over seventy degrees Fahrenheit in fifteen hours in winter. My journal records a rise of 42° in six hours, of 32° in five hours, and of 12° in one hour; a fall of 38° in thirteen hours, and one of 20° in four hours. These great and rapid changes usually occur in winter—dur-

---

* Report of Adirondack Survey, Verplanck Colvin, Superintendent, 1880, pp. 324-6.

ing January, February, and March. Notwithstanding these facts, diseases of the lungs are rare among the inhabitants, and even the severe winters have proved of benefit to those consumptives that have remained here throughout the entire year.

The mean annual rain-fall exceeds that of most portions of the State, and is estimated by Mr. Colvin, from the available data, to be 45.18 inches (1,149 mm.) for the entire region. The mean annual rain-fall over the whole State is 41.94 inches (1,063 mm.).*

There are two elements that tend to increase the humidity of this region : 1st, its mountainous character, for mountains always act as condensers of moisture; and 2d, its heavy covering of forests, for dense vegetation protects the underlying soil and rock from the direct action of the sun, and keeps the temperature lower—thus favoring condensation and the precipitation of excess moisture.

"A deciduous tree, during the season when in foliage, is constantly drawing from the earth and giving off from its leaves a considerable amount of moisture, and in some cases this amount is very great. This change of state, from a fluid to a gaseous condition, is a cooling process, and the air near the surface, being screened from the sun and from the winds, becomes by this means so humid, that a rank succulent vegetation often springs up and thrives, which in an open field would wither and perish in an hour."†

Now it is well known that there is, in nature, no such thing as a perfectly dry atmosphere, for at all times, and in all places, it is laden with less or more aqueous vapor in a state of suspension. The higher the temperature the greater the capacity for carrying moisture, and consequently the more moisture required to produce saturation—by which term we understand the maximum quantity of watery vapor that a definite amount of atmospheric air can contain at any given degree of temperature. No evaporation whatever can take place from any surface in a saturated atmosphere, and any cooling of such an atmos-

---

* Meteorology of New York State, Second Series, F. B. Hough, 1872, p. ix.
† Hough's Report on Forestry, 1878, p. 289.

phere produces instant precipitation of the excess of moisture above the degree to which the temperature has been lowered. Therefore, the temperature and dew point being low in this great wilderness, and a large amount of moisture being given off, both from the dense forests themselves, and from the multitude of lakes and swamps scattered over its surface, the atmosphere is often saturated, and showers during the summer season are of frequent occurrence. The conformation of the country, too, favors precipitation within its own borders, for a wind, from whatsoever direction blowing, could not easily convey the lower vapor-laden atmosphere away without coming in contact with some cool area or mountain side that would so lower its temperature as to cause instant precipitation. Clouds carried over the Adirondacks from a distance would, when sufficiently low, share the same fate, and disappear in showers over the foot-hills.

And such is, in fact, the case; for a long residence overlooking a considerable portion of the western slope of the region has enabled me to observe repeatedly, not only occasional showers, but sometimes even whole days of more or less continuous rain there, when not a drop, or at most a slight shower, fell at the point of observation, only twelve or fifteen miles distant.

## 5.—GENERAL FEATURES.

We have found, then, that the atmospheric and general climatic conditions, over this area, favor the production of a luxuriance of vegetation; and, on the other hand, the conformation of the land and the density of the forests and undergrowth tend to lower the temperature and increase the humidity—interacting causes whose effect upon floræ and faunæ has hardly received the attention it deserves.

The deep beds of moss upon the mountain tops consist chiefly of species of *Sphagnum* and the "Shining Feather Moss" (*Hypnum splendens*), over which runs, in various places, the pretty Creeping Snow-berry (*Chiogenes hispidula*) and the lovely twin bell-flowers of *Linnæa borealis*. Other still more characteristic marsh plants grow upon these elevated summits, for, in the language of our State Botanist, Mr. Charles H. Peck, " the frequent rains, the investing clouds, and the low temperature which retards evaporation, all conspire to produce that prevalence of moisture which imitates the condition of the marshes."* On the open summit of Mt. Marcy (altitude 5,344 feet, or 1,628 metres) Mr. Peck found *Cassandra calyculata, Ledum latifolium, Kalmia glauca, Habenaria dilatata, Veratrum viride, Carex irrigua*, and *Calamagrostis Canadensis*—all swamp plants. There are no trees here to protect them from the sun, for they grow upon the *open summit "above timber line"*—which is about 4,800–4,900 feet (1,463.04–1,493.52 metres) above tide-level.

Many of the valleys are occupied by extensive balsam and tamarack swamps, which are always carpeted with dense mats of wet *Sphagnum*, into which one sinks half a foot or more and yet rarely leaves a trail—so perfectly does the spongy mass resume its former shape. These places are the homes of the Spruce Grouse or Canada Partridge, the Blue Yellow-backed Warbler that builds its pensile nest of the gray tamarack lichen (*Usnea*), the Canada Fly-catching Warbler, and several other species.

Most of the mountains are covered with a tolerably dense growth of coniferous trees, but there are quite a number whose summits have been laid bare by tornadoes. These devastating winds every now and then uncover a mountain so effectually that not only the trees and undershrubs, but even the soil itself, and all life upon it, are hurled together into the valley below—forming vast and lasting " windfalls " to bar the path of inquisitive man.

Fire, also, too frequently overruns and lays waste tracts of large extent, that, for years afterwards, constitute marked features in the make-up of the country, and exert a decided influence upon the minor local distribution of life over its surface. The charred stubs of the larger trees long remain as favorite haunts for several species

---

* Report of Adirondack Survey, Albany, 1880, pp. 405–6.

of Woodpeckers, while the dense growth of blackberry and rasp-
berry bushes, dotted over with the large showy flowers of the Willow
Herb (*Epilobium angustifolium*), is well known to the ornithologist
as the summer home of the Mourning Warbler.

Here is a sparkling trout stream, perhaps the outlet of a mountain
lake ; let us follow its winding course through yonder thicket of
alders. Working our way through the tangled bushes we soon
emerge into the open grassy bottom of one of the most beautiful and interesting of nature's many adornments—a Beaver meadow.
Here, less than a century ago, might have been heard the splash and
seen the hut of the sagacious Beaver. But, like the Moose that once
roamed these mighty forests, they have, excepting a few isolated
individuals, been exterminated or driven beyond our borders, till
now these green meadows, with occasionally the buried ruin of an
ancient dam, are about all that remain to remind us of the former
existence here of one of the most curious, interesting, and typical of
North American mammals.

The dam has long since disappeared, and as it gave way the pond
again became a narrow stream, spreading its way through the broad
muddy bottom, now verdant with marsh grasses that spring from a
thick bed of elastic *Sphagnum*. Upon this moist level now stand
scattered clumps of feathery tamaracks ; and here and there over
the uniform light green of the meadow rise, in marked contrast, the
odd-looking Blue Gentians and the bright scarlet Cardinal Flowers.
These are favorite haunts of the Canada Jay and, in the autumn, of
immense flocks of Robins that come to feed upon the handsome berries of the mountain ash trees that always skirt the open places,
easing the stiff edge of the bordering forest. Here, too, may
be heard the quick snap of the Wood Pewee, as he gobbles
up some passing insect, and the characteristic note of his congener,
the Olive-sided Flycatcher, who is perched upon the topmost
branch of yonder hemlock. Should you possess the keen eye and
stealthy tread of the experienced hunter, you may surprise a red

deer quietly feeding in supposed security, and may rest assured that a nice bit of fresh venison steak will in no way interfere with your investigations.

Crossing from the Beaver meadow to the nearest lake, we find its shores steep and rocky, with a dense border of dark cedars overhanging the water—which is of considerable depth, even close to the shore. A little farther along, the steep rocks are replaced by a more sloping bank, covered with stones of various sizes, and spruce and hemlocks, mingled, perhaps, with a few birches and maples, are substituted for the cedars just passed. Beyond still is a beach of clean white sand, strewn with smooth quartz pebbles, and backed with a grove of tall pines, beneath whose lofty summits a cluster of paper birch saplings casts flitting shadows over the blue huckleberries below. Continuing the circuit, we next come to a marshy bay lined with sedges and covered with lily-pads—a feeding ground, at night, for the much persecuted deer. Finally we reach the outlet, with its dense thicket of alders, and are startled by the splash of a diving Musk-rat, or the sudden flight of a Wood Duck or Heron. In the alders and undershrubs bordering the stream we notice a few Song Sparrows, Rusty Blackbirds, and a solitary Maryland Yellow-throat. Turning from the lake into the adjoining forest, the dark form and yellow crown of a Three-toed Woodpecker arrest our eye, and rounding a rocky knoll we get a glimpse of his princely cousin, the Cock-of-the-Woods. From various quarters may be heard the clear mellow whistle of the Peabody Bird, and the less frequent but sadder note of the Wood Pewee. Winding slowly up the shady ravine that leads to the pass between the mountains that separate us from the valley beyond, a Hermit Thrush silently glides across our path, and we notice here a pair of Slate-colored Snow-birds, and the trim form of a little Winter Wren as she flits from a moss-covered log to the branches of a fallen tree-top, pertly tipping her tail in salute. Nearing the summit a passing flock of noisy Blue Jays excites the wrath of a Red Squirrel who, perched on a neighboring limb, manifests his indignation by chippering saucily, keeping time with vehement jerks of the body and spasmodic flourishes of the tail, which he has by no means neglected to cock up over his arched back. Crossing the crest of the divide the coarse croak of a Raven greets our ears; and, descending into the valley below, the shrill cry of a wary Loon, from the distant lake, melts away into the evening air, and the silence of the fast-approaching twilight is unbroken save by the soft flute-like song of the sombre Thrush.

During winter and early spring the birds one is most apt to find here are the White-winged and Red Crossbills, the Blue and Canada Jays, Black-capped and Hudsonian Titmice, Nuthatches, Ravens, several species of Woodpeckers, the Ruffed and Spruce Grouse, and once in a while an Owl. Sometimes the Pine Grosbeak is common, in flocks; and occasionally, during February, March, and April, the Wilderness literally swarms with Pine Linnets which then breed here in thousands and may hardly be seen again for several years.

In autumn, during the fall migrations, the most marked feature in the bird line consists in what I have for many years designated the " mixed flocks." At this season one may hunt for hours and scarcely see a bird, when, suddenly, he finds himself surrounded by a host of individuals, representing many species and pertaining to widely different families. To illustrate, I quote from my journal under date of October, 1879—a lowery day—the locality being Big Moose Lake in the heart of the Wilderness. " During the afternoon one of those mixed flocks of birds, so characteristic of the Adirondacks at this season, passed slowly by our camp and I stepped out, in the rain, and watched them till all were gone. There were at least fifty Robins and they loaded down a mountain ash, feeding upon its berries and making a most-unnecessary amount of noise—very unlike their conduct at home, where, when similarly engaged in our garden, they are noted for their silence. In the trees overhead were several Blue Jays, and in the undergrowth and amongst the fallen timber were large numbers of Slate-colored Snow-birds, a few White-throated, Song, and Fox-colored Sparrows, a couple of Winter Wrens, and one Nashville Warbler—which I shot. A dozen Chickadees, with an equal number of Yellow-birds and a few Golden-crowned Kinglets, could be seen among the branches of a low spruce near by, while several Red-bellied Nuthatches and a pair of Brown Creepers amused themselves with winding up and down its trunk. Leaving out the Fox Sparrows and the Nashville Warbler, this flock stands as a very fair example of these incongruous assemblages, several of which one falls in with every day at this time of year. It seems strange that the desire for company, always marked during the migrations, should induce such unlike species to collect and wander together over this wilderness. It must be that they have faith in the old adage that ' there is strength in numbers!' I have seen the Purple Finch in some of these mixed flocks; and a few Hairy and Downy Wood-peckers and Hermit Thrushes sometimes hang about their outskirts, but the latter are more commonly seen by themselves in groups of half a dozen or thereabouts."

## 6.—BOTANY.

While the grand scenic effect of any region, the effect that is de-pendent on the general contour and make up of the country and its gross reliefs, is governed by its geology and topography; so is the general aspect, or *physiognomy*, of a region dependent upon the char-acter of the vegetation in which it is clothed. As, in the tropics, the stately Palms, the colossal arborescent Ferns, the solemn Aloes, and the light and feathery Mimosas contribute such striking features to the physiographical areas to which they severally pertain; so do the deciduous hardwood groves of the temperate zone, and the dark co-niferous forests of the north give to these regions their peculiar and characteristic appearance.

The distinctive physiognomic aspect of the Adirondack Wilderness, the dark and sombre evergreen forests, is chiefly the consequence of the large development of a single genus of coniferous trees; for the predominating forms are not only coniferous evergreens, but consist mainly of Spruce, Hemlock, and Balsam—all representatives of the genus *Abies*. Tall Pines, at intervals, rear their lofty summits above the level of surrounding tree-tops, fragrant Cedars overhang the lake-shores and swamps, delicate Tamaracks wave over the soft grassy bottoms of Beaver meadows, dense thickets of tangled Alders border many of the streams and rivers, hardy Birches and light Poplars are scattered sparingly upon the mountain-sides and in the valleys, and areas of hard timber, indicating second growth, mark tracts that have been bared by fire, wind, or the woodman's axe. These hardwood areas are readily distinguished, at a distance, by the marked contrast afforded by the light color and different aspect of the foliage, in summer, and by their nakedness in winter. They are composed, chiefly, of Maple, Beech, and Birch.

The common forest trees of the Adirondacks are: the American Linden or Bass Wood (*Tilia Americana*), Sugar Maple (*Acer saccharinum*), Black Sugar Maple (*A. saccharinum nigrum*), Red or Swamp Maple (*A. rubrum*), Black Cherry (*Prunus serotina*), Beech, (*Fagus ferruginea*), Iron Wood (*Ostrya Virginica*), Cherry Birch (*Betula lenta*), Yellow Birch (*B. lutea*), Paper or Canoe Birch (*B. papyracea*), American Aspen (*Populus tremuloides*), Large-toothed Aspen (*P. grandidentata*), White Pine (*Pinus strobus*), Red or "Norway" Pine (*P. resinosa*—common only in certain localities, not generally distributed), Black Spruce (*Abies nigra*), White Spruce (*A. alba*), Hemlock (*A. Canadensis*), Balsam Fir (*A. balsamea*), Tamarack or Larch (*Larix Americana*), White Cedar or Arbor Vitæ (*Thuja occidentalis*). Besides these occur the following, which are rare, or are common only along the borders of the region: Locust (*Robinia pseudacacia*), White Ash (*Fraxinus Americana*), Black Ash (*F. sambucifolia*), Elm (*Ulmus Americana*), Slippery Elm (*U. fulva*), Butternut (*Juglans cinerea*), Swamp Hickory (*Carya amara*), three or more Oaks (*Quercus*), Balsam Poplar or Tacamahac (*Populus balsamifera*), Pitch Pine (*Pinus rigida*), and Juniper (*Juniperus Virginiana*).

The more common undershrubs (some of them growing to be small trees) are : *Acer Pennsylvanicum, A. spicatum, Prunus pumila, P. Pennsylvanica, P. Virginiana, Spiræa salicifolia, S. tomentosa, Rubus odoratus, R. triflorus, R. strigosus, R. occidentalis, R. villosus, R. Canadensis, Rosa Carolina, Cratægus coccinea, C. tomentosa, C. crus-galli, Pyrus sambucifolia, Amelanchier Canadensis, A. Canadensis botryapium, A. Canadensis oblongifolia, Ribes lacustre, R. rubrum, Hamamelis Virginica, Cornus circinata, C. stolonifera, C. paniculata, C. alternifolia, Lonicera ciliata, Diervilla trifida, Sambucus pubens, S. Canadensis, Viburnum lentago, V. acerifolium, V. opulus, V. lantanoides, Cephalanthus occidentalis, Gaylussacia resinosa, Vaccinium Pennsylvanicum, V. corymbosum, Arctostaphylos uva-ursi, Cassandra calyculata, Andromeda polifolia, Kalmia angustifolia, K. glauca, Azalia nudiflora, Rhodora Canadensis, Ledum latifolium, Apocynum androsæmifolium, Ilex lævigata, Corylus rostrata, Carpinus Americana, Myrica gale, Alnus viridis, A. incana, Salix* (several species), and *Taxus baccata Canadensis.*

Of the smaller flowering plants the following are among the most noticeable: *Clematis Virginiana, Anemone Pennsylvanica, A. nemorosa, Hepatica triloba, Thalictrum dioicum, Ranunculus flammula reptans, R. abortivus, R. recurvatus, Caltha palustris, Coptis trifolia, Aquilegia Canadensis, Actæa spicata rubra, A. alba, Caulophyllum thalictroides, Nymphæa odorata, Nuphar advena, Sarracenia purpurea, Sanguinaria Canadensis, Dicentra cucullaria, D. Canadensis, Dentaria diphylla, D. laciniata, Arabis lyrata, Viola rotundifolia, V. blanda, V. Selkerki, V. cucullata, V. canina sylvestris, V. rostrata, V. Canadensis, V. pubescens, Drosera rotundifolia, D. longifolia, Helianthemum Canadense, Hypericum pyramidatum, H. ellipticum, H. perforatum, Elodes Virginica, Silene inflata, Arenaria Grœnlandica, A. lateriflora, Claytonia Caroliniana, Geranium Robertianum, Impatiens pallida, Oxalis acetosella, Ampelopsis quinquefolia, Celastrus scandens, Polygala paucifolia, Poterium Canadense, Geum macrophyllum, Waldsteinia fragarioides, Potentilla Norvegica, P. Canadensis, P. tridentata, P. palustris,*

*Fragaria vesca, Dalibarda repens, Saxifraga Pennsylvanica, Mitella diphylla, M. nuda, Tiarella cordifolia, Circæa alpina, Epilobium angustifolium, E. palustre lineare, E. coloratum, Œnothera biennis, Œ. pumila, Heraclium lanatum, Archangelica atropurpurea, Osmorrhiza longistylis, O. brevistylis, Aralia racemosa, A. nudicaulis, A. trifolia, Cornus Canadensis, Linnæa borealis, Triosteum perfoliatum, Galium trifidum pusillum, Mitchella repens, Houstonia cærulea, Eupatorium purpureum, E. perfoliatum, E. ageratoides, Tussilago farfara, Solidago thyrsoidea, Bidens cernua, Achillea millefolium, Tanacetum vulgare, Antennaria margaritacea, Senecio aureus, Lobelia cardinalis, L. syphylitica, L. inflata, L. Kalmii, Campanula rotundifolia, Vaccinium macrocarpon, V. cæspitosum, Chiogenes hispidula, Epigæa repens, Gaultheria procumbens, Pyrola rotundifolia, P. chlorantha, P. secunda, Chimaphila umbellata, Monotropa uniflora, Trientalis Americana, Lysimachia ciliata, L. thyrsiflora, Utricularia cornuta, Epiphegus Virginiana, Verbascum Thapsus, Scrophularia nodosa, Chelone glabra, Mimulus ringens, Rhinanthus crista-galli, Pedicularis Canadensis, Monarda didyma, Scutellaria galericulata, S. lateriflora, Symphytum officinale, Cynoglossum officinale; C. Morrisoni, Hydrophyllum Virginicum, H. Canadense, Diapensia Lapponica, Gentiana* (several species), *Asarum Canadense, Laportea Canadensis, Comandra umbellata, Arisæma triphyllum, Calla palustris, Acorus calamus, Scheuchzeria palustris, Saggitaria calycina, Orchis spectabilis, Habenaria tridentata, H. viridis bracteata, H. hyperborea, H. dilitata, H. Hookeri, H. orbiculata, H. blephariglottis, H. lacera, H. psycodes, H. fimbriata, Goodyera repens, Spiranthes latifolia, S. cernua, S. gracilis, Listera cordata, Pogonia ophioglossoides, Calopogon pulchellus, Calypso borealis, Microstylis monophyllos, Cypripedium parviflorum, C. pubescens, C. spectabile, C. acaule, Trillium grandiflorum, T. erectum, T. erythrocarpum, Medeola Virginica, Veratrum viride, Uvularia grandiflora, U. sessifolia, Streptopus roseus, Clintonia borealis, Smilacena racemosa, S. stellata, S. trifolia, S. bifolia, Polygonatum biflorum, Erythronium Americanum, Allium tricoccum, Pontederia cordata,* and *Eriocaulon septangulare.*

Among the Mosses the genera *Sphagnum, Dicranum, Orthotri-chum,* and *Hypnum* are particularly well represented, both in species and individuals; but such a vast number of mosses are found here that an enumeration of even the more common or characteristic would be out of place.

The so-called " Iceland Moss" (*Cetraria Islandica*) and "Reindeer Moss" (*Cladonia rangiferina*), together with the common gray *Usnea,* are worthy of special mention from out the host of Lichens that thrive upon the moist atmosphere of the Wilderness.

## 7.–FAUNAL POSITION.

There remains to be considered the Faunal Position of the Adirondacks.

Data are wanting for the determination of exact thermometric means over any considerable portion of the region, but sufficient exist to establish the fact that during the months of May, June, and July (the breeding season of birds) the thermometer shows an average of 57° Fahr. (14° C.), or lower, everywhere within the limits of the Wilderness, and averages below 50° Fahr. (10° C.) throughout much of the interior. The temperature alone, therefore, would indicate that the district pertained to the Canadian Fauna, and a brief study of its characteristic animal and plant life will suffice to confirm the fact.

Amongst the Mammals the following species are eminently northern in habitat : the Lynx, Fisher, Marten, Hudsonian Flying Squirrel, Jumping Mouse, Long-eared Wood Mouse, Porcupine, and Northern Hare.

Of the Birds that breed here many are characteristic of the Canadian Fauna. Such are: the Hermit Thrush, Swainson's Thrush, Redbellied Nuthatch, Winter Wren ; Tennessee, Yellow-rumped, Blackburnian, Black and Yellow, Mourning, and Canada Flycatching

Warblers; White-winged and Red Crossbills, White-throated Sparrow, Junco, Rusty Blackbird, Raven, Canada Jay, Olive-sided Flycatcher, Black-backed and Banded-backed Three-toed Woodpeckers, Spruce Grouse, Goshawk, and Golden-eyed Duck. In addition to the above it is not improbable that the Hudsonian Tit and one (or both) of the Kinglets will be found nesting here.

Mention of the characteristic Reptiles, Batrachians, and Fishes is deferred, and will be made in the chapters pertaining to these groups.

Following is a list of " Subarctic " species of Lepidoptera collected in the immediate vicinity of Beaver Lake (also called " Fenton's," and " Number 4") in Lewis County, by Mr. Hill, and identified by Prof. J. A. Lintner, late State Entomologist : *Agrotis Chardinyi*, *A. conflua*, *A. astricta*, *Plusia bimacalata*, *P. u-aureum*, *Thamnonoma brunneata*, *Melanippe hastata*, *M. fluctuata*, *Coremia ferrugaria*, *Cidaria Packardata*, *C. albolineata*, *C. cunigerata*, *C. hersiliata*, *C. truncata*, *Spargamia magnoliata*, *Oporabia cambricaria*, and *Larentia cæsiata*. These were all found in a single locality, and therefore probably constitute but a small proportion of the northern Lepidoptera that occur in the Adirondacks.

Floral limitations are by no means so clearly defined as the boundaries of Faunal areas, and for the reason that plants are much more easily than animals affected by minor physiographical conditions. They are more susceptible to the influences of local topographical and climatic conditions, such as altitude, humidity, etc., and are also affected by the nature of the soil, and by association with one another. This is seen in the influence which certain kinds of forests exert in determining the character of the more humble plants that grow in their shade. For example, it is well known that the destruction of an evergreen coniferous forest is commonly followed, in the course of nature, by a growth of hard timber—maple, beech, and birch (all deciduous trees) usually predominating. Coincident with this change of forest is an equally radical change in the kinds of small plants that spring up underneath.

3

Many plants that are quite characteristic of northern latitudes are found in greater or less abundance in isolated localities, such as high mountain sides and cool shaded ravines or deep swamps, far southward of their usual homes; and, on the other hand, representatives of many southern species find their way far northward along suitable water-courses, and warm valleys, that penetrate regions clothed in vegetation of a very different type. These seeming peculiarities of distribution are dependent on definite physiographical conditions and are not difficult of explanation, however annoying they may be to those engaged in the determination of distributional areas. Nevertheless there are species that are more or less distinctive of certain tolerably well-defined areas, and I present the following as a provisional list, fairly characteristic of a CANADIAN FLORA : *Ranunculus flammula reptans, Coptis trifolia, Dicentra Canadensis, Viola rotundifolia, V. Canadensis, Arenaria Grœnlandica, Claytonia Caroliniana, Geranium Robertianum, Impatiens pallida, Oxalis acetosella, Acer spicatum, Polygala paucifolia, Poterium Canadense, Geum macrophyllum, Waldsteinia fragarioides, Potentilla tridentata, Dalabarda repens, Ribes lacustre, Mitella diphylla, M. nuda, Tiarella cordifolia, Epilobium alpinum, E. palustre lineare, Circea alpina, Aralia trifolia, Cornus Canadensis, Linnœa borealis, Aster acuminatus, Solidago thyrsoidea, S. Virga-aurea alpina, Nabulus nanus, N. Boottii, Campanula rotundifolia, Vaccineum uliginosum, V. cæspitosum, V. Vitis-Idæa, Chiogenes hispidula, Cassiope hypnoides* (Dr. Parry), *Cassandra calyculata, Kalmia glauca, Rhododendron Lapponicum, Rhodora Canadensis, Ledum latifolium, Pyrola rotundifolia, Chimaphila umbellata, Trientalis Americana, Empetrum nigrum, Betula glandulosa, Salix Cutleri, Pinus strobus, Abies nigra, A. Canadensis, A. balsamea, Thuja occidentalis, Diapensia Lapponica, Orchis spectabilis, Habenaria hyperborea, H. dilitata, Goodyera repens, Listera cordata, Microstylis monophyllos, Cypripedium pubescens, C. spectabile, C. acaule, Trillium grandiflorum, T. erectum, T. erythrocarpum, Streptopus roseus, Clintonia borealis, Smilacena trifolia, S. bifolia.*

# CHAPTER II.

# MAMMALIA.

In the following pages forty-two species of mammals are enumerated as occurring in the Adirondack region, and it is not probable that future investigation will greatly augment this number. With the exception of one or two additional Shrews, and two or three Bats, I know of no others that are likely to be found. The Harbor Seal and the Fox Squirrel are accidental stragglers, but the remaining forty are permanent residents. Among them are several of considerable economic value. These are : the Marten, Fisher, Ermine, Mink, Skunk, Otter, Bear, Deer, Beaver, and Muskrat; and it is not many years since the Moose could have been reckoned with the rest, for it was formerly abundant here, and large numbers were killed for their flesh and hides.

The great majority of our mammals move both by day and night, few being either strictly nocturnal or exclusively diurnal. The only species that can fairly be called nocturnal are the Skunk, the Raccoon, the Bats, and the Flying Squirrels ; and even these are occasionally seen abroad during cloudy days, and do much of their hunting in the twilight. Of strictly diurnal forms the number is still smaller, for I know of but two, the Gray Squirrel and the Chipmunk, that have not been seen after nightfall. The truth of the matter seems to be that very few mammals range about much during the brightest part of the day, or darkest part of the night, these being the times when most of them do the greater part of their sleeping. It is between the dark and the daylight, before sunrise in the morning and in the dusk of evening, when the faint light obscures their outlines and hides their movements, that the larger number do their hunting. Many of them are also out during cloudy days and moonlight nights; and in winter, when the ground is white with snow, they apparently circumambulate all night long.

The phenomenon of hibernation, which enables many mammals to endure a climate to the severity of which they would inevitably succumb were they to remain active throughout the year, and to thrive in regions where they would starve during certain seasons but for their ability to become dormant when scarcity of food prevails, is well exemplified in a number of our species. The following are known to pass a greater or less period of the winter season in a condition of lethargy : the Bear, Raccoon, Bats, Gray Squirrel, Chipmunk, Woodchuck, and Jumping Mouse. Of these the Woodchuck affords the most remarkable example. With astonishing regularity and precision, and utterly regardless of the state of the weather or condition of his food supply, he sinks into his burrow about the 20th of September, and is rarely seen again before the middle of March. It frequently, indeed usually, happens that the time chosen for entering upon the execution of this singular proclivity is during fine warm weather and at a time when the fields are clothed with a luxuriant growth of his favorite food, clover. In fact the Woodchuck retires to the cold dank recesses of his cheerless subterranean abode to commence a period of voluntary seclusion, to enter upon a state of complete oblivion and absolute lethargy, at the very time when one would naturally suppose he would most enjoy himself above ground.

The Gray Squirrel, on the other hand, remains out nearly the entire winter and withdraws to its nest, in some hollow tree, only during the severest weather. The Raccoon and the Bear furnish examples of animals whose dormant periods are intermediate in duration between those above cited.

Hibernation is, after all, merely a profound sleep, intensified and protracted. During ordinary sleep respiration is slackened and the temperature of the body is lower than when the animal is awake.

The longer the sleep continues the less frequent do the respirations become and the lower does the temperature fall, till finally the condition of deep and continued sleep—the true lethargy of hibernation—is attained. This apparent phenomenon, then, is a genuine physiological process, differing in degree only from ordinary sleep. It is the result of conditions of environment, and has become an hereditary habit, enabling certain mammals to exist during a period when their usual food supply is cut off. The dormant state is sometimes brought on by extremes of temperature, but this is not often the case.

Few mammals are commonly seen by those who traverse the forests of the Adirondacks, and it is a fact that the average sportsman, during his annual "trip to the North Woods," rarely sees any save Red Squirrels, Chipmunks, a few Mice, and perhaps a Deer or Porcupine. This is in part due to the nature of their haunts, partly because they do not roam about much in broad daylight, but chiefly because of their shy dispositions and wary habits. The experienced hunter, more familiar with their haunts and ways, falls in with a larger number; still, by far the greater portion go unobserved. Of the forty-two kinds found here I have myself seen living, and in the wild state, all but three; therefore the remarks upon their habits, in the following biographies, are, when the contrary is not stated, drawn largely from the results of personal observation.

---

Order FER&AElig;. FISSIPEDIA. Family FELID&AElig;.

## FELIS CONCOLOR Linnæus.

*Cougar; Panther; Mountain Lion (of the West); Puma (of South Am.).*

It is not many years since the Cougar or Panther, second largest of American *Felidæ*, was a common inhabitant of the primeval forests of the Adirondacks; but, since the State offered a bounty* for their

---

* The law granting this bounty was passed April 26, 1871. It reads as follows: "A State bounty of thirty dollars for a grown wolf, fifteen dollars for a pup wolf, and twenty dollars for a panther,

destruction, so many more have been killed than born that they are now well nigh exterminated. However, a few still remain, and some years may yet elapse before the last Panther disappears from the dense evergreen swamps and high rocky ridges of this Wilderness.

For many of the facts related in the following narrative of the habits of this gigantic "Cat," I am indebted to the experienced hunter and guide, Mr. E. L. Sheppard, who has himself killed, or been instrumental in killing, twenty-eight Panthers in the Adirondacks.

Cougars are either particularly fond of porcupines, or else are frequently forced by hunger to make a distasteful meal, for certain it is that large numbers of these spiny beasts are destroyed by them. Indeed, it often happens that a Panther is killed whose mouth and lips, and sometimes other parts also, fairly bristle with the quills of this formidable rodent. Porcupines are such logy, sluggish creatures, that in their noctivagations they fall an easy prey to any animal that cares to meddle with them.

But the Panther feeds chiefly upon venison, which he captures by "still-hunting," in a way not unlike, save in the manner of killing, that practised by its greatest enemy—man. Both creep stealthily upon the intended victim until within range, when the one springs, the other shoots.

Panthers hunt both by day and by night, but undoubtedly kill the larger part of their game after nightfall. When one scents a deer he keeps to the leeward and creeps stealthily toward it, as a cat does after a mouse. With noiseless tread and crouching form does he

---

shall be paid to any person or persons who shall kill any of said animals within the boundaries of this State. The person or persons obtaining said bounty shall prove the death of the animal so killed by him or them, by producing satisfactory affidavits, and the skull and skin of said animal, before the supervisor and one of the justices of the peace of the town within the boundaries of which the said animal was killed. Whereupon said supervisor and justice of the peace, in the presence of each other, shall burn and destroy the said skull, and brand the said skin so that it may be thereafter identified," etc.—thus ruining many valuable specimens. (Laws of 1871, chap. 721, § 39.) When the game laws were repealed, in 1879, this section became a part of the new law, and it may be found in the Laws of 1879, chap. 534, § 31.

May 5, 1874, a law was passed providing the sum of $500, or so much thereof as might be necessary for the payment of bounties in pursuance of the requirements of the above law of April 26, 1871, chap. 721, § 39. (See Laws of 1874, chap. 323, § 2.) But nearly double this amount has already been paid on Panthers alone (see p. 39).

pass over fallen trees and ragged ledges, or through dense swamps and tangled thickets, till, if unobserved, within thirty or forty feet of his intended victim. If he can now attain a slight elevation and a firm footing he springs directly upon his prey, but if upon level ground makes one or two preliminary leaps before striking it. The noise thus made frightens the deer, who makes a sudden and desperate effort to escape. But, if lying down, several seconds are necessary to get under full headway, and the Panther follows so rapidly, in a series of successive leaps, that it often succeeds in alighting upon the back of its unhappy quarry. Its long claws are planted deep into the quivering flesh, and its sharp teeth make quick work with the ill-fated sufferer. If, however, the deer sees him in season, and can get a good footing for a sudden move, it commonly escapes, and the Panther rarely follows it more than a few rods, for as soon as he finds that the deer is gaining on him he at once gives up the chase. In fact, a Panther rarely secures more than one out of every four or five deer upon which he attempts to spring. Then, too, it not infrequently happens that he strikes a deer when it is under such headway that it escapes; and when Panthers were more plenty here than they now are it was no uncommon thing to shoot a deer bearing deep scars upon its flanks—scars that were clearly made by the claws of this powerful beast. The female is by far the better hunter and does not lose so many deer as the male.

The deer that furnish the most nutriment to our Panthers are generally under two years of age. This is not because this beast is afraid to attack a full-grown animal, but because young deer are less wary, and therefore more easily captured.

The distance that a Panther can pass over in a single leap is almost incredible. On level ground a single spring of twenty feet is by no means uncommon, and on one occasion Mr. Sheppard measured a leap, over snow, of nearly forty feet. In this instance there were three preliminary springs, and the Panther struck his deer on the fourth. The longest leap measured by Mr. Sheppard was one of sixty feet, but here the Panther jumped from a ledge of rocks about twenty feet above the level upon which the deer was standing.   He struck it with such force as to knock it nearly a rod farther off.

Under certain conditions of the deep snows the deer cut in so deeply that the poor animals can make but slow progress.   At such times a Panther, by spreading the toes of his great broad paws, simulates a man on snow-shoes and sinks but a short distance in the snow.   He thus gains a vital advantage over his prey, and will now give chase to and capture one that he missed on his first spring. Under no other circumstances will a Panther pursue a deer, for he is too well aware of the uselessness of an attempt to overtake so fleet an animal.   Immediately upon killing one he drags it bodily into some dense thicket or windfall, where he will not be likely to be observed.   He has thus been known to drag a full-grown deer considerably over a hundred feet before reaching a satisfactory covert. Unlike the wolf, he makes the most of his prey and devours it all before killing another.   One deer generally lasts a Panther a week or ten days, and during this time he may usually be found within a mile of the carcass, hidden under some log or uprooted tree. Sometimes, but very rarely, does he partially bury it, after each meal, by scraping leaves and brush over it.   When all but enough for one or two meals has been eaten, the Panther, especially if a female with young, will often make another hunt, but if unsuccessful returns to the remains of the old carcass.

The young follow the mother till nearly two years old—that is until about two-thirds grown.   She leaves them when hunting, and, after having killed a deer, returns and leads them to it.

It is often stated that Panthers hunt in pairs, but on one occasion only has Mr. Sheppard found an adult male and female in company. This was early in December and the tracks on the snow indicated that they had been sporting considerably, and were probably rutting. He killed them both.

The range of these animals, as individuals, is very extensive, and is only limited by the confines of the Adirondacks. They are, indeed, famous travellers, and when not hunting, roam far and wide, following the highest ridges of the Wilderness, and finding their path along the steepest and most inaccessible ledges. During the winter of 1877–78 J. W. Shultz killed one near Lake Terror that he, in company with E. L. Sheppard, had followed over the summit of Lake Terror Mountain. They sometimes make use of trees to aid in the ascent and descent of steep rocky cliffs, and generally take refuge in a spruce or hemlock when pursued by dogs ; but under no other circumstances do any but the young sporting kittens ever climb trees.

Panthers are hunted during the deep snows of winter, when the hunter, on snow-shoes, makes wide circuits in various directions till he finds a track. This he follows, leading the dogs, till he comes to the carcass of a deer which the Panther has recently killed and partially devoured. Knowing that the animal is not far off he now "lets loose" the dogs, and as a rule the cowardly beast is soon "treed" and shot. Out of the twenty-eight Panthers in the killing of which Mr. Sheppard was concerned, four refused to "tree," and were shot while on the ground. When attacked they never spring after the dogs, but merely act on the defensive. When a dog makes bold to come too near he receives such an energetic "cuff" from the Panther's paw that he rarely solicits another.

Though possessed of great strength and power, and naturally quick in his movements, the Panther is a positive coward. For all that, when seriously wounded, without being entirely crippled, all his latent ferocity is aroused, and he rushes fiercely at his assailants. But even at such times, when in an attitude of supreme anger and rage, and while lashing the snow impetuously with his long tail, anything thrust into his open mouth serves to divert his wrath from the enemy to his weapon. Thus on two occasions, once with an axe, and once with the muzzle of his gun, has Mr. Sheppard saved himself and his dogs from mutilation, if not from a horrible death.

The hunter commonly follows a Panther for many days, and sometimes for weeks, before overtaking him, and could never get him were it not for the fact that he remains near the spot where he kills a deer till it is eaten.    When the hunter has followed a Panther for days, and has, perhaps, nearly come up with him, a heavy snow-storm often sets in and obliterates all signs of the track.    He is then obliged to make wide detours to ascertain in which direction the animal has gone.    On these long and tiresome snow-shoe tramps he is of course obliged to sleep, without shelter, wherever night overtakes him. The heavy walking makes it impossible for him to carry many days' rations, and when his provisions give out he must strike for some camp or settlement for a new supply—this of course consumes valuable time and enables the Panther to get still farther away.    When the beast is finally killed the event is celebrated by a feast, for Panther meat is not only palatable, but is really very fine eating.

Most mammals are larger at the north than at the south, but with the present species the reverse is true.    Individuals from various parts of the south and southwest average considerably larger than those found in the Adirondacks.    This is in obedience to the law, clearly defined by Mr. J. A. Allen, that : " The maximum physical development of the individual is attained where the conditions of environment are most favorable to the life of the species." *

In the Adirondacks, it is an uncommonly large Panther that measures eight feet from the end of its nose to the tip of its tail, and an unusually heavy one that weighs a hundred and fifty pounds.    Still, on the 15th of February, 1877, Mr. Verplanck Colvin, Superintendent of the Adirondack Survey, shot a male on Seventh Lake Mountain, in Hamilton County, that weighed about two hundred pounds. This is the heaviest Panther concerning which I have been able to procure trustworthy information.    It was killed near a deer " yard," and the carcasses of two of its victims were found hard by.    Hence it is fair to infer that he had been for some time lurking in this vi-

* Bulletin of the U. S. Geol. Survey, Aug., 1876, Vol. II, No. 4, p. 310.

cinity, feasting and fattening upon the deer that were unable to escape in the deep snow.

An adult Panther stands about two and a half feet high at the shoulders and is so slender that it generally appears to be very thin and gaunt when in reality it may be quite fat. Either the old males kill the young males (which I do not think probable), or the females greatly preponderate at birth; for out of twenty-eight killed by, or through the instrumentality of E. L. Sheppard, only five were males.

The mother commonly has two kittens at a birth, sometimes one, three, or even four. The period of gestation was ascertained to be ninety-seven days in a female observed by the Zoological Society of London. The young are brought forth late in the winter or in early spring, and the lair is usually in a shallow cavern on the face of some inaccessible cliff or ledge of rocks. It is probable that they do not, with us, have young oftener than every other year.*

## SOME COMMON FALLACIES CONCERNING PANTHERS.

### 1st. Concerning the alleged Fierceness of the Panther.

Not only is it customary for the community at large to speak of the terrible danger of encountering one of these dreadful and savage animals, but even many very respectable works upon Natural History contain the most detailed and heart-rending accounts of the loss of human

---

* William A. Conklin, Esq., Ph. D., has had the kindness to favor me with the following very valuable note concerning the breeding of a female Panther, during a series of years, at the Central Park Menagerie, of which he is director, in New York city. Mr. Conklin writes: "In my experience the period of gestation is thirteen weeks (91 days), and it occasionally, but rarely, exceeds that time by one or two days. I have one Panther that has bred seven times, as follows:

| | | | | | |
|---|---|---|---|---|---|
| In her 1st litter were 4 kittens. | | | In her 4th litter were 4 kittens. | | |
| " 2d " " 4 " | | | " 5th " " 3 " | | |
| " 3d " " 2 " | | | " 6th " " 2 " | | |
| | In her 7th litter was 1 kitten. | | | | |

Her age, 16 years, at the time of her last litter, and the fact that this female came from Texas, may have some bearing on the number of young produced at a birth. The cubs are born with the eyelids closed; they open after eight or nine days. The incisors and canine teeth cut through the gums in eighteen or twenty days. The body is at first spotted, the spots disappearing in about six months. They are weaned when three months old. The mother carries the young about in her mouth in the same way that a cat does her kittens."

life by the brutal attacks of these ferocious beasts.   Even as cautious
and reliable a naturalist as Zadock Thompson quotes the following
appalling and blood-curdling tale as an authentic narrative: "Two
hunters, accompanied by two dogs, went out in quest of game, near
the Catskill Mountains.   At the foot of a large hill, they agreed to
go round it in opposite directions, and when either discharged his
rifle, the other was to hasten toward him to aid him in securing the
game.   Soon after parting, the report of a rifle was heard by one of
them, who, hastening toward the spot, after some search, found nothing but the dog, dreadfully lacerated and dead.   He now became
much alarmed for the fate of his companion, and, while anxiously
looking round, was horror-struck by the harsh growl of a Catamount,
which he perceived on a large limb of a tree, crouching upon the
body of his friend, and apparently meditating an attack on himself.
Instantly he levelled his rifle at the beast, and was so fortunate as to
wound it mortally, when it fell to the ground along with the body of
his slaughtered companion.   His dog then rushed upon the wounded Catamount, which, with one blow of its paw, laid the poor creature dead by his side,"* et cetera.   The illustrious Audubon, in his
great work upon the Quadrupeds of North America, cautions the reader not to credit the legends of the vulgar in regard to the ferocity of
this animal, and its propensity to attack man, and then goes on to
picture midnight encounters and hair-breadth escapes almost as thrilling and improbable as the story above quoted.   Oh, the inconsist-
ency of man!

It is now so well known that the Panther is one of the most cowardly of beasts, never attacking man unless wounded and cornered,
that it is unnecessary to do more than contradict the popular impression to the contrary.

### 2d. Concerning the Method of Capturing its Prey.

It is commonly and widely believed, and frequently and boldly as-

---

* Natural and Civil History of Vermont, 1842, p. 38.

serted in print, that the Panther lurks in ambush for its prey; that it lies in wait beside the runways of the wary deer, hidden by some rock or thicket, or crouching upon an overhanging limb, and falls, like a thunderbolt from heaven, upon the back of its hapless and un-suspecting victim. Such romances, however gratifying to the nar-rator, and entertaining to the community, are without foundation in fact, and could only have originated in the over-fertile imagination of a conscienceless fabricator:

> " ———— a false creation,
> Proceeding from the heat-oppressed brain."

### 3d. Concerning the Screams of the Panther.

Who has not heard of the piercing cries and startling screams of the Panther? Who has listened, about the evening camp-fire, to the tales of hunters and woodsmen, but has felt his blood run cold, and his hat lighten on his head, as the earnest speaker, perhaps in a whisper, and uninterrupted save by the sputtering of the fire, told of the time when alone in the solitudes of the deep forest, and at the dead of night, he was suddenly awakened by a piercing scream that burst upon his weary ears. It seemed like the shriek of a woman in distress, or the pitiful cry of a lost child. Half asleep, bewildered, and amazed, he starts to his feet to render assistance, when the glar-ing eyeballs of a fierce Cougar meet his horrified gaze and acquaint him with the nature of his unwelcome guest!

An attack of indigestion, the cry of a Loon, or the screech of an Owl, a piece of phosphorescent wood, and a very moderate imagination, are all that are necessary, in the way of material and connections, to build up a thrilling tale of this description. Indeed, the writer once had a bit of personal experience in this line that is not yet forgotten.

In conversing with honest hunters upon this point it has been my uniform experience to find that those who have had most to do with Panthers are the most skeptical in regard to their cries; and I have yet to find the man, whose statements on this point are of any value, that has ever heard a wild Panther scream.  This is negative evidence it is true, but it is by no means without value ; and it is certainly safe to assert that at least ninety-nine per cent. of the so-called " Panther screams" emanate from a widely different source.

### 4th. Concerning the Size of the Panther.

In talking with border hunters of a certain type, and in perusing the literature of the subject, one is every now and then confronted with the most fabulous statements concerning the size of the beast now under consideration.  Some would have us believe that Panthers have been killed and measured with a " two-foot rule" that were eleven, twelve, and even thirteen feet in length.  Formidable beasts, indeed!  No less an authority than James De Kay tells us, in apparent good faith, that one was killed on an island in Fourth Lake (of the Fulton Chain) in Herkimer County, that, when recently killed, " had a total length of eleven feet three inches."*  To those that are inclined to credit such statements I have only to say : measure off eleven feet on your floor ; place the largest Panther you ever saw on this measured line, and then tell me on what part of the beast you would " annex " or " splice on " the three or more additional feet.

### 5th. Concerning the way a Panther carries its Prey.

We often see statements to the effect that a Panther has killed a deer or a young bullock, " slung it over his back," and marched off (perhaps up an embankment, or even climbed a tree) with it.  A Panther drags a deer along the ground just as a dog drags a sheep, or a cat a big piece of meat, and if he is a large one he may be able to lift the deer so high that only its hinder parts drag.

---

* Zoology of New York, Part I,  Mammals, 1842, p. 48.

# Bounties paid on Panthers under the Law of 1871.

Data concerning Panthers killed in the Adirondacks from June, 1871, to August, 1882, on which bounties have been paid by the State.* (From official records on file in the Comptroller's office, at Albany.)

| Locality where killed. County. | Town. | Date of killing. | By whom killed. | No killed. | Amt. paid. |
|---|---|---|---|---|---|
| Essex, | Newcomb, | Nov. 10, 1871, | J. C. Farmer, | 1 | $20 |
| " | " | Dec. 11, 1871, | J. C. Farmer, | 3 | 60 |
| " | " | Feb. 25, 1880, | Wm. H. Cullen, | 1 | 20 |
| Franklin, | Dickinson, | Aug. 29, 1873, | Chas. A. Merrill, | 1 | 20 |
| " | " | Dec. 4, 1872, | Milo H. Ober, | 1 | 20 |
| Hamilton, | Lake Pleasant, | Feb. 29, 1872, | Aaron B. Sturges and B. Page, | 1 | 20 |
| " | Long Lake, | Feb., 1878, | J. W. Shultz, | 1 | 20 |
| " | Wells, | Dec. 19, 1876, | Silas Call, | 1 | 20 |
| Herkimer, | Wilmurt, | Dec. 11, 1877, | Edwin L. Sheppard, | 1 | 20 |
| " | " | Dec. 12, 1877, | Edwin L. Sheppard, | 1 | 20 |
| " | " | Dec. 13, 1877, | Edwin L. Sheppard, | 1 | 20 |
| " | " | Feb. 26, 1878, | E. N. Arnold, | 1 | 20 |
| " | " | March 8, 1878, | E. N. Arnold, | 1 | 20 |
| Lewis, | Diana, | May 23, 1882, | George Muir, | 1 | 20 |
| " | " | June 10, 1882, | George Muir, | 1 | 20 |
| " | " | June 27, 1882, | George Muir, | 1 | 20 |
| " | " | July 13, 1882, | George Muir, | 1 | 20 |
| St. Lawrence, | Fine, | June 7, 1871, | Spencer B. Ward, | 1 | 20 |
| " | " | June 22, 1871, | Spencer B. Ward, | 1 | 20 |
| " | Township, No. 11, | Oct. 24, 1871, | Michael Duffy, | 1 | 20 |
| " | Fine, | June 15, 1872, | John Muir, | 1 | 20 |
| " | " | June 26, 1872, | John Muir, | 1 | 20 |
| " | " | June 29, 1872, | John Muir, | 1 | 20 |
| " | Hopkinton, | Nov. 19, 1873, | Noah A. Gale, | 1 | 20 |
| " | Fine, | June 8, 1873, | John Muir, | 1 | 20 |
| " | " | Oct. 23, 1872, | Wm. Henry Marsh, | 1 | 20 |
| " | Hopkinton, | Nov. 4, 1874, | Norman E. Wait, | 1 | 20 |
| " | " | Dec. 26, 1876, | Charles W. Gale, | 1 | 20 |
| " | Fine, | Jan. 24, 1877, | Webster Partlow, | 1 | 20 |
| " | Colton, | Feb. 15, 1878, | Hiram Hutchins, | 1 | 20 |
| " | Fine, | May 1, 1879, | George Muir, | 1 | 20 |
| " | Hopkinton, | Oct. 12, 1879, | Peter Burreau, | 1 | 20 |
| " | Fine, | June 15, 1880, | George Muir, | 1 | 20 |
| " | Colton, | Jan. 15, 1881, | Hiram Hutchins, | 1 | 20 |
| " | " | Nov. 23, 1880, | Hiram Hutchins, | 1 | 20 |
| " | Fine, | Oct. 7, 1881, | George Muir, | 1 | 20 |
| " | " | Oct. 6, 1881, | George Muir, | 1 | 20 |
| " | " | Aug. 26, 1881, | George Muir, | 1 | 20 |
| " | " | July 16, 1881, | George Muir, | 1 | 20 |
| " | " | May 23, 1881, | George Muir, | 1 | 20 |
| " | " | April 26, 1881, | George Muir. | 1 | 20 |
| " | " | Sept. 10, 1881, | George Muir, | 2 | 40 |
| " | " | Nov. 7, 1881, | George Muir, | 1 | 20 |
| | | | | 46 | $920 |

*It is impossible to obtain, even with approximate accuracy, any satisfactory estimate of the total number of Panthers that have been killed in the Adirondacks, even during the past fifty years. Mr. Byron P. Graves, of Boonville, N. Y., shot three in Herkimer and Hamilton Counties during February and March, 1871, four were killed about the same time in Franklin County, and others in other parts of the Woods. A year or two previous to this several Panthers, one of which I skinned, were shot on the extreme western confines of the Wilderness—in the town of Greig, in Lewis County. As near as I can reckon, from the data that I have been able to procure, nearly an hundred Panthers have been killed in the Adirondacks since the year 1860.

## LYNX CANADENSIS (Desm.) Raf.

*Canada Lynx.*

The Lynx is, and so far as I can learn, has always been a rather rare inhabitant of this region. It is most often met with on the Champlain or eastern side of the Woods, but is nowhere common.

The Lynx is called "Loup Cervier" by the French Canadians, and has been erroneously termed Carcajou, or Wolverine, by some of the older hunters in this State.

It preys upon the northern hare, and such other small mammals as it can catch, and upon the Ruffed Grouse and Spruce Partridge. It has also been known to devour pigs, lambs, and young fawns, but the accounts of its attacking full-grown deer are not to be credited.

Its haunts are in the deep forests and burnt districts, remote from the paths of man; and consequently it rarely intrudes upon the barn-yard.

Its ordinary gait when in a hurry is a long gallop, like that of the hare, and it is said to swim well.

The female commonly has two young at a birth, her lair being usually located in a cavern or hollow tree.

The older naturalists, having little or no personal acquaintance with the animals of which they wrote, were often led into grave errors when treating of their habits, and even Thomas Pennant, writing in 1770, said, of the present species, that it " is long lived : climbs trees : lies in wait for the deer which pass under, falls on them, and seizing on the jugular vein soon makes them its prey : will not attack mankind, but is very destructive to the rest of the animal creation : the furs of these animals are valuable for their softness and warmth :  .  .  . The ancients celebrated the great quickness of its sight; and feigned that its urine was converted into a precious stone." *

---

* Synopsis of Quadrupeds, 1771, pp. 187-188.

# LYNX RUFUS (Gmelin) Raf.

*Wild Cat; Bay Lynx; "Chat Cervier."*

The Wild Cat is, for some reason, an extremely rare animal in the Adirondacks. It may be that our climate is too severe for it, since it is much more common farther south.

It frequents rocky hills and ledges, and does not show that antipathy to civilization so marked in its congener, the Lynx. In fact it is often quite common in thickly settled portions of the State, and sometimes proves of much annoyance to the farmer by carrying off lambs, little pigs, and poultry—ducks, geese, turkeys, and chickens proving alike acceptable. Away from the farm-yard it feeds upon rabbits, squirrels, mice, grouse, and what small birds it is fortunate enough to capture. It generally makes its nest in a hollow tree or log, and lines it well with moss. From two to four young constitute a litter, the most frequent number being three.

In 1873 or 1874, I shot a grouse as it was flying along the north side of Mt. Tom, in Massachusetts. Scarcely had it touched the rocky slope when a Wild Cat sprang upon it, from behind a neighboring bush, and, in a succession of rapid leaps, started up the side of the mountain with the grouse in its mouth. The contents of the other barrel of my gun caused him to change his mind as well as direction.

I have eaten the flesh of the Wild Cat, and can pronounce it excellent. It is white, very tender, and suggests veal more than any other meat with which I am familiar.

When enraged, this animal is the most ferocious-looking beast I have ever seen, and hisses, spits, and growls in the most unattractive manner imaginable.

The term " Wild Cat" is sometimes also applied to certain erratic individuals of the domestic cat kind, that have become wild and make their homes in the forest, bringing forth their young in hollow logs,

4

old stumps, and caves, and preying upon poultry and eggs as well as upon wild game. With these the present species must not be confounded.

## Family CANIDÆ.

## CANIS LUPUS Linnæus.

*Wolf.*

Comparatively few Wolves are now to be found in the Adirondacks, though twelve years ago they were quite abundant, and used to hunt in packs of half a dozen or more.

They have hard work to get a living here, and are always gaunt and hungry. They cannot catch deer with any certainty except in deep snow, and are, therefore, during the greater part of the year, forced to subsist upon skunks, hares, mice, frogs, carrion, and such other food as they are able to procure. In times past they were a great enemy to the settlers of this region and within fifty years have caused our border farmers much annoyance by destroying their sheep and pigs; they have also been known to kill calves and young colts.

In summer they sometimes drive a deer into a lake and follow it along the shore, from time to time jumping high in the air in order to sight it and determine the direction in which it is swimming. If the lake is a small one and there are enough Wolves, they are occasionally able to pounce upon it as it emerges from the water; but this rarely happens, and the deer almost always escapes. In September, 1870, I saw a pack of Wolves drive a deer into the head of Seventh Lake, Fulton Chain. It escaped the Wolves to be slain by a man with a shot-gun!

Within my recollection Wolves were so common here that scarcely a night passed when they could not be heard howling in various parts of the forest. So bold and impudent were they that they often came about camp while the inmates were sleeping and stole any venison, or other meat, that chanced to hang within reach.

The amount of noise that a single Wolf is capable of producing is simply astonishing, and many amusing episodes of camp lore owe their origin to this fact. More than one "lone traveller" has hastily taken to a tree, and remained in the inhospitable shelter of its scrawny branches for an entire night, believing himself surrounded by a pack of at least fifty fierce and hungry Wolves, when, in reality, there was but one, and (as its tracks afterwards proved) it was on the farther side of a lake, a couple of miles away.

The Wolf is one of the most cowardly and wary of our mammals, always taking good care to keep out of sight; and he is so crafty and sagacious that it is almost impossible to allure him into any kind of a trap.

When opportunity affords he is one of the most destructive and wasteful of brutes, always killing as much game as possible, regardless of the condition of his appetite, and he used to be the greatest enemy that our deer had to contend with. During the deep snows a small pack of Wolves would sometimes kill hundreds of deer, taking here and there a bite, but leaving the greater number untouched.

In the year 1871 the State put a bounty* on their scalps, and it is a most singular coincidence that a great and sudden decrease in their numbers took place about that time. What became of them is a great and, to me, inexplicable mystery, for it is known that but few were killed. There is but one direction in which they could have escaped, and that is through Clinton County into Lower Canada. In so doing they would have been obliged to pass around the north end of Lake Champlain and cross the River Richelieu, and before reaching any extensive forests would have had to travel long distances through tolerably well-settled portions of country. And there is no evidence that they made any such journey.

The Wolf makes its nest in rocky caverns, under the upturned roots of fallen trees, and in hollow logs; and where suitable shelter

---

* The law granting this bounty has already been given in a foot note under the Panther. See pp. 29–30.

cannot be found, it digs holes in the ground for its home. From six to ten pups constitute a litter, and they are usually produced in April or May. The period of gestation is said to be sixty-three days.*

## BOUNTIES PAID ON WOLVES UNDER THE LAW OF 1871.

Data concerning Wolves killed in the Adirondacks from June, 1871, to July, 1882, on which bounties have been paid by the State. (From official records on file in the Comptroller's office, at Albany.)

| Locality where killed. County. | Town. | Date of killing. | By whom killed. | No. killed. | Amt. paid. |
|---|---|---|---|---|---|
| Essex, | Minerva, | Sept. 6, 1872, | Wesley Rice, | 2 | 60 |
| Franklin, | Duane, | July 4, 1874, | James H. Bean, | 1 | 30 |
| " | Brandon, | June 12, 1875, | Calvin Wait, | 1 | 30 |
| " | " | June 17, 1875, | Calvin Wait, | 1 | 30 |
| Herkimer, | Ohio, | Jan. 28, 1882, | Henry Sheldon, | 1 | 30 |
| " | " | Feb. 2, 1882, | Henry Sheldon, | 1 | 30 |
| Oneida, | Forest Port, | Feb. 14, 1882, | Henry Dunan, | 1 | 30 |
| " | " | March 15, 1882, | Henry Dunan, | 1 | 30 |
| " | " | March 19, 1882, | Henry Dunan, | 1 | 30 |
| Lewis, | Greig, | Nov. 10, 1881, | George Botchford, | 1 | 30 |
| " | Diana, | June 27, 1882, | George Muir, | 1 | 30 |
| St. Lawrence, | Fine, | Oct. 17, 1871, | John Muir, | 1 | 30 |
| " | Hopkinton, | Aug. 17, 1871, | George Spear, | 1 | 30 |
| " | " | Aug. 17, 1871, | George Spear, | 1 Pup | 15 |
| " | " | Oct. 6, 1871, | Joseph Whitney, | 1 | 30 |
| " | Fine, | Nov. 7, 1872, | John Muir, | 1 | 30 |
| " | " | May 26, 1872, | John Muir, | 1 | 30 |
| " | Pitcairn, | Nov. 4, 1872, | Aaron Thomas, | 1 | 30 |
| " | " | Dec. 12, 1873, | Aaron Thomas, | 1 | 30 |
| " | Brasher, | Dec. 21, 1872, | Timothy Desmond, | 1 | 30 |
| " | Fine, | May 22, 1875, | John Muir, | 1 | 30 |
| " | " | May 24, 1875, | John Muir, | 1 | 30 |
| " | " | May 15, 1876, | John Muir, | 1 | 30 |
| " | Hopkinton, | Oct. 9, 1876, | George Peck, | 1 | 30 |
| " | Fine, | April 8, 1878, | George Muir, | 1 | 30 |
| " | " | May 5, 1877, | George Muir, | 1 | 30 |
| " | " | July 14, 1877, | George Muir, | 1 | 30 |
| " | " | April 29, 1879, | George Muir, | 1 | 30 |
| " | " | Sept. 16, 1878, | George Muir, | 1 | 30 |
| " | " | April 26, 1880, | George Muir, | 1 | 30 |
| " | " | Oct. 3, 1880, | George Muir, | 1 | 30 |
| " | Parishville, | Nov. 13, 1880, | Henry C. Hibbard, | 1 | 30 |
| " | Colton, | Nov. 5, 1880, | Abram Barkley, | 1 | 30 |
| " | Hopkinton, | Nov. 6, 1880, | Jonathan Baldwin, | 1 | 30 |
| " | Fine, | Sept. 25, 1881, | George Muir, | 1 | 30 |
| " | " | Aug. 24, 1881, | George Muir, | 1 | 30 |
| " | " | July 20, 1881, | George Muir, | 1 | 30 |
| " | " | June 11, 1881, | George Muir, | 1 Pup | 15 |
| " | " | June 11, 1881, | George Muir, | 1 | 30 |
| " | " | April 28, 1881, | George Muir, | 1 | 30 |
| " | " | Nov. 8, 1881, | George Muir, | 1 | 30 |
| " | Hopkinton, | Sept. 20, 1881, | Henry Hibbard, | 1 | 30 |
| Washington, | Dresden, | Feb., 1882, latter part, | Rollin Gamby, | 1 | 30 |
| " | " | March, 1882, early part, | Rollin Gamby, | 1 | 30 |
| | | | | 45 | $1,320 |

* Fauna Americana, by Richard Harlan, M.D., 1825, p. 81.

# VULPES VULGARIS PENNSYLVANICUS (Bodd.) Coues.

*Fox; Red Fox; Cross Fox; Silver Fox; Black Fox.*

The common Fox is a tolerably abundant resident in the "North Woods," and its short bark is often heard, after nightfall, by parties encamped about our lakes.

He is both nocturnal and diurnal in habits, and preys upon skunks, woodchucks, muskrats, hares, rabbits, squirrels, mice, and small birds and eggs. He is a well-known and much-dreaded depredator of the poultry-yard, destroying, with equal alacrity, turkeys, ducks, geese, hens, chickens, and doves ; and has been known to make off with young lambs. He will also eat carrion, and even fish, and is said to be fond of ripe grapes and strawberries.

The cunning of the Fox is proverbial. Wily, crafty, and sagacious, to a degree almost beyond credibility, he defies the superior skill and intelligence of man, and meets, with shrewd manœuvre and subtle stratagem, all attempts at his extermination. He lives and thrives and multiplies in our very midst, and is as common in many of the thickly settled portions of the State as in the remotest depths of the primeval forests.

He is hunted both for pleasure and profit, and for the gratification of a malicious spite that seems to be inherent in man for his destruction. He is trapped for where his presence is suspected, hounded when his foot-prints are seen on the snow, dug out when found in his subterranean burrow, and shot at when surprised at any of his tricks, from the first hour of his youthful gambols till the time that he finally succumbs before man's combined and persistent efforts toward his annihilation. Nevertheless, his race survives, and I have yet to be convinced that his numbers have undergone any very material diminution during the last hundred years.

The influence of *natural selection* in developing hereditary habits for the protection of the species is well exemplified in this animal, for he seems familiar, from earliest infancy, with the multifarious contri-

vances devised by man for his capture, and avoids them all, eluding
and circumventing his pursuer with an intelligence and promptness
that command our wonder and respect.

The pastime (?) of Fox hunting is largely practised everywhere along
the border-lands of our Wilderness, and two or three men, with one
or two fox-hounds, commonly constitute a hunting party. As soon
as a fresh track is found the dog is allowed to follow it, which he
does with great joy and alacrity. The men now separate, each proceeding, without further delay, to some ravine, hill-side, or other
point that is known to be one of the " run-ways" of the Fox. Occasionally the Fox, on being started, makes a round on one of these
courses, and is shot while passing the first station. More commonly,
however, he makes off, taking a tolerably straight course, and runs
several miles before commencing to circle and wind about among the
hills. Therefore the hunter is, on these interesting excursions, generally
obliged to walk many miles over the deep snow, and night frequently
overtakes him, tired and hungry, far from the cheerful fireside of his
pleasant home. And he may, or may not, have been rewarded by
securing the object of the chase.

It sometimes happens, especially during a thaw, when the snow
" slumps," that the dog catches up with the Fox. At such times both
pursuer and pursued are commonly well-nigh exhausted, and the weary
hunter lags far behind. The resulting scene, to which I have myself
been an eye-witness, is so graphically depicted by Audubon and
Bachman that I take pleasure in reproducing their account of it here :
". . . . every bound and plunge into the snow, diminishes the distance between the Fox and his relentless foe. . . . . One more
desperate leap, and with a sudden snappish growl he turns upon his
pursuer, and endeavors to defend himself with his sharp teeth. For
a moment he resists the dog, but is almost instantly overcome. He
is not killed, however, in the first onset; both dog and Fox are so
fatigued that they now sit on their haunches facing each other, resting, panting, their tongues hanging out, and the foam from their lips

dropping on the snow. After fiercely eyeing each other for a while, both become impatient—the former to seize his prey, and the latter to escape. At the first leap cf the Fox, the dog is upon him; with renewed vigor he seizes him by the throat, and does not loose his hold until the snow is stained with his blood, and he lies rumpled, draggled, with blood-shot eye, and frothy open mouth, a mangled carcass on the ground."*

Not infrequently the Fox, after leading his pursuers a long and tiresome chase, betakes himself to his hole. If this chances to lie within a ledge of rocks it is the safest of retreats, but if it be merely a burrow in the earth he is by no means secure, for the hunters (provided they have enough energy and ambition left) repair to the nearest farm-house for spade and pick with which to dig out the luckless beast.

Hence Fox hunting, with us, can hardly be ranked among the most fascinating of sports; and those that indulge in it must have good pluck and hard muscle or they are apt to come out the worse for wear. *Sic transit gloria mundi !* Having "killed my Fox" I am not now easily seduced into this form of recreation.

Foxes make rather pretty pets, and, when taken young, are easily tamed; but they are so deceitful and treacherous that they are not apt to gain one's affection.

The Fox makes its nest in caverns and ledges of rocks, in burrows in the earth, and occasionally in old stumps and hollow logs. From four to nine young are brought forth at a time, the usual period being, with us, the latter part of March or first of April.

### Family MUSTELIDÆ. Subfamily MUSTELINÆ.

NOTE.—The Wolverine (*Gulo luscus*) is not now an inhabitant of the Adirondacks, and I have been unable to find among the hunters and trappers of this region anyone who has ever seen it in our Wilder-

---

* Quadrupeds of North America, Vol. I, 1846, p. 48.

ness.   Dr. DeKay, writing in 1842, said: "Although we have not met with this animal, yet hunters who have killed them repeatedly, and knew them well, have assured us that they are still found in the districts north of Raquet Lake."*

Dr. Bachman killed one, about the year 1811, in its den in a ledge of rocks, in Rensselaer County.†

This animal is the *Carcajou* of the Canadians.

## MUSTELA PENNANTI Erxleben.

*Fisher; Pekan; Pennant's Marten; " Black Cat;" " Black Fox."*

Though not so common as formerly, the Fisher, as it is here termed, is by no means a rare inhabitant of these mountains.

The name Fisher is somewhat of a misnomer, for these animals commonly frequent deep swamps and wooded mountain-sides, away from the immediate vicinage of water, and are not known to catch fish for themselves as do the Mink and Otter.   However, they are fond of fish and never neglect to devour those that chance to fall in their way.   They prey chiefly upon hares, squirrels, mice, grouse, small birds, and frogs, and are said to eat snakes.   They also catch and feed upon their own congener, the Marten, and make a practice of devouring all that they discover in dead-falls and steel-traps, thus proving almost as great a nuisance to the trapper as the Wolverine.   It is said to be less objectionable than the Wolverine in one particular: *i. e.* it leaves the traps where it finds them, while the other blackleg often lugs them off and hides them.

Sir John Richardson tells us that "its favorite food is the Canada Porcupine, which it kills by biting in the belly."   This habit, which has been questioned, has recently received additional confirmation from the pen of Corporal Lot Warfield, who writes of this animal, from Weston, Vermont, stating his experience as follows:  " I agree with ' Penobscot' that they are not plenty, but account for it on

* Zoology of New York, Part I, Mammals, 1842, p. 28.
† Quadrupeds of North America, Vol. I, 1846, pp. 207–208.

different grounds, namely, its fondness for the flesh of the porcupine, whose quills often prove fatal to it. I have several times found the quills buried in their bodies, besides quantities of flesh, hair, and quills in the stomach and excrements, and from this gained a point in baiting them; let other trappers try it. They are an agile, muscular animal, jumping from tree to tree like a squirrel, clearing a distance of forty feet in a descending leap, never failing a secure grip."[*]

During a recent visit to the north shore of the Gulf of St. Lawrence I was informed, both by an agent of the Hudson's Bay Company and by the trappers themselves, that porcupines constitute a large and important element in the food supply of the Pekan. Mr. Nap. A. Comeau, of Godbout, who secured for me a large and handsome male of this species, tells me that its intestine contained hundreds of porcupine quills, arranged in clusters, like so many packages of needles, throughout its length. In no case had a single quill penetrated the mucous lining of the intestine, but they were, apparently, passing along its interior as smoothly and surely as if within a tube of glass or metal. Mr. Comeau could not discover a quill in any of the abdominal viscera, or anywhere in the abdominal cavity, excepting as above stated. A great many, however, were found imbedded in the muscles of the head, chest, back, and legs, and it was remarked that their presence gave rise to no irritation, no products of inflammation being discovered in their vicinity. In examining the partially cleaned skeleton of this specimen I still find some of the quills in the deep muscles and ligaments about the joints. A knee, in particular, shows several in its immediate neighborhood. One is deeply imbedded in the dense ligament alongside the patella; three lie parallel to and close against the tibia, and two can be seen between it and the fibula.

It is probable that all of these quills entered the body of the animal while engaged in killing and devouring the porcupine, for those swal-

---

[*] Forest and Stream, Vol. XII, No. 21, June 26, 1879, p. 405.

lowed seemed to have caused no trouble after having fairly entered the alimentary canal. Therefore there remains no question whatever that the Fisher feeds upon the porcupine, but I do not agree with Corporal Warfield in the belief that the "quills often prove fatal to it."

It is indeed remarkable that an animal no larger than the one now under consideration should habitually feed upon a beast in whose capture he must be pierced with numbers of large and sharp needles, many of which exceed two and a half inches (64 mm.) in length— needles that are destined to penetrate to the remotest parts of his body.

That it, at times, attacks so large and tough an animal as the Raccoon is evident from the following : Dr. Coues, in his valuable Monograph of North American Mustelidæ (pp. 73–74), quotes a letter from Peter Reed to Prof. Spencer F. Baird, to the effect that the writer once followed, on the snow, the bloody trail that marked the progress of a fierce and desperate contest between a Fisher and a 'Coon. This was in Washington County, New York, near the southeastern border of the Adirondack region. Mr. Reed further stated that as the Fisher became rare in that section the Raccoon greatly increased in abundance, and he regards these circumstances as cause and effect.

When pressed by hunger the Pekan is said to subsist upon beech-nuts. This could hardly be true in the Adirondacks, for here a good yield of beech-nuts is almost invariably followed by an abundance of small game—grouse, squirrels, chipmunks, and mice alike fattening upon the mast. " Beech-nut years," too, are apt to be followed by mild winters; while it is during the deep snows of our severest winters, when there are few or no beech-nuts, and a consequent scarcity of small game prevails, that Pennant's Marten is likely to be pinched for food.

The Pekan is a large and powerful mammal, with resemblances pointing both toward the Marten and the Wolverine. Individuals have been killed that stood a foot high and measured three and a half feet in length, but this is much above the average size. As there are "giants among men," and "giant wolves," so are there giants among Fishers. They are always males. About twenty years ago E. L. Sheppard caught one on Seventh Lake (Fulton Chain) that was estimated to weigh about forty pounds and whose skin was larger than that of a good-sized Otter! In my Osteological Cabinet reposes the skull of a Fisher that measures five inches in length. It was presented to me by Mr. John Constable, who killed it between Stony Lake and "The Hollow," near Independence River, during the early part of the winter of 1840. Mr. Constable tells me that it ascended a gigantic dead pine, the tip of which had broken off. The "stub" of this tree was more than six feet through at the base, and upwards of an hundred and fifty feet in height. The Fisher climbed to the very top and lodged in a depression where the tip had broken off. He was shot but was so lodged that he did not fall, and the tree had to be felled before he was secured. The pine was an unusually fine one—a straight pillar, tapering uniformly to the top, and so perpendicular and well balanced that when the side choppings met it did not fall, and was with great difficulty overthrown. When it did finally tumble, and the cloud of snow that filled the air as it came crashing and thundering to the ground had cleared away, the Fisher was found to be dead. It proved to be in keeping with the tree it had climbed, for it was as large as an Otter and by far the biggest Fisher that Mr. Constable, or the old hunter with him, had ever seen.

Though chiefly nocturnal they sometimes hunt by day. They are expert climbers and have been known to leap from one tree to another when in pursuit of their prey, and also when badly frightened.

Their nest is made in the hollow of some standing tree, generally thirty or forty feet from the ground, and from two to four young are commonly brought forth about the first of May.

## MUSTELA AMERICANA   Turton.

*Marten; American Sable; Pine Marten; Hudson's Bay Sable.*

The Marten is a common resident of the dark evergreen forests of the Adirondacks, and hundreds of them are trapped here every winter for their fur.   Like the Fisher, it is chiefly nocturnal, but is occasionally seen abroad by day.   They prey upon partridges, rabbits, squirrels, chipmunks, mice, shrews, and any other "small game" that they are smart enough to catch.   Birds' eggs and young birds are greedily devoured, and frogs and toads, and even our larger insects, do not come amiss.   It is said that they are exceedingly fond of honey, but on how good authority I am unable to attest.   They are arboreal to such an extent that they are never found in districts devoid of timber, and seem to show a predilection for coniferous forests. Not only are they expert climbers, but they sport about amongst the tree-tops, both in pursuit of game and pleasure, with the ease and grace of squirrels.   Preferring moss-covered logs and the seclusion of deep evergreen woods to the beaten paths and stir of the settled districts, or even the rude civilization of the hardy frontiersman, the Marten avoids the clearings and habitations of man, and cannot be reckoned among the depredators of the poultry-yard.

It is one of the prettiest of North American mammals, but its disposition is sadly out of harmony with its attractive exterior.   Mr. John Constable has narrated to me a most interesting and vivid account of an affray that he once witnessed, in company with his brother, Mr. Stevenson Constable, between a Marten and a Great Northern Hare.   The Marten, generally so meek and docile in appearance, assumed the savage mien and demeanor of a fierce tiger, as it attacked and slew the luckless hare—an animal of several times its own size and weight.   And even after the poor hare was dead the Marten's fury did not abate, and he angrily jerked and twisted the lifeless body from side to side, as if to reek vengeance, for sins never committed, upon the defenceless body of his innocent victim.   So intent was he upon this deed of carnage that he was utterly oblivious to the human spectators, who put an end to the scene by driving a bullet through his obdurate pate.

Audubon said of it : " Let us take a share of the cunning and sneaking character of the fox, as much of the wide-awake and cautious habits of the weasel, a similar proportion of the voracity (and a little of the fetid odor) of the mink, and add thereto some of the climbing propensities of the raccoon, and we have a tolerable idea of the attributes of the little prowler."*

Mr. Constable tells me that when the hunter discovers a Marten climbing about amongst the tree-tops he has only to whistle, and the inquisitive animal will stop and peer down at him, affording an excellent shot.

I have no personal knowledge of the size of a litter of Martens, and the number of young produced at a time is variously stated (2 to 8 being the extremes given) by different authors. The assertion that from four to six constitute an average litter would probably hit pretty close to the truth. The nest is placed in a hollow tree or log, rarely in the ground, and the young are brought forth in April.

The fur of this species, which is one of the most valuable of fur-bearing animals, becomes prime early in November. As long ago as 1770, Pennant said that their skins were " a prodigious article of commerce "; † and Richardson, in 1829, stated that " Upward of one hundred thousand skins have long been collected annually in the fur countries." ‡ Dr. Coues tells us that : " Even in Nova Scotia a thousand skins are said to have been exported annually within a few years, and they may justly be regarded as among the most important of the land fur-bearing animals." And goes on to say, " Respecting their comparative scarcity at times, Mr. Ross has recorded a remarkable fact of periodical disappearance. ' It occurs in decades,'

* Quadrupeds of North America, Vol. III, 1854, p. 177.
† Synopsis of Quadrupeds, 1771, p. 216.
‡ Fauna Boreali Americana, Vol. I, 1829.

he says, 'or thereabouts, with wonderful regularity, and it is quite
unknown what becomes of them. They are not found dead. The
failure extends throughout the Hudson's Bay Territory at the same
time. And there is no tract or region to which they can migrate
where we have not posts, or into which our hunters have not penetrated.'" *

## PUTORIUS VULGARIS (Aldrov.) Griff.

### *Least Weasel.*

Having been reared in the rural districts of northeastern New York,
I early became acquainted with this interesting little animal, and have
always watched its habits with a great deal of pleasure. It is the commonest Weasel in the Adirondack region, and always turns white
shortly after the first fall of snow. It inhabits all parts of the Wilderness, being found alike along water-courses, in deep swamps, and on
rocky ledges and mountain sides. It preys upon mice, moles, shrews,
small birds and eggs, and insects—chiefly *Coleoptera.* I have never
known it to attack larger mammals or poultry.

Numbers of mice make their homes under the heaps of brush and
rubbish and piles of stones that accumulate along the borders of clearings and in neglected pastures. Such places, together with old
tumbled-down stone walls and log heaps constitute, therefore, the
favorite haunts of the Least Weasel in the semi-civilized districts.
It is not wary and will suffer man to approach within a few feet of it
before withdrawing from view. It is curious and inquisitive and will
soon stick its head out of some hole near by to see what has become
of the intruder. Ever on the alert it moves backwards and forwards
generally keeping near some object, behind, into, or under which it
can disappear at a moment's notice, and is never still for any appre-
ciable length of time—a fact which can easily be demonstrated by
attempting to hit one of them with a rifle ball.

----

* Fur-Bearing Animals, 1877, p. 94

They are said to be nocturnal in habits, but those that I have seen, and their number is not small, all seemed very much at home in broad daylight. I have often surprised them in the woods and fields, and have observed that on such occasions they usually make for some convenient covert and, when within reach of its shelter, immediately turn about to view the stranger, who is now an object of curiosity rather than of alarm. Once, while sitting quietly on the end of an old log, in the woods, I noticed one of these pretty little Weasels coming obliquely toward me, in a series of leisurely leaps, stopping every now and then to look about. Perceiving me he stood bolt upright, his head bent at right angles to his slender body, and eyed me for a moment without moving a muscle; he then betook himself to the roots of the nearest tree, and under the quasi-protection of this open retreat, commenced a more deliberate survey of my peculiarities. Many times did he advance toward me, and as many back up to the tree again, with his head elevated, and constantly sniffing the air in my direction. He finally gathered sufficient courage to cross over to the log upon which I was sitting, and under the shelter of its shadow scrutinized me still more closely.

The Least Weasel is so small and slender that it can easily enter the burrows of a large proportion of the animals that constitute its prey. When they take to the open fields and outrun their pursuer, he is not discouraged, but follows their tracks by the scent, like a hound, and overtakes them in their securest retreats; thus are his ill-fated victims attacked in their own homes, and thus are they deprived of any haven to which they may fly to escape from the eager pursuit of this indefatigable and inexorable little beast.

I have never found the nest of the Weasel, and therefore transcribe the following account of its breeding habits from the pen of Thomas Bell : " The female Weasel brings forth four, or more frequently five young, and is said to have two or three litters in a year. The nest is composed of dry leaves and herbage, and is warm and dry, being usually placed in a hole in a bank, in a dry ditch, or in a hollow tree.

She will defend her young with the utmost desperation against any assailant, and sacrifice her own life rather than desert them; and even when the nest is torn up by a dog, rushing out with great fury, and fastening upon his nose or lips." *

## PUTORIUS ERMINEA (Linn.) Cuvier.

*Ermine; Stoat; Large Weasel; "White Weasel"; "Brown Weasel."*

The Ermine is a common resident and, like the preceding species, becomes white at the approach of winter. Like it also, it wanders over different kinds of territory, and is frequently taken in traps set for more valuable fur. In addition to the small game mentioned as constituting the larder of the Least Weasel, the Ermine attacks and slays animals many times its own size and weight. Thus the house rat, squirrels, rabbits, and even the great northern hare fall easy victims before its superior prowess. It is very fond of the ruffed grouse, and its proneness to depopulate the poultry-yard is notorious. Audubon tells us that he has "known forty well-grown fowls to have been killed in one night by a single Ermine." And on our own premises a Stoat once killed fifteen doves in a single night! Rats and mice also it slays by dozens when opportunity presents. Unlike others of its tribe it does not, when game is plenty, devour the flesh of its victims, but merely eats their brains or sucks their blood; and when feasted to satiety continues its work of carnage till scarcity of material, or bodily fatigue, induce it to take a temporary respite.

Ever victorious, of pre-eminent assurance, reliant on its own superiority and power, and confident of success, this indomitable little animal is, in courage and ferocity, insatiate bloodthirstiness, and bold audacity, almost without parallel in the history of mammalia. Hunger plays but little part in the slaughter, the war of destruction and extermination, waged against its multifarious prey by this terrestrial vampire, but pitiless, relentless, wasteful in the extreme, it kills for

---

* Quoted in Coues' Fur-Bearing Animals, 1877, p. 109.

the mere sake of killing, and its entire existence is almost one continuous course of bloodshed.

Dr. Coues speaks thus of its general aspect : " A glance at the physiognomy of the Weasels would suffice to betray their character. The teeth are almost of the highest known raptorial character; the jaws are worked by enormous masses of muscles covering all the side of the skull. The forehead is low, and the nose is sharp; the eyes are small, penetrating, cunning, and glitter with an angry green light. There is something peculiar, moreover, in the way that this fierce face surmounts a body extraordinarily wiry, lithe, and muscular. It ends a remarkably long and slender neck in such a way that it may be held at a right angle with the axis of the latter. When the creature is glancing around, with the neck stretched up, and flat triangular head bent forward, swaying from one side to the other, we catch the likeness in a moment—it is the image of a serpent."*

The foregoing forcible picture fits the Weasel well when under conditions of excitement and anger; but there are times when its appearance in no wise suggests its sanguinary propensities. In certain states of pelage it is very beautiful, and when at rest a more innocent and harmless looking creature can hardly be found. On the approach of any of the animals that constitute its prey, however, its bearing is instantly changed, and its fiendish nature is soon revealed.

I once put a very large rat into a square tin cage with a Weasel of this species. The rat had been caught in a steel trap, by the toes of one of its hind feet, and was in no way injured. He was very ugly, biting fiercely at the trap and the stick with which I assisted him into the cage of the Weasel. No sooner had he entered the cage than his whole manner and bearing changed. He immediately assumed an attitude of abject terror, trembled from head to foot, and crawled into the nearest corner. The Weasel advanced toward

---

* Fur-bearing Animals, 1877, p. 129.

5

him at once, and as he did so the rat raised on his hind legs, letting his fore paws hang helplessly over his breast, and squealed
piteously.   Not only did he show no disposition to fight, but offered
no resistance whatever, and did not even attempt to defend himself
when molested.   The Weasel did not seize him at first, but cuffed
him with his fore paws and drove him from one corner of the cage to
another, glaring at him continuously.   Then, with a sudden move, he
sprang upon his victim, already paralyzed with fear, laid open the
back of his head with a single bite, ate the brains, and left the quivering carcass untouched.

The Ermine hunts both by day and by night, and climbs trees with
great ease and celerity.   I have often "treed" them myself by running after them in the woods, and have also seen them chase chipmunks up trees.   Twice have I seen them run up the smooth trunks
of the beech.   They are not very timid and will allow a near approach before taking fright.

The much lamented Robert Kennicott, whose untimely death on
the icy shores of the Yukon* deprived the world, prematurely, of one
of her most indefatigable and conscientious naturalists, gave us such an
interesting and truthful account of the habits of this species, that I
take pleasure in reproducing brief portions of it here.   He said : "A
more fierce and cruel mammal does not exist in America than this
little Weasel.   The courage and sanguinary disposition of the panther are insignificant in comparison, having regard to the strength of
the two.   Without hesitation, the Weasel attacks animals five or ten
times its own size; and, not content with killing enough for food,
wantonly destroys whatever life it can, . . . . . When a Weasel has
gained access to a poultry-yard, it will frequently kill every fowl within its reach in a single visit. . . . Fortunately, however, this animal,
even when abundant, does not enter the farm-yard so frequently as
might be expected, appearing to prefer a free life in the woods to

---

* Mr. Kennicott died of heart disease, May 13, 1866, aged thirty. (Dall's Alaska, 1870, p. 70.)

easy but dangerous feasts on domestic fowls. . . . I have observed for several years the presence of a number of these Weasels in a grove near a farm-yard well stocked with poultry, which they never appeared to enter, though repeatedly visited by minks and skunks. Indeed, I am inclined to think that, notwithstanding their occasional predatory inroads, they should not be killed when living permanently about meadows or cultivated fields, at a distance from the poultry; for they are not less destructive to many of the farmer's enemies in the fields. Meadow-mice are certainly the greatest pests among mammals in northern Illinois; and of these the Weasel destroys great numbers. I am informed that, upon the appearance of a Weasel in the field, the army of mice of all kinds begins a precipitate retreat. A gentleman of Wisconsin related to me that, while following the plough, in spring, he noticed a Weasel with a mouse in its mouth, running past him. It entered a hollow log. He determined to watch further, if possible, the animal's movements, and presently saw it come out again, hunt about the roots of some stumps, dead trees, and log-heaps, and then enter a hole, from which a mouse ran out. But the Weasel had caught one, and carried it to the nest. Upon cutting open this log, five young Weasels were found, and the remains of a large number of mice, doubtless conveyed there as food. . . .

"Stacks and barnfuls of grain are often overrun with rats and mice; but let a Weasel take up his residence there and soon the pests will disappear. A Weasel will, occasionally, remain for some time in a barn, feeding on these vermin, without disturbing the fowls. But it is never safe to trust one near the poultry-yard, for, when once an attack is made, there is no limit to the destruction. When the animal has entered stacks or barns, it has the curious habit of collecting in a particular place the bodies of all the rats and mice it has slain; thus sometimes a pile of a hundred or more of their victims may be seen which have been killed in the course of two or three nights."*

---

* The Quadrupeds of Illinois injurious and beneficial to the Farmer. By Robert Kennicott. Report of the Commissioner of Patents for the year 1857, Agriculture, 1858, pp. 104–106.

And in another place Mr. Kennicott tells us that an Ermine "destroyed nearly fifty chickens, several of which were adults and many half grown, in a single night, and the early part of the following evening; and it was so bold as to kill several young chickens in a coop beside which a man was standing, watching for it. I finally shot it while it was running near me in pursuit of a chicken, though a few minutes before we had chased it into a retreat under a haystack. This extreme boldness could not have been the result of hunger, as it had already, during the same evening, killed a large number of fowls."[*]

Their nests are usually made in an old stump or log-heap, or under some outbuilding, and from four to six young are commonly brought forth early in May. The young are apt to remain during the summer in the vicinity of the nest.

### *The Ermine as a Ferret.*

That the Ermine can be successfully employed as a Ferret is amply proven by the following narrative, from the pen of Dr. John Bachman: "Whilst residing in the State of New York many years ago, we were desirous of preserving a number of rabbits during the winter from the excessive cold and from the hands of the hunters, who killed so many that we feared the race would be nearly extirpated in our neighborhood; our design being to set them at liberty in the spring. At this period we had in confinement several Weasels of two species existing in that part of the country. . . .

"We bethought ourselves of using one of each species of these Weasels instead of a Ferret, to aid in taking the rabbits we wanted, and having provided ourselves with a man and a dog to hunt the rabbits to their holes, we took the Weasels in a small tin box with us, having first tied a small cord around their necks in such a manner as to prevent them from escaping, or remaining in the holes to eat the rabbits, whilst it could not slip and choke them.

---

[*] Ibid., 1858, p. 244.

" We soon raced a rabbit to its hole, . . ." and the Ermine "although we had captured the individual but a few days before, entered readily; but having his jaws at liberty, it killed the rabbit. Relinquishing the Weasel to our man, he afterwards filed its teeth down to prevent it from destroying the rabbits; and when thus rendered harmless, the Ermine pursued the rabbits to the bottom of their holes, and terrified them so that they instantly fled to the entrance and were taken alive in the hand; and although they sometimes scrambled up some distance in a hollow tree, their active and persevering little foe followed them, and instantly forced them down. In this manner the man procured twelve rabbits alive in the course of one morning, and more than fifty in about three weeks, when we requested him to desist." *

### Concerning the Change in Color in the Ermine.

It is eminently proper that a subject which has attracted so much attention, and occasioned so much controversy, as the seasonal change in color in this and other species, should receive, in the present connection, the consideration that its importance demands. Audubon and Bachman, who observed the spring moult in an individual kept in confinement, give, with much detail, full notes (taken at the time) concerning the progress and nature of the change, as it advanced from day to day. The result of their observations is thus stated : "As far as our observations have enabled us to form an opinion on this subject, we have arrived at the conclusion, that the animal sheds its coat twice a year, i. e., at the periods when these semi-annual changes take place. In autumn, the summer hair gradually and almost imperceptibly drops out, and is succeeded by a fresh coat of hair, which in the course of two or three weeks becomes pure white; while in the spring the animal undergoes its change from white to brown in consequence of shedding its winter coat, the new hairs then coming

---

* Quadrupeds of North America, Vol. I, 1846, pp. 177–178.

out brown."* On this point Dr. Coues writes as follows: "The question practically narrows to this: Is the change coincident with renewal of the coat, or is it independent of this, or may it occur in both ways? Specimens before me prove the last statement. Some among them, notably those taken in spring, show the long woolly white coat of winter in most places, and in others present patches— generally a streak along the back—of shorter, coarser, thinner hair, evidently of the new spring coat, wholly dark brown. Other specimens, notably autumnal ones, demonstrate the turning to white of existing hairs, these being white at the roots for a varying distance, and tipped with brown. These are simple facts not open to question. We may safely conclude that if the requisite temperature be experienced at the periods of renewal of the coat, the new hairs will come out of the opposite color; if not, they will appear of the same color, and afterwards change; that is, the change may or may not be coincident with shedding. That it ordinarily is not so coincident seems shown by the greater number of specimens in which we observe white hairs brown-tipped. As Mr. Bell contends, temperature is the immediate controlling agent. This is amply proven in the fact that the northern animals always change; that in those from intermediate latitudes the change is incomplete, while those from farther south do not change at all."†

Dr. Coues, it will be observed, states, without qualification, that "temperature is the immediate controlling agent" in this change of color, and remarks: "This is amply proven in the fact that the northern animals always change," etc. Now the facts with which I am familiar lead me to take a very different view of the case, and I am of opinion that temperature, *per se*, has very little to do, either with the time of the change, or the fact of the change; and in support of this view I adduce the following facts—and let it be understood that my observations pertain to the species as found in the

---

* Quadrupeds of North America, Vol. II, 1851, pp. 62–63.
† Fur-bearing Animals, 1877, p. 123.

Adirondack region only, for I have not seen it elsewhere during the transition. It has been my experience, and the experience of the many hunters and trappers that I have consulted on this point (an experience resulting from the examination of upwards of an hundred specimens caught at about the time of the first snow) that the Ermine never assumes the white coat till after the ground is covered with snow, which is generally late in October or early in November. It frequently happens that the temperature of the atmosphere is many degrees lower during the week or ten days preceding the first fall of snow than at, or immediately subsequent to, the time of its deposition. Notwithstanding these facts, it is equally true that Ermine caught up to the very day of the first appearance of snow bear no evidence of the impending change. Within forty-eight hours, however, after the occurrence of this snow-storm (provided enough has fallen to remain and cover the ground; and regardless of the temperature, which commonly rises several degrees soon after the storm sets in) the coat of the Ermine has already commenced to assume a pied and mottled appearance (often symmetrically marked and strikingly handsome), and the change now commenced progresses to its termination with great rapidity. In early spring, the period for the reversal of this process, the changing back from the white coat of winter to the brown summer coat is determined by the same cause—the presence or absence of snow.

It may be asked "what induces the change in individuals kept in confinement?" My reply is: *certainly not temperature*, for it has taken place when the animal was caged in a warm room, indoors. The transition is more tardy in confinement than in a state of nature, and may be coincident with the moult. In any case, we find the explanation of its occurrence in the inevitable influence of hereditary habit; and it is not rational to suppose that the temporary effect of different conditions of environment would, in a single season, nullify a tendency that is the outgrowth of causes that have been operating for ages to bring about and perpetuate certain fashions for the protection of the species.   And this leads us to the consideration of of an important element in the discussion, to wit, the cause, or causes, which, acting through a long period of years, resulted in establishing this seasonal change in color.   If the Ermine is the direct descendant of a dark-colored animal, and was, originally, an inhabitant of the temperate zone, it would have found, upon extending its range northward, and indeed, wherever snow covers the ground in winter, that its dark color, by rendering it conspicuous on the white surface, proved a disadvantage to it, both in the pursuit of its prey, and in the escape from its natural enemies.   Therefore, by individual variation, and by the effect of light upon the snow, aided and directed by the laws of natural selection, it finally got to assume, during the winter season, a dress that is in harmony with the objects among which it moves—a garb well adapted for the maintenance and preservation of the species.

Mr. Bell's theory, that the object of the white color is, by retarding radiation, to increase the amount of heat retained by the animal, is not only inadequate to account for the facts in the case, but, it seems to me, arises from straining a point (and an imagination as well!) to invent an improbable hypothesis for the explanation of a phenomenon the rationale of which is almost self-evident.   The cause cited must have played the part of a very subordinate factor.


## PUTORIUS VISON (Brisson) Gapper.

### Mink.

The Mink is a well-known and tolerably abundant inhabitant of this region, frequenting water-courses, and preying upon muskrats, rats, mice, birds and their eggs, fish, frogs, turtle's eggs, cray-fish, and fresh-water mussels.   It occasionally enters the poultry-yard of the border farmer and thins out his stock of ducks and chickens.   It also feeds upon the rabbit; and on the salt-water marshes of the South kills great numbers of the clapper rail and the sharp-tailed and seaside finches.

The Mink is an excellent example of an amphibious mammal, for it not only swims and dives with facility, but can remain long under water, and pursues and captures fish by following them under logs or other places from which there is not a free escape. It has thus been known to secure as swift and agile a fish as the brook-trout, and Audubon says that he has seen a Mink catch a trout upwards of a foot in length! It is remarkably strong for so small an animal, and a single one has been known to drag a mallard duck more than a mile, in order to get it to its hole, where its mate joined in the feast.

They are partially nocturnal, and hunt both at night and in broad daylight, like most of their tribe. I once saw three together on the banks of the outlet of Seventh Lake, and have many times met them singly about our water-courses, both in summer and in winter. They prowl about the lakes after nightfall and devour any fish that have been left on shore near the camps.

As an enemy to the farmer, in point of destructiveness in the poultry-yard, the Mink ranks next to the Ermine; and I sometimes incline to the opinion that, in the long run, more fowls and ducks are slain by him than by the last-named animal. He does not, it is true, make those occasional devastating raids, slaughtering everything that falls in his way, that constitute a chapter in the life-history of the Ermine, but takes one victim at a time, commonly devouring it before killing another. Still, the wholesale butchery sometimes carried on by the Ermine occurs at long and irregular intervals, whilst the depredations of the Mink are apt to be more frequent and continuous. Taking up his abode in, or in proximity to, the poultry-yard, or duck-pond, he is pretty sure to remain for weeks, helping himself, daily, to as many birds as his voracious appetite enables him to dispose of. His small size and partially nocturnal habits tend to conceal his movements, and the daily loss of a fowl is commonly laid at the door of the skunk, fox, or owl, long before the true marauder is suspected.

I find that many hunters and trappers believe that the Mink does not make long journeys, but remains in the vicinity of its nest, to

which it returns every twenty-four hours or thereabouts. My experience, in certain cases at least, proves the contrary. On the banks of a
stream, along which I once had a line of traps, I noticed at intervals
of two or three weeks, the tracks of an unusually large Mink. After
a long while I succeeded in tracking him to an old bridge, in a pasture, and on lifting the planks at one end discovered his nest (or one
of them). It consisted of a mass of dead leaves, a foot or more in
thickness, well lined with feathers. Alongside it were the remains of
a muskrat, a red squirrel, and a downy woodpecker, but the Mink
was not there—he had gone on up the stream. Concealing a good
Newhouse steel trap in the approach to his nest, I replaced the old
planks and went away. This was about the middle of October.
Two weeks passed without any indication of his return, but the time
had arrived when he might be expected to "happen around" almost
any day. I therefore made daily visits to the stream to search for
his tracks, taking care to avoid the immediate neighborhood of the
bridge. A heavy snow-storm now set in and next morning a foot of
newly fallen snow covered the ground. During this storm the Mink
returned and was caught. He was the largest and handsomest Mink
I have ever seen, and I regret to have lost the record of his dimensions, taken at the time. Some idea, however, of his size and the
quality of his fur may be had from the fact that his pelt sold for fourteen dollars.

This, and other more or less similar experiences, have convinced
me that the Mink frequently, if not commonly, makes long excursions,
like the Otter, following one water-course and then another, and returning over the same route; and I believe that they have a number
of nests scattered at convenient intervals along these circuits. This
habit may be confined to the old males, but whether it is so or not
remains to be proven.

Concerning its manner and actions when caught we have the following graphic account from the facile pen of Dr. Coues: " One who
has not taken a Mink in a steel trap can scarcely form an idea of the

terrible expression the animal's face assumes as the captor approaches. It has always struck me as the most nearly diabolical of anything in animal physiognomy. A sullen stare from the crouched, motionless form gives way to a new look of surprise and fear, accompanied with the most violent contortions of the body, with renewed champing of the iron, till breathless, with heaving flanks, and open mouth dribbling saliva, the animal settles again, and watches with a look of concentrated hatred, mingled with impotent rage and frightful despair. . . . As may well be supposed, the creature must not be incautiously dealt with when in such a frame of mind." *

When taken sufficiently young he is easily domesticated, and makes one of the very best of " ratters." He follows these common pests into their holes, and destroys large numbers of them. The remainder are so terrified that they leave the premises in great haste and are not apt soon to return.

The Mink carries a pair of anal glands that secrete a fluid of an extremely fetid and disgusting odor. It cannot be ejected to a distance, like that of the skunk, but is poured out under sexual excitement, and when the animal is enraged. It is commonly emitted when the beast is trapped, and sometimes becomes insufferably sickening while removing the skin. It is the most execrable smell with which my nostrils have as yet been offended, and is more powerful and offensive in some individuals than in others—the difference probably depending upon season and age. In one specimen the fetor was so intolerably rank and loathsome that I was unable to skin it at one sitting; and I am free to confess that it is one of the few substances, of animal, vegetable, or mineral origin, that has, on land or sea, rendered me aware of the existence of the abominable sensation called *nausea*.

The fur of the Mink being valuable, the species has been extensively trapped and is consequently not nearly so abundant here as formerly. It is prime early in November.

---

* Fur-Bearing Animals, 1877, p. 176.

They rut during the latter part of February or early in March, and during this season their tracks may be seen everywhere—along rocky ridges, over high mountains, and in all sorts of places. Dr. Bachman tells us that at this time the Mink "seems to keep on foot all day as well as through the whole night," and says further : " Having for several days in succession observed a number of Minks on the ice hurrying up and down a mill-pond, where we had not observed any during a whole winter, we took a position near a place which we had seen them pass, in order to procure some of them.

" We shot six in the course of the morning, and ascertained that they were all large and old males. As we did not find a single female in a week, whilst we obtained a great number of males, we came to the conclusion that the females, during this period, remain in their burrows." *

From four to six young constitute an ordinary litter, and they are brought forth early in May. The nests are in burrows or hollow logs and are usually well-lined with feathers, and sometimes, it is said, with the fur of the female. The young follow the mother till the fall, and then generally disperse to look out for themselves.

The famous *"Minkery"* of Mr. H. Resseque, at Verona, Oneida County, New York, has afforded rare facilities for the study of the breeding habits of this species, and from the accounts of it that have been published in the Fanciers' Journal and Poultry Exchange, and Forest and Stream, and summarized by Dr. Coues, I quote the following: "At this time [early in March] the males fight desperately, and if not soon separated one always gets the mastery. . . . . The females reproduce when one year old. The duration of gestation scarcely varies twelve hours from six weeks. There is but one litter annually. The litters run from three to ten in number; the young are born blind, and remain so for five weeks. When newly born, they are light-colored, hairless, and about the size and shape of a little finger.

---

* Quadrupeds of North America, vol. I, 1846, ·p. 258.

By the time the eyes are open, they are covered with a beautiful coat of glossy hair. The young females develop sooner than the males, attaining their stature in ten months, while the males are not full-grown until they are a year and a half old. It is noted that in every litter one or the other sex predominates in numbers, there being rarely half of them males and the other half females." *

Subfamily MEPHITINÆ.

## MEPHITIS MEPHITICA (Shaw) Baird.

*Skunk; Polecat; "Alaska Sable."*

The Skunk is very common in the clearings and settled districts bordering this region, and is found, sparingly, throughout the Adirondacks.

He preys upon mice, salamanders, frogs, and the eggs of birds that nest on, or within reach from, the ground. At times he eats carrion, and if he chances to stumble upon a hen's nest the eggs are liable to suffer; and once in a while he acquires the evil habit of robbing the hen-roost. Still, as a rule, Skunks are not addicted to this vice, and it is with them very much as it is with dogs and cats; for every now and then a dog will get into the habit of killing sheep, and a cat of killing chickens and sucking eggs, and yet we do not wage a warfare of extermination against them, collectively, on account of the sins of a few of their number.

Of all our native mammals perhaps no one is so universally abused, and has so many unpleasant things said about it, as the innocent subject of the present biography; and yet no other species is half so valuable to the farmer. Pre-eminently an insect eater, he destroys more beetles, grasshoppers, and the like than all our other mammals together, and in addition to these devours vast numbers of mice.

He is not fond of extensive forests, but seeks the clearings and pastures that surround the habitations of man, and not infrequently

* Fur-bearing Animals, 1877, pp. 182–183.

takes up his abode under one of the outbuildings ; or, retiring to a neighboring grove, may make his nest under an old stump, or dig a hole into some wooded knoll or side-hill hard by.  Being loath to intrude the presence of man, he sleeps away the day, and at nightfall comes forth to wander through the garden, orchard, and meadow, to prey upon the insects that feast upon the product of man's toil.

He is of the greatest practical value to the hop-grower, for he frequents the hop-yard with great regularity, and greedily devours the insect pests that, from their numbers and destructiveness, always injure, and sometimes ruin the crop.  Such is the extent and importance of the services rendered in this direction that, at a recent Session of our State Legislature, a bill was introduced for his protection.  Indeed, the benefit that accrues to the farmer from the occupancy of his premises by a family of these useful animals can hardly be over-estimated.  They are large eaters and subsist almost exclusively upon his greatest enemies—insects and mice.  Of the truth of this assertion he may easily convince himself by merely taking the trouble to examine any bit of " Skunk sign" that he happens to come across; for, in the summer season, their dejections consist wholly of the indigestible chitenous coverings of beetles, grasshoppers and other insects.  The raids that some of their numbers occasionally make upon his poultry-yard are more than compensated for by the constant and unremitting services of the entire family in ridding his fields and garden of the vermin that destroy his crops.  In fact, I do not hesitate to assert that a single Skunk nets the farmer more, in dollars and cents, each year, than he loses from their depredations during his entire life-time.  And yet so short-sighted is he, that he rarely lets slip a chance to kill one; and were they more diurnal in habits their race would doubtless, ere now, be well-nigh exterminated.

Many of our mammals are noted for their beauty and attractive appearance, but amongst them it would be difficult to find a prettier beast than the Skunk.  He was not built after the most graceful of patterns, to be sure, and it must be acknowledged that his snout is strongly suggestive of the pig's ; still, his *tout ensemble* is decidedly pleasing. There is nothing obscure in his color or markings. The handsome black body, the narrow white stripe running up the forehead, the clear white crown from which a broad band of the same color commonly extends down the nape, splitting into two as it passes along the back, contrasting handsomely with the glossy black of the surrounding fur, and the large, bushy tail, terminating in a tuft of creamy white, combine to produce an exterior of unusual attractiveness. His fur is long, thick, and glossy, and makes an elegant centre for a robe. During the past few years prime pelts (those lacking the white back stripes) have been largely employed in the manufacture of fine furs, and are sold under the *nom de guerre* of " Alaska Sable."

Excepting alone the weasels, the Skunk is the least wary, not only of the *Mustelidæ*, but of all our Carnivores. He is not suspicious, and may be taken in almost any kind of a device contrived for the purpose—box-traps, steel-traps, and dead-falls being most commonly employed in his destruction. To the trapper he often proves a source of great annoyance, by getting into toils set for the fox and other more valuable fur.

He does not evince that dread of man that is so manifest in the vast majority of our mammals, and when met during any of his circumambulations rarely thinks of running away. On the contrary, his curiosity is aroused, and he is full as apt to come towards one as to make off in the opposite direction. He is slow in movement and deliberate in action, and does not often hurry himself in whatever he does. His ordinary gait is a measured walk, but when pressed for time he breaks into a low, shuffling gallop. It is hard to intimidate a Skunk, but when once really frightened he manages to get over the ground at a very fair pace.

He is an inquisitive beast, and will often take much trouble to examine anything peculiar about the premises. One evening, while sitting near the open door of my museum, one came and peeped in at me.  As I remained motionless he climbed up and rested his fore-paws on the threshold, so near that I could easily have reached him with my hands.  After carefully scrutinizing me with his keen, black eyes, he began to stamp and scold saucily, and then backed slowly off, keeping his eye on me all the while.  Scarcely had he commenced this quasi-retreat, when he chanced to back into a beech-tree that stood near by.  Evidently thinking that someone had at-tacked him from the rear (risky business!) he whirled about in a jiffy, with his tail up and hair on end, growling excitedly, and scampered away into the bushes.

Skunks are so slow to get out of the way that they are often run over by vehicles in the evening, and are liable, under such circum-stances, to perfume the establishment unapproachably.  I have had many such experiences.

When engaged in the nefarious business of plundering the poultry-yard (an iniquity to which he rarely descends) he makes no provision for escape, and, in the terse language of Dr. Coues, "even after dis-covery, the Skunk seems to forget the propriety of making off, and generally falls a victim to his lack of wit."

Skunks remain active throughout the greater part of the year, in this region, and hibernate only during the severest portion of the winter.  They differ from most of our hibernating mammals in that the inactive period is, apparently, dependent solely upon the temper-ature ; in this respect they resemble the gray squirrel.  That the amount of snow has no influence upon their movements is evident from the fact that they are frequently out, in numbers, when its average depth exceeds a metre and a half (a trifle over five feet) on the level.  Neither can it be a difference in food supply that affects them, for at this season they subsist almost wholly upon mice and shrews, and I have repeatedly noticed these little beasts scamp-ering about on the crisp snow when the thermometer indicated a temperature below $-30°$ C. $(-20°$ F.)  With us there is apt to be a month or six weeks of very cold weather in January or February, and during its continuance I have never seen evidence of their presence ; for it is at such times that they " den up." The length of time that they remain in their holes depends entirely upon the duration of the period of low temperature, and they are always out and active with the first thaws of March. The occurrence of a thaw, at any time, commonly brings them to the surface, but a recurrence of the severe cold suffices to drive them back to their burrows.

Skunks, particularly when young, make very pretty pets, being attractive in appearance, gentle in disposition, interesting in manners, and cleanly in habits—rare qualities indeed! They are playful, sometimes mischievous, and manifest considerable affection for those who have the care of them. I have had, at different times, ten live Skunks in confinement. They were all quite young, measuring from 100 to 150 mm. (approximately 4 to 7 in.) only, in length, when first taken. Some were dug out of their holes, and the rest caught in box traps. Two were so young that they could walk but a few steps at a time, and had to be brought up on milk, being fed with a spoon. The others ate meat and insects from the start. From some of them I removed the scent bags, but the greater number were left in a state of nature. None ever emitted any odor, although a couple of them, when half grown, used to assume a painfully suggestive attitude on the too-near approach of strangers—so suggestive, indeed, that their visitors commonly beat a hasty retreat. These same Skunks, when I came within reach, would climb up my legs and get into my arms. They liked to be caressed, and never offered to bite. Others that I have had did not show the aversion for strangers evinced by this pair, and I believe the difference to be due to the way in which they are brought up. If accustomed to the presence of a number of people they are familiar and friendly toward all; while if kept where they habitually see but one or two persons they will not permit a stranger to touch them.

Two summers ago I was the happy master of the cleverest young Skunk that I have thus far chanced to meet. For a name he receiv-

6

ed the title of his genus, and we called him " Meph." for short.   By
way of precaution I removed his scent sacs, and he made a rapid
and complete recovery, after a few days of temporary indisposition.
While driving about the country, in the performance of professional
duties, he usually slept in my pocket.   After supper I commonly took
a walk, and he always followed, close at my heels.   If I chanced to
walk too fast for him, he would scold and stamp with his fore-feet,
and if I persisted in keeping too far ahead, would turn about, disgust-
ed, and make off in an opposite direction ; but if I stopped and called
him he would hurry along at a sort of ambling pace, and soon overtake me.   He was particularly fond of ladies, and I think it was the
dress that attracted him; but be this as it may he would invariably
leave me to follow any lady that chanced to come near.   We used
to walk through the woods to a large meadow which abounded in
grasshoppers.   Here " Meph." would fairly revel in his favorite food,
and it was rich sport to watch his manœuvres.   When a grasshopper
jumped he jumped, and I have seen him with as many as three in
his mouth, and two under his fore-paws, at one time !   He would eat
so many that his over-distended little belly actually dragged upon the
ground, and when so full that he could hold no more, would still catch
and slay them.   When so small that he could scarcely toddle about he
never hesitated to tackle the large and powerful beetle known as the
" horned bug," and got many smart nips for his audacity.   But he
was a courageous little fellow and it was not long before he learned
to handle them with impunity, and it was very amusing to see him
kill one.   Ere many weeks he ventured to attack a mouse, and the
ferocity displayed in its destruction was truly astonishing.   He devoured the entire body of his victim, and growled and stamped his
feet if anyone came near before the repast was over.

His nest was in a box near the foot of the stairs, and before he
grew strong enough to climb out by himself he would, whenever he
heard me coming, stand on his hind legs with his paws resting on the
edge of the box, and beg to be carried up-stairs.   If I passed by

without appearing to notice him he invariably became much enraged and chippered and scolded away at a great rate, stamping, meanwhile, most vehemently. He always liked to be carried up to my office, and as soon as strong enough, would climb up of his own accord. He was very sprightly and frolicsome, and used to hop about the floor and run from room to room in search of something to play with, and frequently amused himself by attempting to demolish my slippers. I have often given him a bit of old sponge, with a string attached, in order to keep him out of mischief. During the evening he occasionally assumed a cunning mood, and would steal softly up to my chair, and standing erect would claw at my pants once or twice, and then scamper off as fast as his little legs could carry him, evidently anxious to have me give chase. If I refused to follow, he was soon back, ready to try a new scheme to attract my attention.

I have heard many persons, who reside in the country, say that they had never seen a live Skunk. This must be because they are not much in the fields and groves at dawn of day, or dusk of evening, for at these times they are frequently seen. The farmer's boy, in going after his cows early every morning, meets plenty of them.

Skunks have large families, from six to ten young being commonly raised each season; and as a rule they all live in the same hole till the following spring. A steel trap, set at the mouth of this hole, will often capture the entire family, at the rate of one per night. In winter half a dozen or more may sometimes be taken in a single night, in the following manner : the hunter treads a narrow path in the snow, leading from the mouth of the hole away in the direction of some favorite resort and, at intervals along this path, the traps are set in the snow. At nightfall, when the Skunks come out, they march, single file, down the path, the mother usually taking the lead. The head one is generally caught in the first trap, and the others climb over the resulting obstruction and move on till a second is taken, and a third, and so on.

The flesh of the Skunk is white, tender and sweet, and is delicious eating. It is not unlike chicken, but is more delicate, and its taste is particularly agreeable. Being, happily, free from any of that " squeamishness" which Audubon and Bachman lament as preventing them from tasting the meat of this animal, I am able to speak on this point from ample personal experience—having eaten its flesh cooked in a variety of ways, boiled, broiled, roasted, fried, and fricasseed—and am prepared to assert that a more " toothsome bit " than a broiled Skunk is hard to get, and rarely finds its way to the table of the epicure.

The fore-feet of the Skunk are provided with long claws, which he employs in excavating his burrows and in digging after mice, which latter occupation consumes a large share of his time. He is also armed with a fine set of sharp teeth, that are capable of inflicting severe wounds; still, his chief weapon of defence lies in the secretion of a pair of anal glands, that lie on either side of the rectum, and are imbedded in a dense, gizzard-like mass of muscle which serves to compress them so forcibly that the contained fluid may be ejected to the distance of four or five metres (approximately 13 to 16½ feet). Each sac is furnished with a single duct that leads into a prominent nipple-like papilla that is capable of being protruded from the anus, and by means of which the direction of the jet is governed. The secretion is a clear limpid fluid of an amber or golden yellow color, has an intensely acid reaction, and, in the evening, is slightly luminous. On standing, in a bottle, a flocculent, whitish precipitate separates and falls to the bottom. The fluid sometimes shows a decided greenish cast, and it always possesses an odor that is characteristic, and in some respects unique. Its all-pervading, penetrating, and lasting properties are too well known to require more than passing comment. I have known the scent to become strikingly apparent in every part of a well-closed house, in winter, within five minutes' time after a Skunk had been killed at a distance of an hundred metres (about twenty rods)! The odor generally remains noticeable for weeks, and sometimes for months, about the place where one has been killed. The condition of the atmosphere has much to do in determining this matter, for the more humid the air and the higher the temperature, the farther is the scent discernible, and the longer does it last. Under favorable conditions it is certainly distinctly recognizable at the distance of a mile, and DeKay quotes a statement from the Medical Repository that a Dr. Wiley, of Block Island, "distinctly perceived the smell of a Skunk, although the nearest land was twenty miles distant"!*

There is a marked difference in the intensity of the scent in different Skunks, and I am persuaded that it is due, chiefly, to the age of the animal whence it emanates. It is not impossible that there may also be a difference due to the length of time that the secretion has been retained, i. e., that it is not so rank and overpowering when recently secreted as when there has been no discharge for some time— when it seems to have become concentrated.

When recently ejected the fumes from this liquid are overpoweringly pungent, and extremely irritating to the air passages; and, I have no doubt, are as capable of producing œdema of the glottis as the fumes from stronger ammonia. When inhaled without the admixture of a large amount of atmospheric air the unhappy victim loses consciousness and breathes stertorously, the temperature falls and the pulse slackens, and if the inhalation were prolonged the result would doubtless prove fatal.†

---

* Zoology of New York, Mammals, 1842, p. 30.

† In connection with the foregoing remarks, I introduce the following clipping, which has gone the rounds of the Medical press :

"SKUNK PERFUME AS AN ANÆSTHETIC.—Dr. W. B. Conway (*Virginia Medical Monthly*, August, 1881) reports a case where roguish school-boys caused one of their number to inhale from a two-ounce phial an unknown quantity of Skunk perfume. The effects produced were total unconsciousness, muscular relaxation, a temperature of 94 and pulse of 65, together with cool extremities. The respiration and pupils were normal. The patient soon recovered under hot pediluvia and stimulants. The Skunk perfume is rather an unpleasant substance to experiment with, still, those endowed with anosmia might obtain results of value from similar experiments with it."

Dr. Conway (of Blacksburg, Va.) further stated that the patient "remained for one hour" in a state of "total unconsciousness." During that time the Doctor "administered small quantities of whiskey at short intervals," having "some difficulty in getting him to swallow. . . . He was finally aroused, suffering no inconvenience from its effects except a slight headache, which passed off after a good night's sleep." (Virg. Med. Month., Vol. VIII, No. 5, Aug., 1881, pp. 359–360.)

The evidence is pretty conclusive that the peculiar substance under consideration is an efficacious remedy in certain spasmodic affections of the air passages, such as asthma, hooping-cough, and spasmodic croup. It certainly deserves more extended trial, but, unfortunately, its offensive odor is a practical bar to its general employment. Still, to my nostrils, it is not half so disagreeable as many less wholesome smells. It is powerful, pungent, and penetrating, to be sure, but is not one-tenth part so disgustingly nauseating as the secretion from the corresponding glands of many other members of the *Mustelidæ*, and particularly of the mink and weasel.

If any of this acrid liquid finds its way into the eye it produces intense pain and sets up an acute conjunctivitis, which commonly runs its course in a week or ten days. I have myself met with this misfortune, but suffered no permanent injury therefrom. However, we have reliable accounts of the entire loss of vision from this cause, and it is reasonable to suppose that attendant circumstances would have much to do with the result.

The scent glands of the Skunk may be removed, bodily, without in any way affecting the health or happiness of the animal. The gizzard-like mass of muscle in which they are imbedded completely surrounds the gut, just at the outlet of the pelvis, and is attached to the tuberosities of the ischium. The chief danger attending the operation is the liability of wounding the rectum, or of creating so much irritation about it that the subsequent inflammation and cicatrization will result in stricture of that important viscus. Care must also be exercised in order to avoid wounding the genito-urinary passages. I have operated, with complete success, both with and without antiseptic precautions. A much simpler operation, where the end in view is merely to disarm the animal, is that performed by Dr. J. M. Warren, of Boston, in the year 1849.* It consists in making an incision through the skin, directly in front of the anus, and in snipping the ducts of the glands, at the bases of the nipple-like

* "Proceed. Bost. Soc. Nat. Hist., vol. III, p. 175, 1849."

papillæ which project into the gut, just within the sphincter. Adhesive inflammation follows and permanently occludes the ducts at the points of division. Therefore, although the glands themselves are left in situ, the animal is, forever after, incapable of ridding himself of their contents.

The Skunk is a sort of "little lord" of the domain over which he roams, for there are few enemies, save short-sighted man, that care to dispute his right of way. It is true that the wolf, fox, and great-horned owl occasionally dine upon his tender flesh, but the details of the struggle, inevitable to his capture, are not altogether pleasant; hence he is not often interfered with, and becomes as bold as he is abundant. Concerning his confidence in the efficacy of his over-powering weapon, and the effect of this assurance upon his disposition and habits, Dr. Coues makes the following pertinent remarks—condensing into one brief sentence thoughts that suggest whole chapters in the history of this interesting animal : " Its heedless familiarity, its temerity in pushing into places which other animals avoid as dangerous, and its indisposition to seek safety by hasty retreat, are evident results of its confidence in the extraordinary means of defence with which it is provided." And further on observes : "the abundance of the animal in most parts of the country, and its audacity in the face of danger, show that its confidence in the singular means of defence it possesses is not misplaced."*

Dr. Coues expresses the belief in which I cannot concur, that the scent of the Skunk is not only used as a means of defence, but also serves as a means or bringing these animals together—that they are attracted to one another by it—and goes on to say : " Burrows are sometimes found to contain as many as a dozen individuals, not members of one family, but various adult animals drawn together." Now, as previously stated, the Skunk is a very prolific animal, commonly bringing forth from six to ten at a birth, and these young, with their parents, remain in one hole for the ensuing year. Before the expira-

---

* Loc. cit., p. 215.

tion of this period the young Skunks have grown up and several of
them, at least, have attained the full dimensions of their parents, so
that it is impossible to distinguish between them except by a careful
examination of their teeth and claws; and even these means sometimes fail, as when the parents themselves are but a year older than
their offspring, and nothing short of a comparison of their skulls affords positive evidence of their ages. I have dwelt thus at length
on this point in order to show how easy it is to be mistaken in the
ages of Skunks after the first six or eight months, so rapidly do they
attain their growth; and I have yet to see satisfactory evidence that
more than two adult Skunks have been found in the same hole at
any one time.

### How to Kill a Skunk.

When we bear in mind that thousands of Skunks are slain each
year for their fur, it is indeed surprising that so few hunters, trappers, and naturalists should know how to kill them, without provok-
ing a discharge from their scent reservoirs. And yet there is a
method, *safe, sure, and simple,* by which they may be killed without
the emission of a single drop of the much dreaded secretion. This
method depends upon the well-known physiological fact that an injury to the spinal cord produces immediate paralysis or loss of
power of the muscles supplied by the nerves that are given off below
the point of injury. Hence, loss of control over the posterior extremities (a condition technically known as *paraplegia*) may be produced, in any mammal, by a blow across the back that is sufficiently
forcible to destroy the integrity of the cord opposite the injured point.
The back must generally be broken to insure this result.

Therefore, to kill a Skunk without permitting the evacuation of
its peculiar perfume, it is only necessary to deal it a smart rap across
the back. If the animal is in a trap he should be approached slowly
and cautiously, for, under these circumstances it is prudent not to be
in too much of a hurry, and to avoid making sudden moves. If you go

too fast he will elevate his tail, present his rear, and assume an uncomfortably suspicious attitude. Give him a little time and he will about-face and peer at you again with his little keen black eyes. Now advance a little nearer and be sure of your aim; and when you strike, *strike hard.* The main thing is to keep cool and not strike too soon. On receiving the blow his hinder parts settle helplessly upon the ground, and the tail, which was carried high over the back, now straightens out behind, limp and powerless. As a rule the head soon droops and the animal expires. If he does not die directly he is easily dispatched, being effectually disarmed. The common causes of failure, in this mode of killing, are two: 1st, in using too long a pole, and consequently striking when so far off that the beast has time to jump forward (in attempting to dodge the blow) and is hit too far aft—often on the tail; and 2d, in not striking hard enough to break the back. When properly done this method never fails, and it is the safest, surest, and simplest way to kill a Skunk without occasioning a discharge from his battery. I speak with some confidence on this point, having myself killed upwards of an hundred Skunks in the manner above recommended. Out of this number were six failures, due to the causes above specified.

It has been asserted, on high authority, that if the Skunk is shot in a vital part he will die without discharging his scent. This is an error, as I have demonstrated repeatedly to my entire satisfaction. I have put the muzzle of my double-barrelled shot-gun within a foot from the head of a Skunk, that was in a steel-trap, and literally blown his whole head off; under similar circumstances have I tried the effect of both shot and ball upon his heart and lungs; and further, on one occasion, I severed the head from the body with one blow from a sharp axe, and in each instance was the death struggle accompanied by a discharge of the scent. These remarks may seem to conflict with the writings of Audubon and Bachman, who state: "We had one of their burrows opened to within a foot of the extremity, where the animals were huddled together. Placing ourselves a few yards off, we suffered them successively to come out. As they slowly emerged and were walking off, they were killed with coarse shot aimed at the shoulders. In the course of half an hour, seven (the number contained in the burrow) were obtained; one only was offensive, and we were enabled without inconvenience to prepare six of them for specimens." * But it is explicitly mentioned that " they were killed with coarse shot aimed at the shoulders," and this fact explains why six out of seven did not smell, for some of the shot doubtless hit the cord.

Skunks caught in dead-falls rarely ever emit scent, and for the simple reason that their backs are broken and their hinder parts paralyzed.

A veteran fox-trapper, Mr. C. L. Whitman, of Weston, Vermont, rids his traps of Skunks by slipping a wire noose over their heads and choking them to death. He claims that they rarely smell when thus dealt with.†

When caught in the vicinity of water, they are easily drowned, and when so treated never smell.

### SOME COMMON FALLACIES CONCERNING SKUNKS.

#### *1st. What the Scent is.*

It was for many years believed, even amongst naturalists, that the scent of the Skunk was its urine, and this belief is still widely prevalent with the masses of our population. The urine of the Skunk has no offensive or even characteristic odor, the scent being the secretion of a pair of highly developed and specialized anal glands, which have already been sufficiently described. (See p. 76.)

#### *2d. How it is Scattered.*

The vulgar notion that the Skunk scatters its scent with its tail was formerly so universal and wide spread that no less renowned a

---

* Quadrupeds of North America, vol. I, 1846, p. 324.

† Forest and Stream, Feb. 17, 1876. Quoted by Coues in Fur-bearing Animals, 1877, p. 217.

zoologist than the accurate and sagacious Dr. Richard Harlan was (mis-) led to write that these animals emit, " particularly when disturbed, a most nauseous, detestable odor, proceeding from the liquor of the anal glands, which they mix with the urine; with this fluid they wet the tail, and scatter it to a considerable distance."* No statement could have less foundation in fact. The Skunk is a very cleanly beast, and, when about to discharge his scent, arches his tail high over his back so that it may not be defiled by the fluid. The scent is thrown by the contraction of the thick muscular tunic in which the glands are imbedded.

### 3d. When do they part with it?

It is commonly believed, by the community at large, that a Skunk is always ready to spatter anyone that chances to come within range. Nothing could be wider from the truth. A Skunk generally waits till he is hurt before discharging his battery, and I have more than once seen a dog get fairly hold of the beast before the emission occurred. Indeed, I have never known one to eject a single drop of the precious fluid except when hard pressed and very much excited— and it takes considerable to excite an adult Skunk. When caught in steel traps not more than one in twenty will smell, and the remaining nineteen suffer themselves to be tormented to an astonishing degree before " opening the valve." One may, with considerable confidence, approach one when in a trap, take hold of the chain, and drag the trap and contents to any convenient place, provided he goes slowly and makes no sudden move. Never but once has my confidence been betrayed while thus engaged. It was when attempting to drag a young Skunk out of its hole, into which it had retreated with the trap; and I was well sprinkled in the operation. These unsophisticated juveniles, when harassed, get excited far more easily than their parents, and sometimes " squirt " upon insufficient provocation.

* Fauna Americana, 1825, p. 69.

It is supposed by many that the Skunk empties his scent sacs at other times than during the excitement of danger; that it is done to attract the opposite sex, or for practice, or for some other reason than the annoyance of his enemy.   This is contrary to my experience, and is also, I believe, at variance with the facts of the case, so far as known.

### 4th.  Does one Discharge empty the Sacs ?

It is frequently asserted, by those having little or no personal acquaintance with these animals, that the Skunk completely empties his scent reservoirs at the first discharge, and becomes, immediately thereafter, " as harmless as a cat."   To such as entertain this opinion I extend a cordial invitation to accompany me to the presence of a Skunk, whom I will provoke to make several distinct and separate discharges, and will then step aside and be pleased to see them pick up the " harmless " animal !

### 5th.  When held by the Tail, what ?

I have been told, and have likewise seen the statement in print, that a Skunk, when held up by the tail, cannot eject his scent.

Having in early childhood been the unhappy victim to a sufficiently satisfactory demonstration to the contrary, I will relate the result of a somewhat humiliating experience, for the benefit of those who are in doubt on this point.   It was in the fall of the year, and a light snow enabled me to track a Skunk to his hole in the woods, where I set a box trap, baited with meat.   Next morning I found the trap sprung, but, hearing no noise within, opened the lid. Before I had time to see what was there my little dog rushed in, and as I reached out my arm to pull him back, I somehow got hold of the Skunk's tail by mistake.   My chin dropped with astonishment as I held the affrighted beast up before me, and the dog seized him by the head.   Scarce had I realized the peril of the situation when I was blinded and stifled by the terrible discharge, which hit me full in the face, entering my gaping mouth and one of my eyes. Nearly suffocated by the overpowering stench, and screaming with pain, I rushed into the house, where, in the efforts to wash the fluid from my eye, my head was crowded into a pail of water, and I was well nigh drowned. I had read that a single drop of the secretion was sufficient to produce total blindness, and consequently expected nothing less than to lose the sight in this eye. The resulting inflammation, however, subsided in about a week, leaving no ill effect.*

### 6th. Skunk Bites and Hydrophobia.

Under this head I take the liberty to reproduce an article that I wrote for *Forest and Stream* in July, 1880 :

" Ever since the Rev. Horace G. Hovey, M. A., took it upon himself to notify the civilized world (through the medium of the *American Journal of Science and Arts* for May, 1874, pp. 477–483) of the terrible consequences attending the bite of our common Skunk (*Mephitis mephitica*), the columns of your valuable paper, together with those of various other publications, have been much of the time pregnant with more or less extended remarks upon the subject.

" The Rev. Mr. Hovey announced that the bite of the Skunk was usually fatal, and produces in the human subject a peculiar kind of hydrophobia, which he named *Rabies Mephitica*. In the *New York Medical Record* for March 13, 1875, Dr. John S. Janeway, U. S. A., proves that the disease is nothing more nor less than ordinary hydrophobia as derived from the dog, cat, or other rabid animal.

" Dr. Elliott Coues deems the subject of sufficient importance to reproduce both articles (Rev. Hovey's and Dr. Janeway's), but

---

* Since penning the above I have again had the misfortune to get a charge of this fluid into one of my eyes. It was due to carelessness on my part, and occurred August 10, 1882, while removing the scent glands from a young Skunk. The contents of one of the sacs was suddenly and unexpectedly discharged, striking me full in the right eye. For a time the pain was intense, but I immediately and thoroughly washed out the fluid by pumping water into the open eye, and the conjunctival congestion that ensued subsided in a few hours. But in this case the fluid was not nearly so strong and irritating as that from the adult animal.

unfortunately without comment, in his most admirable and valuable monograph of our Fur-bearing Animals (pp. 223–235).

" Dr. Janeway states that the disease ' is evidently epidemical, no cases of it having been reported previous to 1870 in this region,' which is unquestionably the fact.

" Now it strikes me that there is a good deal of first-class ' poppycock' in the Rev. Mr. Hovey's article, and in most of the contributions that have appeared since

" Let us take a rational view of the case, and glance, for a moment, at the history of an average outbreak of hydrophobia. Here is a rabid dog. Before succumbing to the disease, or to the hand of man, he has probably bitten at least one or two other dogs or cats, which in their turn bite others, and so on, till the community becomes aroused; and scarcely enough of these animals are left to propagate their kind.

" Now, suppose a 'mad dog' should, in his wild delirium, chance to run across and bite a Skunk, and in a region where Skunks happened to abound, would not the natural result be that this Skunk would bite others and so communicate the disease to them, and they to others still, and so on till most of the Skunks of that neighborhood had been infected? During a certain stage of the disease, should any of these hydrophobic Skunks, by any accident fall in with a man sleeping on the ground, that man would certainly be very liable to be bitten, and if bitten, to die of this terrible malady. Exactly such a state of things, apparently, came to the notice of Mr. Hovey, who published the facts in the *American Journal of Science and Arts*, as above stated. But instead of confining his remarks to a simple, truthful narration of facts, he indulges in the wildest speculations and empty theories concerning the fatal nature of Skunk bites in the abstract.

" To suggest, as does the Rev. Hovey, that the bite of a healthy Skunk is followed by hydrophobia is, to speak mildly, the height of irrational nonsense. Equally insane is his idea that Skunks, in the normal state, are aggressive animals and habitually bite those persons whom they find sleeping upon the ground. Indeed nothing could be more contrary to the known habits and disposition of these beautiful and useful little animals.

"As to the effect of Skunk bites in general I will only state my experience. Twelve or fifteen years ago, when hunting and trapping Skunks, I was twice bitten by adult animals and never suffered therefrom more than from equally severe bites from any other of our common mammals. About the same time Dr. C. L. Bagg was also bitten, but nevertheless he still lives and is practising medicine in New York City. Last summer I was again bitten by a Skunk—this time by a half-grown one that I had alive for several months—and have as yet experienced no evil consequences from the bite.[*] Our dogs have many times been bitten, and were never seriously injured thereby."[†]

## Subfamily LUTRINÆ.

## LUTRA CANADENSIS Turton.

### *Otter.*

The Otter is a common inhabitant of the Adirondacks and, from the nature of its habits, and its sagacity, is likely to remain after most of the other representatives of the Mustelidæ have been exterminated. It is thoroughly amphibious, making long journeys through the forest, and swimming the lakes and rivers. It can remain under water almost as long as a Loon, and I have known one to swim nearly a quarter of a mile without showing its head above the surface. Its food consists chiefly of various species of fish, and the lobster-like fresh water Decapod called the cray-fish. When unable to procure these in sufficient quantity it devours frogs, and is said to depopulate

---

* While these pages have been passing through the press I have again been bitten by a half-grown Skunk. The bite was inflicted upon the end of my left thumb, and healed kindly in the course of three or four days, leaving no scar.

† Forest and Stream, Vol. XVI, No. 24, p. 473, July 14, 1881.

the poultry-yard, and even to prey upon young lambs. It can dive and swim under water with such speed and agility, that it can overtake and secure, with great ease and certainty, almost any of our fresh-water fishes. In confinement it will eat meat, and is said to prefer it boiled. The number of cray-fish (*Cambarus*) that the Otter destroys in the course of a summer is almost incredible. The Otter "sign" that one finds so abundantly about our lakes and streams, on rocks and logs, often consists wholly of fragments of the chitenous exoskeleton of this Crustacean. At other times fish bones are mingled with the broken cray-fish shells. Otters are restless creatures, always on the move, and are constantly roaming about from lake to lake, and river to river. They sometimes go from place to place "just as it happens," so to speak; while at other times they travel in definite routes, following one water course for a number of days or weeks, and returning by another. For example: an Otter will start from, say, Seventh Lake, and work down the Fulton Chain to Moose River, down Moose to Black River, and down this to the mouth of Independence or Beaver River; thence, turning up stream, it finds its way back along either of these rivers, perhaps stopping to fish in adjacent lakes on the way up, and finally crossing to Big Moose and thence back to the Fulton Chain. Or, starting from the same point, an Otter may leave the Fulton Chain near the foot of Fourth Lake, cross to North Branch of Moose River, thence to Big Moose, visiting the Saffords and West Pond on the way. From Big Moose it may work up into the big marsh and over to First and Second Gull Ponds, cross to Lake Terror and follow its outlet through Rose Pond to Beaver River, and down the latter to Black River, making the return trip up Independence to Big Moose, and across, by way of Constable Pond, May's Lake, and Queer Lake, to the Fulton Chain; or it may follow up Moose River directly to the Fulton Chain. These routes are not mere creations of my imagination, but have in great measure been verified by hunters who have followed their tracks on the snow. Otters travel great distances in winter, and go so fast that a man has great difficulty in overtaking them. On the ice they proceed by a series of what small boys call " a run and a slide," that is, they make several jumps and then slide ahead, flat on their bellies, as far as their impetus and the smoothness of the ice permit, and then do the same thing over again, and so on. And this mode of progression suggests a curious trait in the character of the Otter, *i. e.*, its fondness for sliding down hill. Dr. John D. Godman, in his well-known work on " American Natural History," speaks thus of the habit: " Their favorite sport is sliding, and for this purpose in winter the highest ridge of snow is selected, to the top of which the Otters scramble, where, lying on the belly with the fore-feet bent backwards, they give themselves an impulse with their hind legs and swiftly glide head-foremost down the declivity, sometimes for a distance of twenty yards. This sport they con-tinue apparently with the keenest enjoyment until fatigue or hunger induces them to desist." This statement accords with the observations of Cartwright, Hearne, Richardson, Audubon, and others, and the last-named author goes on to say that he once witnessed a pair of Otters engaged in this pastime, only they were sliding down a mud-bank instead of a snow-bank, and remarks: " we counted each one making twenty-two slides before we disturbed their sportive occupation." * The borders of the lakes and streams of the Adirondacks afford numerous examples of these slides, and also of their wallowing places, which are either level beds, or slight depressions, in which they play and roll. May's Lake, a small and secluded body of water, abounding in trout, is fairly surrounded by them.

On the morning of October 27, 1881, the Big Marsh at the head of Big Moose Lake was frozen over, with the exception of a narrow strip along its north shore. While working our boat up between the ice and the shore E. L. Sheppard and I noticed three Otters sporting in the open water ahead. They were diving and chasing one another after the manner of so many seals. Several times did they jump so

---

* Quadrupeds of North America, Vol. II, 1851, p. 8.

high that more than half the length of their bodies showed above the water. On firing at one of them all instantly disappeared; one stuck his head up through a hole in the ice to take a parting peep at us, and this was the last we saw of them. Otters are playful creatures and when taken young are easily domesticated, and have frequently been taught to catch fish for their masters. In growing old, however, they are apt to become ugly, and have been known to bite those who attempted to play with them. At all times and on all occasions they manifest an insatiate and uncontrollable desire to break the peace with any dog that chances to cross their path—and woe be to the unfortunate brute! Being compactly built and possessing great strength, and an immense store of endurance, they are quick in movement and make fierce and powerful assailants. Moreover, there is usually such a thick layer of fat under the skin that it slips freely upon the body and renders it well-nigh impossible for a dog to secure a firm hold on them. If the misunderstanding occurs in the vicinity of water, as it commonly does, there is a strong tendency for the participants to drift nearer and nearer the shore, for thitherward the Otter artfully draws his antagonist. I have never witnessed one of these little altercations, but am told that a drowned dog is generally the result.

Thomas Pennant, in his " Synopsis of Quadrupeds," published in 1771, says (p. 239) that the Otter " hunts its prey against the stream; frequents not only fresh waters, but sometimes preys in the sea; but not remote from shore: is a fierce animal; its bite hard and dangerous: is capable of being tamed, to follow its master like a dog, and even to fish for him, and return with its prey."

The fur of the Otter, which is more valuable than that of any other of our fur bearing animals, becomes prime in November, remains good throughout the winter, and is best in spring.

Their skins were formerly much employed by the Indians as material for their garments. In " Wassenaers Historie Van Europa," printed at Amsterdam, 1621–32, occurs the following : " The

Tribes are in the habit of clothing themselves with them; the fur or hair inside, the smooth side without, which, however, they paint so beautifully that, at a distance, it resembles lace. It is the opinion that they make use of the best for that purpose; what has poor fur they deem unsuitable for their clothing. When they bring their commodities to the Traders, and find they are desirous to buy them, they make so very little matter of it, that they at once rip up the skins they are clothed with and sell them as being the best."*

The nest of the Otter is generally placed under some shelving bank or uprooted tree, and has been found in a hollow stub. The young are commonly brought forth about the middle of April, and two (rarely one or three) constitute a litter. Three Otters, the female with her two young, are usually seen together during the summer and fall.

## Family PROCYONIDÆ.

## PROCYON LOTOR (Linn.) Storer.

### *Raccoon.*

Raccoons are common everywhere about the borders of the Adirondacks, but they do not like dense evergreen forests and are therefore rather rare in the interior; still, they are occasionally met with in all parts of the Wilderness.

They are omnivorous beasts and feed upon mice, young birds, birds' eggs, turtles and their eggs, frogs, fish, cray-fish, mollusks, insects, nuts, fruits, corn, and sometimes poultry.

Excepting alone the bats and flying-squirrels, they are the most strictly nocturnal of all our mammals, and yet I have several times seen them abroad during cloudy days. They like to play in shallow water, along the banks of ponds and streams, and find much of their food in these places. They overturn stones and catch the cray-fish that lurk beneath, and also gather the fresh-water mussels (*Unio* and *Anodon*) that live on sandy and muddy bottoms. They also catch

---

* Translated in The Documentary Hist. of the State of New York, Vol. III, 1850, p. 36.

and devour the hapless fish that chance to get detained in any of the little pools along shore; but are unable to dive and pursue their prey under water, like the Otter and Mink. They are good swimmers and do not hesitate to cross rivers that lie in their path.

Although excellent climbers, making their nests in a hollow, high up in some large tree, they cannot be said to be arboreal in habits. They do not pursue their prey amongst the tree tops, after the manner of the martens, nor make a practice of gathering nuts from the branches, like squirrels; nor do they, like the porcupine, browse upon the green foliage. Trees constitute the homes in which they rest and bring forth their young, and to which they retreat when pursued by man or beast; but their business is transacted elsewhere. At nightfall they descend to the ground to prowl through groves, fields, and swamps, and follow streams and lake shores in search of food.

Their fondness for fresh corn has brought many a luckless 'Coon to an untimely end, for " 'Coon hunting, by the light of the harvest moon," has long been a favorite sport. The method of procedure is simple : several men, with dogs, meet together, generally about midnight, near some maize field which is known to be frequented by these animals. If a Raccoon happens to be present he is soon treed by the dogs, and is either shot, or the tree upon which he hides is felled and he is destroyed by the dogs. An old 'Coon is a tough match for an average dog, and many a plucky cur bears lasting scars of their sharp teeth. The 'Coon first invades the corn fields while the tender kernels, not yet full grown, consist of a soft milky pulp, and he continues to feast upon the maize till fully ripe, and even after it is cut and stacked. He is very expert in breaking down the stalks and stripping the husks from the ear, using his fore-paws as we do our hands.

Raccoons are clever beasts, and in certain directions their cunning surpasses that of the fox. The familiar epithet, " a sly 'Coon," owes its origin to certain of their proclivities. Still they do not exercise their cunning for self-preservation; they are not sufficiently suspicious of unusual objects, and are easily taken in almost any kind of a trap. They are not swift runners and if pursued take to a tree and are readily killed.

They make, when taken young, intelligent and interesting pets, being easily tamed, and evincing considerable affection for their master. But they cannot be allowed their liberty, like tame skunks, because of their innate propensity for mischief. If not closely watched they will slyly enter the house through some open door or window, and are liable to do considerable damage, for their natural curiosity prompts them to examine everything within reach, and anything out of reach of a 'Coon must be inaccessible indeed. They invariably manifest an insatiate desire to investigate the pantry shelves, and rarely neglect to taste every edible thing that happens to be there. They have a special *penchant* for sweetmeats and greedily devour preserves, honey, molasses, sugar, pies and cakes; and even bread, butter, lard, milk etc., are by no means disregarded. They remove the covers from jars and pails, and uncork bottles, with as much ease and facility, apparently, as if they had been instructed in this art from earliest infancy. Doors that latch, as they do in most old country houses, are soon opened, even by unsophisticated 'Coons, and it takes them but a short time to acquire the method of opening knob doors. Their fore paws are employed as hands, and can be put to almost as great a variety of uses as those of the monkey—which animal they further resemble in the propensity for mischief-making.

The Raccoon hibernates during the severest part of the winter, retiring to his nest rather early, and appearing again in February or March, according to the earliness or lateness of the season. Disliking to wade through deep snow he does not come out much till the alternate thawing and freezing of the surface, suggestive of coming spring, makes a crust upon which he can run with ease. He does not usually walk many miles during a single night, and consequently is soon tracked to the tree, in some hole of which he has retired for the day. If the tree is too large to be easily felled, a trap set at its foot, and baited with a bit of toasted cod-fish or an ear of corn, is pretty sure to secure him before the next morning.

It is unusual to find a Raccoon alone, for they commonly live and travel in small companies, consisting of the several members of a single family. They do not return to the same nest every morning, but often make little excursions in various directions, being gone several days at a time, and taking refuge, about daylight, in any convenient aboreal shelter. Though preferring a hollow limb high up on some giant elm, ash, or basswood, they will put up with almost any kind of a hollow trunk. I have known them to spend the day in old stubs, in hollow logs, and even in the poor shelter afforded by the angle where a falling tree had lodged in a crotch.

In tracking Raccoons upon the crust I have sometimes observed a family to separate and go in different directions, spending the day in different trees, to come together again on the night following. At this season (before there is any bare ground) they have considerable difficulty in procuring sufficient food.

As already stated, the Raccoon makes its home high up in a hollow of some large tree, preferring a dead limb to the trunk itself. It does little in the way of constructing a nest, and from four to six young are commonly born at a time—generally early in April in this region. The young remain with the mother about a year.

The flesh of young 'Coons is very fair eating, but that of the adult animals is tough and rank, and suggests the meat of old Woodchucks.

More than an hundred years ago Thomas Pennant wrote, in his quaint style, that the Raccoon was "an animal easily made tame, very good-natured and sportive, but as unlucky as a monkey, almost always in motion; very inquisitive, examining everything with its paws; makes use of them as hands: sits up to eat: is extremely fond of sweet things, and strong liquors, and will get excessively drunk: has all the cunning of a fox: very destructive to poultry; but will eat all sorts of fruits, green corn, &c. at low water feeds much on oysters, will watch their opening, and with its paw snatch out the fish; sometimes is caught in the shell, and kept there till drowned by the coming in of the tide: fond also of crabs: climbs very nimbly up trees: hunted for its skin; the fur next to that of the beaver, being excellent for making hats." *

## Family URSIDÆ.

## URSUS AMERICANUS Pallas.

### Black Bear.

This plantigrade mammal, the largest and most powerful of the inhabitants of the Adirondacks, is still abundant in most parts of the Wilderness. His proper home is within the deep evergreen forests, but he is something of a rover and at certain seasons, particularly in autumn, makes numerous excursions into the surrounding country.

Notwithstanding the carnivorous position of the Bear he is *par excellence* an omnivorous beast, and his larder consists not only of mice and other small mammals, turtles, frogs, and fish; but also, and largely, of ants and their eggs, bees and their honey, cherries, blackberries, raspberries, blueberries and various other fruits, vegetables, and roots. He sometimes makes devastating raids upon the barn-yard, slaying and devouring sheep, calves, pigs, and poultry. In confinement he shares with the inmates of the hog-pen whatever is left from his master's table.

He delights in tearing open old stumps and logs in search of the ants that make their homes in such situations,† and digs out the nests of the " yellow-jackets," devouring both the wasps themselves and the comb containing their honey and grubs. So fond is he of honey that he never misses an opportunity to rob a " bee tree," manifesting

---

* Synopsis of Quadrupeds, 1771, pp. 199–200.

† While fishing in the North Bay of Big Moose Lake, during the summer of 1881, Mr. Harry Burrell Miller, of New York city, heard a Bear tearing down an old stump that stood on a point in the bay. His guide, Richard Crego, noiselessly paddled him to the spot and he killed the Bear with one ball from his rifle. Its stomach contained about a quart of ants and their eggs.

no fear of the bees that angrily swarm about him, his thick hair and tough hide protecting him from their stings. When plundering the apple orchard he is said to touch only the sweetest fruit.

He must relish prussic acid, for no article of his comprehensive bill-of-fare is more certain to secure his consideration than a tree laden with ripe black-cherries. Here he will spend hours at a time, glutting upon the handsome fruit, which he leisurely collects from the branches, and is apt to return again and again so long as the supply holds out. Fields of ripe blackberries also claim a large share of attention, and his excessive fondness for them often overcomes his natural prudence, and he is sometimes surprised, in broad daylight, indulging his appetite in such situations.

The senses of smell and hearing are so acute in these brutes that under ordinary circumstances it is impossible to approach even within rifle range of them. But in the fall of the year, during their expeditions through the clearings, they sometimes wander for miles through quite thickly settled portions of country, when, owing to the open nature of the ground, they are frequently seen and occasionally shot.

In Lewis County, about twenty miles west of the western border of the Wilderness, is an uninhabited tract of evergreen forest, covering portions of the towns of High Market, Osceola, Montague, and Pinckney. In this forest dwell many Bears, and in the fall they often cross over the intervening valley, a fertile farming country, and enter the Adirondacks. At such times they occasionally pass through our own grounds, at Locust Grove, in the town of Leyden; and during one October, about five years ago, no less than nine Bears were killed within six miles from my residence.

Though good climbers, Bears are unable, on account of their great weight, to ascend to the tree tops or climb far out on the branches. They are excellent swimmers, crossing with ease not only rivers, but even large and broad lakes. Many have been surprised and killed while swimming the lakes that abound in the " North Woods "; and only last year (in July, 1881) the steamer *Ganouskie,* on Lake

George, ran down one of them, and it was killed with an axe by a drummer from Gotham. This was just above Anthony's Nose.

As a rule our Bears " den up " in winter, but their hibernation is not profound, and it is prudent not to take many liberties with them when in this condition. The exact period when the event takes place is determined by the food supply and the severity of the season. If the beech-nut crop has been a failure and deep snows come early, they generally den near the commencement of winter. If, on the contrary, there has been a good yield of mast, and the winter is a mild one (and it is a fact that, with us, good beech-nut years are commonly followed by open winters), the males prowl about nearly, or quite, all winter, and the females only den a short time before the period of bringing forth their young. Indeed, it can be set down as a rule, that so long as a male Bear can find enough to eat he will not den, be the weather never so severe ; for it is evident that he does not den to escape either the low temperature or the deep snows, but to thus bridge over a period when, if active, he would be unable to procure sufficient food. And the female, under similar circumstances, remains out till the maternal impulse prompts her to seek a shelter for her prospective offspring ; and in this Wilderness they have been found travelling as late as the middle of January.

The den is not commonly much of an affair. It is generally a partial excavation under the upturned roots of a fallen tree, or under a pile of logs, with perhaps a few bushes and leaves scraped together by way of a bed, while to the first snow-storm is left the task of completing the roof and filling the remaining chinks. Not infrequently the den is a great hole or cave dug into the side of a knoll, and generally under some standing tree, whose roots serve as side posts to the entrance. The amount of labor bestowed upon it depends upon the length of time the Bear expects to hibernate. If the prospects point toward a severe winter and there is a scarcity of food, they den early and take pains to make a comfortable nest; but when they stay out late and then den in a hurry, they do not take the trouble to fix up their nests at all.   At such times they simply crawl into any convenient shelter, without gathering so much as a bunch of moss to soften their bed.   Snow completes the covering, and as their breath condenses and freezes into it an icy wall begins to form, and increases in thickness and extent day by day till they are soon unable to escape, even if they would, and are obliged to wait in this icy cell till liberated by the sun in April or May.

The diminutive size, premature appearance, and helpless condition of the young of this species at birth cannot fail to excite surprise. They are not six inches (152 mm) in length, weigh less than a pound (453.6 grams), and are not yet covered with hair.   Their eyes do not open for more than a month.   I know of no other mammal, except among the Marsupials, whose young are so disproportion-ately small, or are born in such an undeveloped condition.   It is necessary for their preservation that the mother should cover them nearly the whole time for the first two months.

Mr. Frank J. Thompson, Superintendent of the Zoological Garden at Cincinnati, has published a thoroughly trustworthy account of the early development of a litter of Black Bears, in confinement; and observations of this nature are so rare that I here reproduce the main part of his communication :

" About the middle of January last, the female Black Bear in the Society's collection refused to come out of her den into the open pit and would not allow the male to approach her.   She was immediately closed in and furnished with an abundance of hay, with which she busied herself in making a nice warm bed.   At 4 P. M. on January 26th, the young ones were born and I did not see them until the third day after, when I was surprised by the keeper informing me that she would allow him to enter the den.   On going with him, he unlocked the door, fearlessly walked in, and quickly began feeding her with bits of bread, which he sliced from a loaf held in his hand. By holding the bread just over her head, he finally tempted her to sit up on her haunches, when I obtained a clear view of the two young ones, lying asleep just back of her front paws. From where I stood, about six feet distant, they did not seem to exceed six inches in length, were a dirty whitish color, and appeared entirely bare of hair. In about ten days their coats began to show and were of a grayish tint, which gradually passed through the various shades until they became a brownish black. It was just forty days before the first one's eyes opened, and two days after the second followed suit. From that time forward I watched very closely to ascertain the exact time that would elapse before the young ones would leave the nest, and on the seventy-first day after birth, when the mother, as was her habit, came to the grating to be fed, one of the youngsters left the nest and followed her. So soon as she found it out she immediately drew it gently back, and on its second attempt, she cuffed it soundly, which put a stop to its wandering propensity. After a few days she allowed them to wander about at will provided no one was immediately in front of the den; but so soon as a visitor put in an appearance, they were driven back into the nest and not allowed to emerge until the strangers were out of sight. For some time she always suckled them in one position, lying over and completely covering them by stretching flat on her belly with her legs drawn up under her and her head tucked down between her front paws. As they grew older and began to run about she would sit on her haunches, lazily lean back against the wall, take a cub on each fore arm and hold them up to her breast until they were satisfied. They soon became expert climbers, taking advantage of the slightest inequalities of the stone walls and the cracks between the heavy oaken planks to reach the ceiling of the den on three sides, whilst the grating in front served capitally for their skylarking. Occasionally they would have a regular sparring bout, standing erect, feinting, countering, and making use of many of the tricks of old votaries of the P. R. These frolics would generally end in a clinch, fall, and a regular rough and tumble fight, when the mother would abruptly put a stop to it, by suddenly knocking both of the contestants completely out of time. In fact, as they grew apace, the parental visitations increased so rapidly I began to fear she would put an end to my Bear investigations by chastising the lives out of them, but of late she has slackened in her attentions, and I am in hopes of following the growth of *Ursus Americanus* from babyhood to adolescence."*

Black Bears commonly have two or three cubs at a birth, and rarely, four. It is doubtful if they have young oftener than every other year.

Early in February, 1878, E. L. Sheppard, J. W. Shultz, and E. N. Arnold, while on a Panther hunt in the country northeast of Big Otter Lake, came across a line cf dimples in the snow that indicated, to their practised eyes, the course taken by a large Bear some time before, and now almost hidden by a heavy fall of snow that had occurred about three weeks previously. Judging that the animal had been searching for winter quarters they determined to follow it; but being out of provisions Sheppard and Shultz returned to camp for a new supply, while Arnold took the track. Owing to the thickness of the forest the snow had not drifted and therefore he had little difficulty in keeping the track, though nearly a foot of snow covered it. He soon reached the den, which was an excavation in the side of a knoll. Not only was the Bear not asleep, but she was extremely lively and earnest in her attempts to get out. Fortunately, however, she was already frozen in, and during her fierce and furious efforts to reach Mr. Arnold he succeeded in shooting her dead. Notwithstanding the fact that he was well armed Mr. Arnold avers that if the Bear had had a free exit from her den he doubts much if he would have lived to narrate the occurrence. After killing the Bear he discovered that there were three living young beneath her in the den. He put them in his pocket, but they died that night. They were very small and helpless, and were probably about two weeks old.

In April of the same year one of the guides found another Bear in her den in a swamp south of Fourth Lake, Fulton Chain. This den,

---

* Forest and Stream, Vol. XIII, No. 4, Sept. 4, 1879, p. 605.

which I have myself seen, was also a hole dug into the side of a knoll, and its presence was betrayed by the young who were playing outside and did not know enough to hide away at the approach of man. In this case also the old Bear was unable to get out and was easily killed.

While hunting, June 10, 1878, Dr. C. L. Bagg and the writer followed the old trail from Fourth Lake across Eagle Creek in the direction of John's Lake. In exploring a hardwood ridge a little to the north of the regular course we were suddenly surprised by a loud and peculiar cry with which we were both unacquainted. It came from the direction of a dense balsam swamp below, and somewhat resembled the squealing of a pig, while at the same time it suggested the noise made by the Great Blue Heron when on its nesting grounds. As the cry was repeated Dr. Bagg imitated it, and succeeded so well that we soon perceived it to be coming nearer. Fearing that it might change its course I ran down the hill and soon saw a dark-colored animal, about the size of a Raccoon, emerge from the swamp and jump upon a log, rushing headlong in the direction towards Dr. Bagg, and squealing at brief intervals as if in great distress. Bringing my gun (loaded only with No. 4 shot) hastily to my shoulder I fired, and the report was followed by a shriek of pain and a plaintive, baby-like, sobbing cry that lasted for nearly a minute. On reaching the spot the animal was found to be a cub Bear, and was then quite dead, one of the shot having passed through both ventricles of the heart. It was very thin, weighing but ten pounds (4536 grams), and had evidently been lost from its mother for some time. Its stomach contained nothing but beech-nuts, and beech-nuts that have lain on the ground all winter, and are still fit to eat in June, are certainly few and far between.

In traversing unfrequented portions of the Wilderness one occasionally meets with a tree whose bark has been scratched and torn, at some little height from the ground, in a manner that cannot fail to excite his attention and surprise. This is the work of the Bear, but the object of it is not known. Hunters claim that whenever a Bear passes one of these trees he stops, stands on his hind-legs and gnaws and scratches it before resuming his journey. The only account of the strange proceeding that I have seen is given by Audubon and Bachman, who state:

"At one season, the Bear may be seen examining the lower part of the trunk of a tree for several minutes with much attention, at the same time looking around and snuffing the air. It then rises on its hind-legs, approaches the trunk, embraces it with the fore-legs, and scratches the bark with its teeth and claws for several minutes in continuance. Its jaws clash against each other until a mass of foam runs down on both sides of the mouth. After this it continues its rambles." *

On the Island of Anticosti, Bears are still numerous, and feed so largely on fish that the inhabitants state that their flesh is, on this account, as unpalatable as that of the Sheldrake. During a recent visit to the west end of this island, I saw the spot, on the beach, where, three days previously, three full-grown Bears had been killed. It was at low water, and they were so busily engaged in capturing and devouring the little fish called Capelin (*Mallotus villosus*) that were detained in the shallow tide-pools on the flat lime-rock shore, that the fishermen approached unobserved and dispatched them without trouble.

Bears are great cowards and never attack man except when wounded, or in defence of their young. When wounded they make desperate and dangerous foes, and more than one hardy hunter has lost his life in encounters with them. In fighting, the large and powerful claws inflict even worse wounds than those made by their formidable teeth, and the bodies of their victims are often frightfully lacerated. If able to "close in" with the luckless hunter they stand upright and hug him tight with their fore-paws, while the hind-claws

* Quadrupeds of North America, Vol. III, 1854, p. 189.

are busy in tearing the flesh from his legs or ripping open his bowels.

Bears are frequently tamed and, being intelligent brutes, make interesting pets; but their dispositions are not of the gentlest type, and in growing old, they are apt, at times, to become obstinate and unruly, if not dangerous, and often have to be killed.

A curious instance of the mischief-making propensity of this animal has recently attracted considerable attention. During the past summer (1882) the Adirondack Survey established a Signal Station on Black Mountain, near the head of Fourth Lake. Returning one day, after a temporary absence, the members of the party were astonished to find their tent torn down, and blankets books, and instruments strewn about upon the ground. The footprints of a Bear revealed the identity of the marauder; and Mr. Colvin, Superintendent of the Survey, afterwards fired at and wounded the beast, but did not succeed in capturing him.

There being no bounty on Bears in New York State, it is impossible to ascertain how many are annually destroyed in this Wilderness. That the average number killed each year exceeds thirty there can be no reasonable doubt, and I have known this number to be killed in Lewis County alone in a single season.

Bear's meat is sometimes very good, and sometimes quite the reverse. I have eaten it when it tasted like fresh pork, and at other times when its flavor was so rank and disagreeable as to render it quite unpalatable. Age, sex, season, and food have to do with this difference.

In Forest and Stream for Dec. 26, 1878, is printed a portion of an original manuscript of one Paul Dudley, written about the year 1718. One paragraph, relating to this species, runs as follows:

" Black Bears—When the snow is deep they den, and don't come out till the snow is so wasted as they can trail their food—nuts, acorns, frogs, berries, crickets, grapes—and preys also. Don't carry food into their dens; generally den alone, unless it be a she with her cubbs of the first year, sometimes in a Hollow Tree, a Hollow Log, under the Root of a Tree, cleft of a Rock. Dog scents them & Barks, then they come out. But if the snow be deep they won't stir. Kill them, nothing in their gutts but slime; they will put fire in the Hole of a Tree then the Bear will come Thundering out whether they are asleep or only mope, for they easily wake. Bear bring forth but once in 3 years. Suckle their young."

PINNIPEDIA. Family PHOCIDÆ.

## PHOCA VITULINA Linnæus.

*Harbor Seal.*

Mention of the occurrence of a Seal, in a treatise upon the Fauna of the Adirondack region, will doubtless occasion surprise in the minds of the majority of my readers. It must be remembered, however, that the eastern limit of this area embraces a portion of Lake Champlain, and that the waters of this beautiful lake are put in direct communication with those of the St. Lawrence, below Montreal, by its outlet, the River Richelieu.

The Harbor Seal breeds regularly both in the Gulf and River of St. Lawrence, and I have seen numbers of them, in July, as far up the River as the Saguenay, and they are still common even within fifty miles of Quebec.

Zadock Thompson has recorded the capture of two of them on Lake Champlain. He says : " While several persons were skating upon the ice on Lake Champlain, a little south of Burlington, in February, 1810, they discovered a living seal in a wild state, which had found its way through a crack and was crawling upon the ice. They took off their skates, with which they attacked and killed it, and then drew it to the shore. It is said to have been 4½ feet long. It must have reached our lake by way of the St. Lawrence and Richelieu;

but it was not ascertained whether the poor (fat) wanderer had lost his way, or having taken *a miff* at society, was seeking voluntary retirement from the world—*of seals*." *

" Another Seal was killed upon the ice between Burlington and Port Kent, on the 23d of February, 1846. Mr. Tabor, of Keeseville, and Messrs. Morse and Field, of Peru, were crossing over in sleighs, when they discovered it crawling upon the ice, and, attacking it with the butt-end of their whips, they succeeded in killing it, and brought it on shore at Burlington, where it was purchased by Morton Cole, Esq., and presented to the University of Vermont, where its skin and skeleton are now preserved." † This is followed by a detailed description of this specimen, which was a female, and by the remark that "At the time the above-mentioned Seal was taken, the lake, with the exception of a few cracks, was entirely covered with ice."

During a recent visit to Lake Champlain I was told that a Seal had been killed on the ice, near Crown Point, within four or five years, but was unable to authenticate the statement.

Dr. DeKay mentioned the occasional occurrence of this species on Lake Ontario, many years ago; and during the past winter one was killed on Onondaga Lake that must have reached this remote inland water by way of Lake Ontario.

I have seen many of these Seals in Long Island Sound, chiefly about the Thimble Islands; and March 25, 1879, I saw one on a rock in the Hudson River, near Sing Sing.

We learn, from Mr. J. A. Allen's excellent "History of the North American Pinnipeds," that the period of gestation, in this restless nomad, is about nine months, and that commonly but a single young is born at a time, though they sometimes have twins.

They breed very late, generally in June and July, and their young are deposited upon the shore instead of upon the ice, as is customary with many species.

---

* Natural and Civil History of Vermont, 1842, p. 38.

† Loc. cit., Appendix, 1853, p. 13.

This species, like most of the Seal kind, feeds chiefly upon fish, squids, shrimps, and the like. They sometimes prove a great nuisance to the fisherman, by robbing his nets of the salmon and other fish that they happen to contain. They have also been observed to catch sea birds while swimming by seizing them from below.

The Harbor Seal, when taken young, is easily domesticated, and soon becomes very tame and fond of its master. It is a very intelligent animal, and may be taught many things. It is said to be particularly fond of music.

Mr. Allen quotes the following from the pen of Dr. Edmonston : "The young ones are easily domesticated, and display a great deal of sagacity. One in particular became so tame that it lay along the fire among the dogs, bathed in the sea, and returned to the house, but having found the way to the byres, used to steal there unobserved and suck the cows."[*]

These Seals make a variety of noises. Their most characteristic cry is a sad, plaintive moan, or a prolonged, dismal howl. When a number unite, as is commonly the case, in a doleful chorus the effect is most depressing. Last summer (in July, 1882), when befogged off the Mingan Islands, I on several occasions observed this performance. It seemed like the lament of a doomed race, bewailing an inevitable fate, and bemoaning, in solemn requiem, the loss of former comrades.

This mournful cadence is usually executed in the night-time, and the darkness certainly does not detract from the general melancholy of the effect. The cold, bleak shores, too, lend an additional element of cheerlessness to the scene. However, it must be remembered that the deep-drawn sighs, the woe-begone moans, and the chorus that suggests a dirge, may all, for aught we know, be expressions of joy and contentment; for it is the impression produced upon us that is melancholy and sad. So little do we comprehend the language of our inferiors.

----

[*] Monograph of North American Pinnipeds, 1880, p. 594.
[From Trans. Linn. Soc. N. Y., Vol. I, Nov., 1882. Paging not changed.]

## Order UNGULATA.  Family CERVIDÆ.

## CARIACUS VIRGINIANUS (Bodd.) Gray.

*Common Deer ; Virginia Deer ; Red Deer ; White-tailed Deer.*

DEER are at present so abundant in most parts of the Adirondacks that they outnumber all the other large mammals together, and this in spite of the fact that during the present century alone hundreds of them have perished of cold and starvation, hundreds have been killed by wolves and panthers, and thousands by their natural enemy, man. And there is every reason to believe that if proper game laws are enforced, their numbers will not materially decrease.

This beautiful and graceful animal, by far the fleetest of our mammalia, roams over all parts of the Wilderness, being found high upon the mountain sides, as well as in the lowest valleys and river bottoms. It frequents alike the densest and most impenetrable thickets, and the open beaver meadows and frontier clearings. During the summer season, which is here meant to apply to the entire period of bare ground, loosely reckoning, from the first of May to the first of November, its food consists of a great variety of herbs, grasses, marsh and aquatic plants, the leaves of many deciduous trees and shrubs, blueberries, blackberries, other fruits that grow within its reach; and, largely, of the nutritious beech-nut. While snow covers the ground, which it commonly does about half the year, the fare is necessarily restricted; and it is forced to subsist chiefly upon the twigs and buds of low deciduous trees and shrubs, the twigs and foliage of the arbor vitæ, hemlock, and balsam, and a few mosses and lichens. In winters succeeding a good yield of nuts the mast constitutes its staple article of diet, and is obtained by following the beech ridges and pawing up the snow beneath the trees.

8

When the first warm winds of approaching spring uncover here
and there in the beaver meadows small spots and narrow strips of
ground between the snowdrifts, the new marsh grass is found already sprouted, and its tender blades afford the Deer a tempting
change from the dry twigs and tough lichens that constitute its winter fare.*

From this time until the latter part of September much of their
sustenance is procured in the immediate vicinage of water. After
the snow has left the forests and the new vegetation has fairly started, they gradually work back into the woods, but return again in
early June to feed upon marsh plants and grasses, and wade or even
swim to procure the lily-pads and other aquatic plants that thrive
in the shallow water near by. During June, July, and August hundreds of Deer visit the water-courses of this Wilderness every night,
and retire at break of day to the deep recesses of the forest.

It has been stated that they do this to rid themselves of black flies
and mosquitoes, but a little reflection will suffice to show the absurdity of this assertion. For nowhere in the entire Wilderness are these
insect pests so abundant and annoying as on the marshes and in the
immediate neighborhood of lakes and streams. And since it is rare
to find a Deer above his thighs in water, the fallacy of this supposition is apparent. The fact is, that, for the sake of obtaining the
plants that grow in such situations, they submit to the annoyance of
swarms of insects most of which they would escape did they remain
amid the mountain fastnesses. It is true, however, that Deer, particularly at the South, do sometimes enter water when not in search
of food, and sink to such a depth that little save the nostrils and eyes
remain in sight; but whether this is done for the riddance of insects,

---

* I was particularly struck with this fact on the 29th April, 1882, while crossing from Big
Moose Lake to Lake Terror, in company with Dr. F. H. Hoadley. Here, along the banks of a
sluggish stream which was still bordered with ice eight to ten inches in thickness, we observed fresh
green grass already over an inch and a half high in small bare spots between snowdrifts two and three
feet in depth. The same day we saw a Deer standing on a mass of ice and snow on the shore of
Lake Terror, doubtless in search of food.

or for the refreshing effects of the bath, is an open question, and for my part I incline to the latter view. Mr. E. L. Sheppard tells me that he has on two occasions seen Deer enter the water and immerse themselves until almost the entire body disappeared from view, and this when not " skulking," or endeavoring to 'elude an enemy. The Rev. John Bachman once witnessed this diversion and described it in these words : " We recollect an occasion, when on sitting down to rest on the margin of the Santee river, we observed a pair of antlers on the surface of the water near an old tree, not ten steps from us. The half-closed eye of the buck was upon us; we were without a gun, and he was, therefore, safe from any injury we could inflict upon him. Anxious to observe the cunning he would display, we turned our eyes another way, and commenced a careless whistle, as if for our own amusement, walking gradually towards him in a circuitous route, until we arrived within a few feet of him. He had now sunk so deep in the water that an inch only of his nose, and slight portions of his prongs were seen above the surface. We again sat down on the bank for some minutes, pretending to read a book. At length we suddenly directed our eyes towards him, and raised our hand, when he rushed to the shore, and dashed through the rattling canebrake in rapid style."*

Early in September our Deer begin to desert the water courses, and before cold weather sets in there is a marked decrease in their numbers in the localities which a short time previously were their favorite feeding grounds. The reason is apparent : the marsh grasses have matured and are now dry; the tender aquatic plants near shore have mostly withered and decayed; and the lily-pads and pickerel weed, cut down by September frosts, no longer remain to tempt their appetites. They retire, therefore, to the higher ground in the forest, which still affords them abundant subsistence.†

---

* Quadrupeds of North America, vol. II, 1851, p. 223.

† The largest and best conditioned Deer I ever saw was a magnificent buck that Dr. F. H. Hoadley shot at Big Moose Lake, October 31, 1881. Its stomach was full, containing a quantity of

A large number of the Adirondack lakes are heavily bordered
with a dense frontage of arbor vitæ (here called "white cedar"),
which so overhangs the water that the lower limbs barely clear
the surface.   Around many of these lakes all the lower branches,
up to a certain height, are dead, so that on viewing the shore
one is struck with the strange appearance of a sharp cut line, about
the height of a man's head, extending partly, or entirely, around the
lake.   Above it the dense foliage presents an almost continuous and
unbroken front, impenetrable to the eye, while below it not a green
sprig can be seen, the dead limbs and branches remaining in the
form of a broad belt.

The cause of this phenomenon long remained a mystery, and many
and amusing theories have been advanced for its explanation.   It
has been supposed that some unusual and unknown agency operated
to produce a great overflow of these lakes, and that the present green
line indicates the high-water mark of this unrecorded inundation, the
branches below it having been killed by the water or ice.   Were there
no other reasons for disbelieving this hypothesis, its absurdity is demonstrated by the fact that on many of the larger lakes the line is
confined to one side.   The only other theory, so far as I am aware,
that is worthy of refutation, was advanced by no less distinguished a
gentleman than Mr. Verplanck Colvin, Superintendent of the Adirondack Survey.   Mr. Colvin's theory is, that the snow which is blown
off from the ice, on some of the larger lakes, and is sometimes piled
in drifts in certain places along the borders, buries the lower limbs
of the cedars; and he thinks that this snow "in some unfavorable
season, becoming compact and icy, had killed the enclosed evergreen
foliage."*   The fallacy of this view is proven, I think, by the following facts : 1st, branches on the opposite or shore side of these very

---

the leaves and stems of the "bunch berry" or dwarf cornel (*Cornus Canadensis*), a small amount of
wintergreen (*Gaultheria procumbens*), and a few leaf-stems of the mountain ash (*Pyrus Americana*)
while throughout the mass were scattered numbers of beech-nuts with the shucks on.

* Report of Adirondack Survey, 1880, p. 162.

trees are usually alive and green, which could hardly be the case were the drift theory true; 2d, the line is often most strongly marked on the shores of ponds that are too small, and too closely hemmed in by hills, to afford the wind a chance to drift the snow about their borders; and 3d, the foliage line is, in all instances where I have observed it, perfectly straight, and exactly parallel to the surface of the water, which could not possibly be the case were it caused by irregularly drifted snow.

Moreover, it is now an ascertained fact that the green line is a result of the wintering of Deer along the shores where it exists, and the evidence on this head may be summed up as follows: In the first place, it is absent from at least half of the cedar bordered lakes, and is only found, of recent origin, in localities where Deer are known to winter. On some of the larger lakes it is confined to one shore and sometimes to a single deep bay, while the cedars about the rest of the lake remain unmarred. Furthermore, it is a fact, which can be verified by any one willing to take the trouble, that where the Deer still winter in these places the snow which covers the ice is literally trodden down by them, a well beaten path follows closely the outline of the shore, and the stumps of newly broken branches may here and there be found. The height of the line shows the distance that a full grown Deer can reach when standing on the snow and ice. And finally, trustworthy witnesses affirm that they have observed the Deer standing on the ice in the act of browsing upon the low branches of cedars overhanging the lake. I regard all this evidence as conclusive.

Though Deer are generally spoken of as nocturnal, they are by no means strictly so, their habits, in this particular, being modified by the environment. In localities that are much frequented by man they keep their beds during the greater part of the day, and feed mostly by night; while in the remoter sections the reverse seems to be true

The spot on which one lies to rest is called its bed. It is generally hidden in some thicket, under the low branches of an evergreen, or by the top of a fallen tree.*

They have no fear of water and, when pressed by wolves or dogs, take to it as a means of escape. They are excellent swimmers, moving with such speed that a man must row briskly to overhaul them. Even the young fawns swim well, and I once caught one alive that had been driven into the lake. It was in the spotted coat, and not more than three months old.†

The extraordinary sagacity of some of these animals, and the temerity, I might even say stupidity, of others is astonishing. As a general thing a Deer is always on the alert; his eyesight is good, his hearing acute, and his sense of smell developed to an unusual degree. Under ordinary circumstances he detects the whereabouts of man at a considerable distance, and even if abundant is seldom seen. At other times, particularly when feeding on the margin of a lake or river, if the wind is right he may be approached in broad daylight by aid of a boat, and will only raise his head from time to time, gazing at the intruder in a vacant sort of a way; but let the wind shift a trifle, so that he gets a whiff from the direction of the boat, and he is off in an instant. Along the borders of the Wilderness a Deer will sometimes join a group of cows or sheep at pasture, and follow them home within gunshot of the house. Not a few have met their death in this way.

During the deep snows of our severer winters Deer are apt to

---

* While on a snow-shoe-tramp from Big Otter to Big Moose lake, in January, 1883, I counted upwards of forty Deer beds—mere depressions in the snow. One only was in an exposed position, being in a little opening alongside a maple sapling. With this single exception, all were under the shelter of small spruce and balsam trees, the space between the bed and the overhanging branches, loaded down with ice and snow, being in most cases barely sufficient to admit the animal.

† In Forest and Stream for Dec. 6, 1883 (vol. XXI, no. 19, p. 362), occurs the following: " Deer at Sea.—Portland, Me., Nov. 29.—The British schooner Howard came in yesterday with one of Howard Knowlton's deer on board, which had been picked up about five miles out at sea. The animal escaped from the garden on Peak's Island last summer, and had not been seen since probably having kept in the woods at the lower end of the island. This is the biggest feat of capturing deer in the water on record."

congregate and remain in one locality till the food supply in the immediate vicinity is exhausted, when they move off to some other place. By working to and fro in search of browse the snow becomes much trampled, and pathways are beaten in various directions. These places are called yards, but they fall far short of the regular enclosures, walled in by deep snow, that we so often read about, and even see pictured under this head. They afford the much persecuted animals no shelter or protection, for if discovered by either the panther or the infamous " crust hunter," they become grave-yards for many. Mr. Verplanck Colvin, speaking of one he found on the south side of Seventh Lake Mountain, February 15, 1877, said : " It was impossible to estimate the number of Deer which had occupied this yard, as they had fled at our approach, plunging into the deep snow below. The ground of this central area resembled a sheep yard in winter, the forms of the Deer being plainly discernible in the beds of snow, in which they had slept, on every side.

" Here we were startled by the sight of the fresh tracks of a panther or cougar, which evidently made his home in this abode of plenty ; and shortly thereafter we found the body of a Deer freshly killed, and shockingly torn and mutilated. The guides were now all excitement, and followed the cougar's trail eagerly. In less than thirty minutes a shout announced that he had been encountered, and rushing forward to the southern front of the plateau I came upon the monstrous creature, coolly defiant, standing at the brow of a precipice on some dead timber, little more than twenty feet from where I stood. Quickly loading the rifle, I sent a bullet through his brain, and as the smoke lifted, saw him struggling in the fearful convulsions of death, till finally precipitated over the cliffs he disappeared from sight in the depths below." *

It is stated by several writers that the Deer delights in destroying snakes. Dr. Harlan thus speaks of this proclivity :—

---

* Report of Adirondack Survey, 1880, pp. 159–160.

"This species displays great enmity towards the rattlesnake, which enemy they attack and destroy with singular dexterity and courage; when the Deer discover one of these reptiles, they leap into the air to a great distance above it, and descend with their four feet brought together, forming a solid square, and light on the snake with their whole weight, when they immediately bound away; they return and repeat the same manœuvres until their enemy is completely destroyed." *

### Antlers.

The branching and gracefully curved antlers which adorn the heads of the bucks, and contribute so largely to the elegant appearance of the animal, are shed and renewed every year. Their growth is so rapid that the full size is usually reached in about three months, and they fall off about four months afterward. They are first seen with us, as a rule, about the middle of May, appearing as soft, dark-colored and rapidly elongating vascular excrescences. They harden from below upwards, and by the time the growth is complete all but the tips is well ossified. The soft, skin-like material, called the velvet, with which they are covered, now begins to peel off in irregular strips and shreds, and by the early part or middle of September the horns are generally clean. The velvet does not come away of itself, but is rubbed and scraped off against shrubs and small trees, as if the antlers itched at the period of maturity. The Hon. Judge Caton, of Ottawa, Illinois, whose facilities for observation in this field have rarely been equalled, makes the following statement, which will, by many, be received with surprise : "The evidence, derived from a very great multitude of observations, made through a course of years, is conclusive that nature prompts the animal to denude its antlers of their covering, at a certain period of its growth, while yet the blood has as free access to that covering as it ever had."†

---

* Fauna Americana, 1825, p. 242.

† The Antelope and Deer of America. By John Dean Caton, LL. D., 1877, p. 172.

## Seasonal Changes in Pelage.

Descriptions of the pelages of our mammals do not fall within the scope of the present work; but the seasonal changes in the coat of the Deer have so much to do with its life history that a brief glance at the distinctive features of these changes is necessary. Our Deer shed their coats twice each year, in June and September; and, from the general appearance of the pelage, are said to be in the *red* coat in summer, and in the *blue* or *gray* coat during the rest of the year. The *gray* is merely the *blue* after it has become old and worn, for in maturing it loses the handsome blue appearance that characterizes the first few weeks of its growth. These seasonal changes are not confined to color alone, for there is an equally radical difference in the length and texture of the hair. In summer it is fine and short, and lacks the wavy look that is always noticeable at other times. In winter it is long and coarse, has a crinkled appearance, and the individual hairs are so large and light that the animal will float in water.*

Judge Caton, whose spacious Deer parks and carefully recorded observations have contributed so largely to our knowledge of this species, has published the most accurate, detailed, and complete account of the changes of pelage, that has ever appeared in print. From his extended remarks upon this subject I quote the following brief passages : " The change from the summer to the winter coat is gradual, the new displacing the old by dislodging the hairs promiscuously, till they become so thin that the new coat is seen through the old. This is not simultaneous over the whole animal, for the neck and shoulders may be clothed entirely with the new dress, while the old still prevails on the thighs and rump; or the winter coat may have replaced the old on the back, while the belly still shows only the summer pelage. When the winter has replaced

---

* It must not be forgotten, however, that Deer are commonly poor in summer, and fat in autumn and early winter. Hence, the later in the season the more nearly will the specific gravity of the animal approach that of water. Consequently, a much smaller amount of buoyant material will suffice to float the animal in October and November, than in July, August, and September.

the summer garb, the hairs are short, fine, and soft; but they rapidly grow in length and diameter, and undergo the changes of color peculiar to the species. At first they lie down smoothly, but presently the diameter becomes so great, that they force each other up to a more vertical position, or at right angles to the skin. As the diameters increase, the cavities within enlarge and become filled with a very light pith, and they become brittle and lose their elasticity, so that the integrity of the walls is destroyed when sharply bent, and they remain in the given position."*

The exact period of shedding and of renewal of the coat varies somewhat from year to year; and it does not always take place at the same time in all the Deer of the region, during the same season. It evidently depends in great measure, if not wholly, upon the condition of the animal at the time of the moult, and this is determined mainly by the way the Deer wintered. After severe winters many are poor and ill conditioned, and they do not put on the *red* coat till late in June, or even till the first of July,—the *blue* being correspondingly delayed. If, on the other hand, the winter has been a mild one, and the supply of beech-nuts large, the Deer have probably wintered well, and come out fat and healthy in the spring. In this case they shed the old *gray* coats early, and the *red* may be seen covering a large part of the animal by the middle of June, or even earlier. These Deer assume the *blue* coat very early, and the change may be well advanced by the last of August.

Deer rut in November, the season commonly extending from the latter part of October till the first week in December. As this period approaches, the necks of the bucks become enormously enlarged,† and their whole demeanor is changed. Instead of treading cautiously through the forest they now rush wildy about, tracking the does

---

* Antelope and Deer of America, pp. 126–127.

† As early as the last week in October I measured the neck of a buck that was 30 inches (762mm) in circumference, only ten inches behind the ears. The maximum development is attained about the middle of November.

by the scent; and when two or more bucks meet, fierce conflicts en-
sue. In these engagements their antlers sometimes become interlocked, so that the combatants cannot free themselves, and both must
inevitably perish. My father has a set of locked horns that were
found, with the carcasses attached, frozen in the ice on Pine Creek,
in Lewis County, several winters ago. The body of the larger buck
was in fair condition, while that of the smaller was much emaciated,
showing that the larger and more powerful had succeeded in forcing
his adversary's head to one side so that he could browse a little.

Audubon and Bachman state that they once saw three pairs of
horns thus interlocked. What a wretched trio this must have been,
slowly starving in the midst of plenty!

At this season the bucks not only fight amongst themselves, but
occasionally attack man, and more than one unfortunate person has
been gored to death by them. In battle they make use of their horns,
and also of the fore feet, whose sharp hoofs are capable of inflicting
terrible wounds. I was once sitting quietly on a log in a Deer park
when a buck approached, and, making a sudden spring, dealt me such
a powerful blow on the head, with the hoofs of his fore feet, as to render me unconscious. No sooner was I thrown upon the ground than
the vicious beast sprang upon me, and would doubtless have killed me
outright had it not been for the intervention of a man who rushed at
him with a club and finally drove him off. Both my father and myself
have been knocked flat upon the ground by being struck in the abdomen by the fore feet of a very harmless looking doe.

As a rule, two fawns are born at a time, one being the exception.
Most of them are brought forth in May, a few being dropped as early
as the latter part of April, while others are postponed until the first
week in June. They are at first spotted, the spots usually remaining
about four months and disappearing in September, when both old and
young change their coats. Before the moult takes place they may
fairly be regarded as one of the most beautiful of North American

mammals, and their graceful and sprightly movements cannot fail to elicit admiration.

The clear white spots are set in a ground of rich bay, and the contrast is heightened, to use the language of Judge Caton, by the animal's " exceedingly bright eye, erect attitude, elastic movement, and vivacious appearance. . . . The highest perfection of graceful motion is seen in the fawn of but a month or two old, after it has commenced following its mother through the grounds. It is naturally very timid, and is alarmed at the sight of man, and when it sees its dam go boldly up to him and take food from his hand it manifests both apprehension and surprise, and sometimes something akin to displeasure. I have seen one standing a few rods away, face me boldly and stamp his little foot, in a fierce and threatening way, as if he would say : ' If you hurt my mother I will avenge the insult on the spot.' Ordinarily it will stand with its head elevated to the utmost; its ears erect and projecting somewhat forward; its eye flashing, and raise one fore foot and suspend it for a few moments, and then trot off and around at a safe distance with a measured pace, which is not flight, and with a grace and elasticity which must be seen to be appreciated, for it quite defies verbal description. A foot is raised from the ground so quickly that you hardly see it, it seems poised in the air for an instant and is then so quietly and even tenderly dropped, and again so instantly raised that you are in doubt whether it even touched the ground, and, if it did, you are sure it would not crush the violet on which it fell."*

Fawns are readily tamed, in fact become tame of themselves, if much handled, in an astonishingly short time; and I have known one to follow its keeper, and even bleat for him, when out of sight, within three or four days after its capture. At this tender age they display neither judgment nor common sense in the selection of food, devouring almost anything that falls in their way which they are able to swallow.

* Antelope and Deer of America, p. 155.

Bits of newspapers, old rags, and pieces of boots and shoes are seized and disposed of with as much apparent eagerness as bread and butter or lily-pads; and I once saw a fawn eat a box of chewing tobacco given it by an unprincipled visitor. It died next day.

The flesh of the Deer is juicy, tender, and well flavored, and is the most easily digested of meats. Its good qualities are too well known to require further comment.

The hide is put to a variety of uses, the most important, with us, being the manufacture of gloves and moccasins.

Our Deer are much larger than those of the South and Southwest, adult well-conditioned bucks averaging from 200 to 225 lbs. Avoirdupois in weight, and exceptionally large ones being much heavier. Hence the Adirondack Deer is more than double the size and weight of the same species in Florida.

I have taken great pains to ascertain, approximately, the number of Deer annually slain in this Wilderness, but with indifferent success. It is a low estimate to state that from five to eight hundred have been killed here yearly for the past ten years. How much longer their numbers can withstand this enormous drain is an open question.

On the 3d of July, 1609, Samuel de Champlain ascended the River Richelieu and entered the lake that now bears his name. In his narrative of this memorable journey he speaks thus of the animals found upon the island at the foot of the lake : " Here are a number of beautiful, but low islands filled with very fine woods and prairies, a quantity of game and wild animals, such as stags, deer, fawns, roe-bucks, bears, and other sorts of animals that come from the mainland to the said islands. We caught a quantity of them. There is also quite a number of Beavers, as well in the river as in several other streams which fall into it. These parts, though agreeable, are not inhabited by any Indians, in consequence of their wars." *

---

* Documentary History of New York, vol. III, p. 5.

Pennant says, that 25,027 hides were exported from New York and Pennsylvania in the sale of 1764. (Arctic Zoology, vol. I, 1792, p. 33.)

### Spike-Horn Bucks.

The matter of " Spike-horn Bucks," though somewhat threadbare, deserves mention in this connection from the circumstance that the supposed variety was first described from the Adirondacks. In a note in the American Naturalist for December, 1869 (vol. III, No. 10, pp. 552–553), a writer observed that he had hunted in the Adirondacks for twenty-one years, and goes on to say : "About fourteen years ago, as nearly as I can remember, I first began to hear of Spike-horn Bucks. The stories about them multiplied, and they evidently became more and more common from year to year. About five years ago I shot one of these animals, a large buck with spike-horns, on Louis Lake. In September, 1867, I shot another, a three year old buck with spike-horns, on Cedar Lakes. These Spike-horn Bucks are now frequently shot in all that portion of the Adirondacks south of Raquette Lake. I presume the same is true north of Raquette Lake, but of this latter region I cannot speak from personal observation, having visited it only once.

" The spike-horn differs greatly from the common antler of the *C. Virginianus.* It consists of a single spike, more slender than the antler, and scarcely half so long, projecting forward from the brow, and terminating in a very sharp point. It gives a considerable advantage to its possessor over the common buck. Besides enabling him to run more swiftly through the thick woods and underbrush (every hunter knows that does and yearling bucks run much more rapidly than the large bucks when armed with their cumbrous antlers [!]), the spike-horn is a more effective weapon than the common antler. With this advantage the Spike-horn Bucks are gaining upon the common bucks, and, may, in time, entirely supersede them in the Adirondacks. Undoubtedly the first Spike-horn Buck was merely an accidental freak of nature. But his spike-horns gave him an advantage, and enabled him to propagate his peculiarity. His descendants, having a like advantage, have propagated the peculiarity in a constantly increasing ratio, till they are slowly crowding the antlered Deer from the region they inhabit." *

The foregoing note contains several inaccuracies of statement, and the writer's deductions are wholly erroneous. It was very justly criticised by Mr. W. J. Hays in the *Naturalist* for May, 1870 (pp. 188–189). Further remarks and discussions may be found in the same Journal, vol. IV, pp. 442–443, 762–763; and vol. V, pp. 250–251. The subject is now well understood, and the Hon. Judge Caton has presented the facts of the case with such accuracy and conciseness that I cannot do better than transcribe his own words :—

"It has long been a prevalent opinion among hunters, and to some extent has been adopted by naturalists, that a race of common Deer, the adults of which have antlers without branches, have established themselves in the northeastern part of the United States and in Canada, whence they are driving out the prong-antlered bucks.

"This is a matter of the greatest scientific importance, and I have taken pains to investigate it to my satisfaction, and am entirely convinced that it is a popular error, founded upon incomplete observations. The *spike bucks* found in the Adirondacks are all yearling bucks with their first antlers. The universal testimony, so far as I have been able to gather it, is, that they are smaller than the average of the prong-antlered bucks, and that their spikes vary in length

---

* The above passage fell under the ever-searching eye of that eminent naturalist and indefatigable collector of facts, the late and much lamented Charles Darwin, whose massive intellect and exhaustive researches have revolutionized Natural Science and mark a new era in the progress of knowledge. Mr. Darwin, misled by this account, part of which he quotes in his masterly work on the Descent of Man, remarks upon it as follows : " A critic has well objected to this account by asking, why, if the simple horns are now so advantageous, were the branched antlers of the parent-form ever developed ? To this I can only answer by remarking, that a new mode of attack with new weapons might be a great advantage, as shown by the case of the *Ovis cycloceros*, who thus conquered a domestic ram famous for his fighting power. Though the branched antlers of a stag are well adapted for fighting with his rivals, and though it might be an advantage to the prong-horned variety slowly to acquire long and branched horns, if he had to fight only with others of the same kind, yet it by no means follows that branched horns would be the best fitted for conquering a foe differently armed." (Descent of Man, New York, 1875, p. 513.)

from eight inches, or ten inches at the very utmost, down to two or three inches in length. It is only the largest of these that any have claimed to be adults. It is very easy for a hunter to say, and even believe that he has killed deer with spikes ten inches long, but did he actually measure them, and make a note of the fact, with time and place, describing its appearance, and take and note the measurements of the animal, or did he preserve the head, so that he could carefully examine it, after the excitement of the chase was over, or so that he could submit it to the examination of others? . . . . .

" Continued observations upon the young deer in my parks have enlightened me much on this subject. For several years, I really persuaded myself that I had the true spike-antlered bucks, and set myself to carefully note their peculiarities, and fondly believed that I was about to add an important chapter to scientific knowledge. But these careful and continued observations soon undeceived and disappointed me. By marking the spike buck of one year, which was as large as one feeding by its side having two or three tines on each antler, I found the next year that his antlers were also branched, and my spike-antlered buck had become a fine specimen of the ordinary kind. And then the early fawn of the year before, dropped from a fully adult vigorous doe, which had furnished him plenty of milk, had now grown to the size of a medium adult, and had fine spike-antlers, resembling in all things his older brother of the preceding year now bearing the pronged antlers. And so I anxiously pursued my ob-servations for a number of years, ever looking in vain for a second antler without prongs. Without this certain means of knowledge, I should have believed that those large spike-antlered bucks were more than yearlings and nearly adult. It is true the dentition might have undeceived me, but this I could not ascertain while the animal was alive, and this test has probably been rarely examined and carefully studied by those hunters who believe they have killed adult deer with spike antlers. I feel quite sure that they had not the means of accurately determining the true ages of the wild deer which they had killed; and what I have already stated may serve to show how very liable all are to be misled in relation to a point, upon a certain knowledge of which the whole question depends." *

The only exception, that has come to my knowledge, to the rule that Spike-horn bucks are always yearlings, is a case that fell under the observation of Mr. E. L. Sheppard : A very old buck, with much gray about its head, was killed in Queer Lake about ten years ago. In addition to its extreme age, it had but three legs and was, consequently, ill-conditioned, having been unable to procure sufficient food. It carried a pair of spike-horns which differed from those of yearling bucks in being much thicker at the base, rougher, more warty, and deeply wrinkled for some distance above the burr. This apparent exception is an illustration of two general laws : (a) that in extreme age there is a tendency for certain parts to revert to a condition resembling that of early life; and (b) that ill-nourished bucks bear stunted and more or less imperfect horns. It is a well-known fact that the largest, handsomest, and most perfect antlers come from middle-aged Deer that have wintered well and are in fine condition; while the few-pronged and unsymmetrical ones are grown by young or very old animals, or by those that have been wounded or from other cause are poor and ill-conditioned.†

All yearlings do not have true spike-horns, and, if the term be made to include all unbranched antlers, I am strongly of the opinion that two-year old bucks sometimes grow them. I have a pair of unbranched antlers that are curved both inward and forward, and are of exceptional length, the separate horns measuring respectively ten and a half and eleven inches (or 267 and 279mm.) over the curve, and

---

* Antelope and Deer of America, pp. 231–232.

† Through the kindness of the well-known guide, Mr. E. L. Sheppard, I possess a specimen of unusual interest that well illustrates this point. The buck, which was an adult, was killed at Big Moose Lake, September 10, 1880, and its horns are imperfect, asymmetrical, and very scraggy. The animal was lank and thin, and was found to be a cripple. Its left humerus had once been broken and the fragments had united at a right angle, so that the fore-leg was directed forward, and the shortening of the humerus was so great (its greatest length being less than six and a half inches, or, exactly, 164mm.) that the foot could not be made to touch the ground.

9

seven and a half and eight inches (190 and 203mm.) in a straight line from the base of the burr to the tip. The longest horn presents a slight enlargement, three inches from the tip, along its upper and posterior border, the greatest thickness of which is three-quarters of an inch (19mm.), thus indicating the point where a prong ought to have grown. I take it that these are the horns of a two-year old, but have no means of determining this very important question. I also have two other pairs of horns from young Deer, that are smaller than those just described and yet one horn of each pair is forked. Whether they came from yearlings or two-year olds I will not venture to decide.

In my opinion the term spike-horn should be limited to the straight and true spike that is known to be characteristic of the yearling buck.

Does sometimes, though rarely, have horns, and they are usually of the "spike" pattern, only more incurved than those of the bucks, and they are apt to be more or less imperfect and unsymmetrical. They are generally covered with the velvet, no matter at what season taken, in this respect resembling those of castrated bucks. Does that bear antlers do not commonly bear young, though they are not always barren.*

### The Chase.

An account of the different ways of hunting the Deer on the plains and prairies of the West, in the canebrakes and swamps of the South, and in other sections remote from the region under consideration, however interesting, does not fall within the scope of the

---

\* Alonzo Wood, Esq., one of the most experienced and competent guides in the Adirondacks, has kindly presented me with a very beautiful pair of spike antlers that were taken from a doe which was killed at Second Lake of North Branch about the first of September, 1876. They are deeply curved, symmetrical, and covered with a very dense coat of "velvet," the individual hairs of which are of unusual length. The measurements of these antlers are as follows :

| | | | |
|---|---|---|---|
| From burr to tip, in a straight line, | 6 | in. | (152 mm.) |
| "        "      around curve, | 8¼ | " | (210 " ) |
| Distance between tips, | 4¼ | " | (108 " ) |
| "      antlers at curve, | 6¼ | " | (159 " ) |

present work ; hence the methods practised in the Adirondacks will alone be described.

There are three principal ways in which Deer are hunted in this Wilderness, namely : by *floating*, by *driving* (hounding), and by *still-hunting*.

*Floating* consists in paddling up to a Deer, at night, with a light called a *jack* fastened above the bow of the boat, and so arranged that it casts the whole light ahead, leaving the boat and contents in exaggerated darkness. The *jack* of our ancestors (used even within the brief period of my own recollection), was a very simple affair, constructed where occasion required. It consisted of a torch, or sometimes a tallow candle, fastened upon a piece of bark, and backed by a bark reflector. This rude illuminator was attached to a stick, three or four feet long, that stood upright in the bow. The stick, or standard of the primitive jack, still remains, and now supports a lantern which is closed in on three sides so that all the light shall be thrown in front. Some sort of a reflector is generally used to concentrate and project the rays to a greater distance. Sometimes the light is fastened to the hat.

Two people constitute a floating party, and the *modus operandi* is as follows : The sportsman sits on the front seat, with his legs tucked under the bow in a position that is, at the start, anything but agreeable, and becomes distressingly uncomfortable as hour after hour drags slowly on. He dare not move lest the noise thus made should alarm the Deer. The guide sits in the stern and must be expert with the paddle, for it is his duty to propel the boat steadily and noiselessly within easy range of the wary Deer.

The locality is usually selected in the day-time, and is generally some marsh-bordered bay, abounding in lily-pads, or a similar place along the banks of a sluggish stream On nearing the feeding ground not a word is spoken, not even in a whisper, and the hunters strain eye and ear to discover the whereabouts of the quarry. The light is turned in such a way that it covers the shore as the boat glides silently on, for the Deer may be gazing at it from the bank, standing motionless and silent. Indeed, he is often seen, not more than a couple of boat lengths away, before any sound has forewarned them of his presence.

Bright moonlight nights are undesirable because the animal can then detect the outline of the boat, and is apt to take to the woods without delay.

Let us note the course of events in an ordinary floating expedition, premising only that the sportsman is somewhat of a novice. Unless there is direct water communication between the camp and the place selected for the hunt, the party eat an early supper and set out at once in order to reach the spot before the gathering darkness obscures the way. The guide, placing the boat upon his sturdy shoulders, takes the lead, following some old trail or blazed line, or, if the spot be unfrequented, finds his way by certain features of mountain or valley that are familiar landmarks to his practised eye. The sportsman follows, carrying the *jack* and gun, as well as a bottle of tar oil for protection against insects.

The start is well timed, for the outlines of near objects have already become indistinct, and the shades of dusk are fast blending the dim forms of the evergreens, transforming the coniferous forest into a uniform mass of darkness, when they emerge upon the open shore of a small and shallow lake and launch the canoe in its black but unruffled water. Night is upon them, and with it the flies and mosquitoes. Tar oil is applied freely to face and hands, the jack is lit and placed, and they step quietly into the boat and move noiselessly off,—the sportsman on the front seat, his overcoat buttoned up to his chin, and his feet crowded uncomfortably under the bow, one on each side of the jack-stick; the guide astern, silently plying his paddle. The nearest marsh-bordered bay is soon reached, and as the light skims along the bank, falling in turn upon clumps of bushes, old logs and stumps, and the dark cone-like forms of the young spruce and balsams, the sportsman's expectation is at its highest pitch; he feels his heart beat faster and faster, and grasps his gun tighter and tighter, imagining that each fantastic shadow will show the white tail of a retreating buck. The suspense is of short duration, for this feeding-ground is passed without so much as the sound of a moving branch to indicate the presence of any animal larger than the flies that swarm about his head. Now comes a pull of half a mile before the next ground is reached, which would afford the sportsman ample time to compose himself, were it not for the armies of pestiferous flies and mosquitoes that demand, and receive, his undivided attention. The bottle of tar oil is produced, and a thorough smearing grants temporary respite. No sooner is this accomplished than the next favorable shore for Deer is fast appearing over the port bow. Another ten minutes of breathless suspense and they turn again into the open lake. A close listener might have detected a half suppressed sigh of submission to the inevitable, from the fore part of the boat, but no other sound disturbs the unbroken silence of the night. The third swampy bay is reached and passed, with like result. A council ensues, in a low whisper, and it is decided to run up the inlet, a marshy stream averaging less than a boat's length in width. Having arrived at its mouth they proceed very slowly, for good feed abounds on both banks, and a Deer may be surprised at any moment. Presently a noise is heard ahead : it is vague and indefinite, but evidently something moving. The boat comes nearer; the noise ceases; it is heard again. The sight is strained to penetrate the bushes along the shore, but nothing is discovered. Hark! something dripping in the water; the eyes are lowered, and there, on a log that projects into the stream, almost within reach from the bow, is seen the form of a large porcupine, lazily eating lily-pads and gazing stupidly at the light. The sportsman is tempted to fire, but controls his disgust and says nothing. A bend in the tortuous channel is passed, and another, and,—*splash, splash, splash:* it is the unmistakable sound of a

Deer wading in the creek.   Then all is still again.   Is the animal standing in the water looking at the light, or has he stepped out upon the bank?   The sportsman hears the faint ripple of water against the bow as the boat moves swiftly on ; he is conscious that the hat is rising on his head ; his heart beats louder and louder, and he feels it knocking violently against his ribs.   The boat is slackened and the light made, in turn, to cover both shores.   Moments seem like hours, and the flies are entirely forgotten.   But what has become of the game?   Inadvertently the gun rubs against the jack-stick when, simultaneously, is heard the sharp shrill whistle of a startled buck, from behind a bush to the right, and the fading sound of crackling branches announce his disappearance in the forest.

The flies now seem worse than ever, and so they really are, for the boat is passing through their very headquarters, and the bright light attracts them to the spot.   Continuing the course up the sluggish stream it is some time before anything occurs to divert the sportsman's attention from these tormenting insects, which constantly get into the eyes, nose, and mouth, till, harassed, exasperated, and well nigh distracted, he applies his only remedy, the tar oil, so freely that he soon feels it trickling slowly down his aching back.   The cramped position of his legs and feet is actually painful, and his back "seems as if it would break."   The hour is past midnight, his lids are heavy, and he has almost determined to request the guide to turn back when a loud plunge alongside the boat gives him a sudden start and elicits the involuntary exclamation : "what's that?" forgetting for the moment the necessity of silence.   "Nothing but a muskrat," calmly replies the guide in a whisper.   "Muskrat? hum!" he retorts in a tone of incredulity, but says no more.

Another hour passes wearily away.   The inlet, which is here so narrow and shallow as scarely to admit the boat, is crossed by a fallen tree that bars farther progress.   The return voyage becomes very monotonous, and finally even the flies fail to keep up the excitement. The drowsy hunter nods, his eyes close, and his head hangs heavily upon his breast. Suddenly an owl, on a low limb overhead, utters one of his loudest and most startling cries. The affrighted sportsman cocks both barrels of his gun, expecting to detect the crouching form of a panther preparing for the fatal spring. On being assured of the harmless nature of his imaginary foe he cannot suppress a groan of mortification and disgust while he endeavors to regain his equanimity. Beads of cold sweat mingle with the oil upon his forehead as he solemnly and silently vows that floating is a diversion into which he will never again be beguiled. He feels chilly, and wonders if this is really a sample of Adirondack sport, or if his guide has been playing him a trick. While his mind is occupied with these meditations they have reached the lake, and the guide, anxious not to return empty-handed, has put the boat into a shallow bay and is working it slowly ahead amongst the lily-pads. The sportsman, now too cold to sleep, feels the boat slacken its headway and stop. He wonders if the guide has dropped off in a doze and is about to turn and investigate when the word " shoot," uttered in a low whisper, falls upon his ears. He doesn't see anything to shoot, but on looking more closely, discovers, partly hidden behind a bush, the form of a Deer, as motionless as a statue, gazing inquiringly at the light. Raising the gun nervously to his shoulder he fires. A desperate leap, a wild plunge ahead, a heavy fall, and a noble buck lies dead upon the bank.

*Driving* consists in chasing a Deer with hounds, and killing it, if possible, when it takes to water. A Deer is not much afraid of a dog, and when the latter commences to bay on the track does not start off at once, but waits till sure that the hound is really chasing it. It then moves away at a brisk pace, rapidly distancing its pursuer, and is apt to run several miles, circling through valleys and over hills, before taking to water. If now a stream of any size is reached, the animal is liable to wade for a considerable distance in order to throw the dog off the scent. It then stops to listen, and if after a while the dog again finds the track, will generally take a pretty straight course for some neighboring lake, and swim it in order to rid itself of the annoyance of being followed. Instead of swimming, it sometimes skulks in shallow water near shore, and in this way baffles the dog.

The details of the hunt having been arranged over night, the participants proceed, soon after daylight, to their respective posts, while the guide puts out the dogs. If the lake about which the hunt centres is a large one, two or more men are stationed at different points to watch it, while the others make portages to adjacent lakes and ponds. The guide commonly starts several dogs, each on a separate track. Each watch-point is provided with a boat, and the hunters keep a sharp look-out, for the Deer is frequently so far ahead that it takes the water before the bay of the hound comes within hearing. If the game is a doe or fawn, and particularly if early in the season, the head alone is commonly seen above the surface, and at a distance it is likely to be mistaken for a duck. A buck swims higher, and the later the date the more of its body shows out of water. Deer killed in September generally sink, but after this month they usually float. This depends upon the state of the pelage; for when in the *red* coat they sink, while, on the contrary, when the *blue* coat, which grows very rapidly, is an inch in length, it will, as a rule, float the Deer that carries it, and this length is generally attained about the first of October.

When a Deer is seen swimming the lake, the hunter waits till it has gone far enough from shore to give him an opportunity to head it off, before launching his boat and starting in pursuit. By exercising a little caution and not hurrying too much, he is often able to approach within easy range without being observed; but, if the animal sights him or hears any suspicious noise, it swims so fast that unless in a large lake and some distance from shore, the hunter has great difficulty in overtaking it. When a large buck is overtaken and unexpectedly finds that he is pursued, he suddenly turns toward the boat, with a look of mingled astonishment and horror, rises high out of water and snorts ; then, facing about, makes a desperate, but usually fruitless, effort to escape.

In September it is not uncommon for a guide to drive the Deer about the lake till well nigh exhausted, and then catch and hold it by the tail, so that it will not sink, while the "sportsman" kills it !

In *driving*, a hunt ordinarily lasts seven or eight hours, and is apt to become a trifle monotonous, particularly for those who do not happen to see a Deer. It commonly has this advantage, however, that there are at this season (autumn) no flies to pester the watchman, who, if he can manage to keep warm, and has enough to eat, may maintain a tolerable degree of complacency.

*Still-hunting*, with us, consists in following a deer, by its tracks on the ground, and in attempting to overtake and shoot it, by daylight, in its home in the forest. It is sometimes, though rarely, practised by our most skilful still-hunters in summer and early autumn, after a recent rain has so moistened the surface that the foot-prints can be traced. But it is when the ground is covered with a few inches of newly fallen snow, in November and December, that this method of hunting is commonly resorted to. A rifle is the weapon usually employed.

In order that he may step as noiselessly as possible, the hunter lays aside his boots, covers his feet with several pairs of woolen stockings, and over them draws a pair of well-made buckskin moccasins. Starting early in the morning, he makes a circuit in search of fresh tracks, and if Deer are plenty, pays no attention to those of does and fawns, but proceeds till the track of a large buck is discovered. This he follows slowly and cautiously, taking care lest he tread on some dead branch or in any way make a noise that might alarm the wary Deer. The animal often takes fright and makes off at full speed before it has been seen at all. This the hunter at once detects by the difference in the track, the long spaces between footprints plainly showing that it was on the run. He now throws off all restraint and strikes into a brisk pace, for the Deer is already likely to be several miles away, and whatever noise is made cannot possibly reach its distant ears. When the tracks indicate that the Deer has slackened its gait into a walk, and has, perhaps, commenced to browse a little, then it is time to advance again slowly and with great circumspection, for having been once alarmed, it is even more on the alert than usual, and can only be approached with the utmost care.

It not unfrequently happens that the Deer enters a swamp where several others are feeding, in which case the snow is apt to be so much cut up that it is impossible to follow the original track unless its size serves to distinguish it; and even then it may cross and recross its own path so many times as to bewilder the hunter, who must now do one of two things: either advance stealthily and noiselessly through the swamp, without regard to the footprints, hoping by chance to get a shot; or he must make a wide detour, circling around it, to see if the track he is after leads away in any direction. If it does not, he knows that the Deer is still in the swamp, and must return and attempt to find it. Appreciating the difficulty of the undertaking, he moves with great deliberation, his practised eye penetrating, at each step, every space and recess that the slight change of position brings in view. To the left he observes a prostrate maple, felled by the wind, and, knowing that Deer are fond of the kind of browse* it

---

* Deer greedily devour the lichens that adhere to the branches of trees that have long been dead, and the buds and twigs of those that were living when they fell. This fact is well-known to woodsmen, who invariably assert that if a tree falls during the night, tracks of Deer can always be found there next morning. And I have heard more than one old hunter affirm it to be his sincere belief that Deer know the cause of the noise produced by a falling tree, and, guided by the sound, at once set out in quest of the spot.

Mr. John Constable tells me that he once shot a Deer in the act of browsing upon the lichens that clung to a fallen tree-top. The animal was standing on its hind-legs, with its fore-feet resting upon a large limb, and was reaching up for the lichens.

affords, works cautiously toward it. The branches are reached
but no live thing is seen, and his eyes are bent in other directions
when,—*crash, crash*, under his very nose, and he is deluged with
a shower of snow that, for the moment, completely blinds him. He
may, or he may not, get his eyes open in time to catch a vanish-
ing glimpse of the affrighted Deer, and, now that it is too late,
discovers the bed of his would-be victim under the fallen tree-top,
at his very feet.

The hunter rarely sees the whole outline of a Deer in still-
hunting. The forests are so thick, and the evergreens so loaded
with snow, that an object is not commonly visible at any great
distance, and a part of the leg or a patch of hair constitute the
target usually presented to his eye. He sometimes fires directly
at what he sees, and sometimes " allows a trifle" aiming a little
ahead or a little behind, as the case may be. If severely wounded,
without being killed outright, the animal is generally left for
several hours, or until the next day; for if pursued it would continue to run as long as its strength held out; while, on the other
hand, if left alone it soon lies down and will probably never rise
again. Judge Caton says: " But few animals will go so far and
so fast, after receiving a mortal wound, as a Virginia Deer," * and
I have myself followed a buck, shot through both lungs with a 44
calibre rifle-ball, more than a mile and a half through the woods !

In localities where Deer are abundant an expert still-hunter
frequently kills two or three in a single day, but such hunts are
very laborious, for the track often leads many miles, in a tortuous
course, over hard-wood ridges, across stretches of spruce and
hemlock, and through dense balsam and cedar swamps. It is a
long distance to camp, but thitherward, at nightfall, the weary
hunter wends his way. His course lies through a swamp in which
the evergreens grow so near together that the eye is unable to
penetrate farther than a few paces in any direction, and are so

* Loc. Cit., p. 383.

loaded with snow that the dark green of the few uncovered branches contrasts markedly with the uniform white of the tent-like cones from which they protrude. The silence is oppressive, and unbroken even by the sighing of the wind. The imagination, aided by the gathering shades of dusk, sees in this picture a primeval forest, amongst whose time-worn trunks stands the long deserted encampment of a bygone race. The well-preserved wigwams of spotless white, bleached by many winters, and pitched upon a floor of alabaster, mark the final bivouac of an unremembered nation.

Of the three methods of hunting heretofore considered, *driving* is the least sportsmanlike, and affords the Deer the smallest chance of escape. It requires neither skill nor cunning on the part of the executioner ; for patience, and a very ordinary amount of common sense, are the only essentials. It has this advantage, however, that the Deer, if wounded at all, is almost certain to be killed outright,—which cannot be said of the other methods.

*Floating* requires one of the actors to be expert in the use of the paddle, and is really quite an exciting diversion. This is partly because it can only be practised by night, and partly because each change of position of the boat, and each curve and bend of the shore brings new objects into the limited field of vision, keeping the expectation in a state of acute tension. But after all, when the novelty has worn off, one cannot help realizing that it is like carrying a lantern, any dark night, through a frontier pasture, and shooting the first unlucky cow that chances to stand in the path.

In *still-hunting*, on the other hand, the hunter is thrown entirely upon his own resources, and it is the only method of taking the Deer in this Wilderness that requires any particular skill or labor on his part. The guide is here superfluous, unless it be to string up the game and find the shortest way to camp when the hunt is over. Still-hunting tends to toughen the muscles, to sharpen the vision, to quicken the hearing, and to impart to the whole system a glow of health and vigor. It calls into play the exercise of functions that are apt to be neglected by the student and man of business, and inspires the lover of nature with a zeal and enthusiasm not easily extinguished.

In addition to the three foregoing legitimate (!) methods of hunting the Deer, there are sometimes practised here two other ways of killing—I might better say butchering—that are too despicable even to be spoken of without a feeling of shame. They are : by means of *licks*, and by *crusting*.

A *lick* is a place where salt is put,* and the supply from time to time replenished. The Deer, being exceedingly fond of salt, after having once discovered the place, repair to it with great regularity. When they have visited the lick nightly for some little time, which is ascertained by examining the ground round about for tracks, the murderous pot-hunter, armed with a double-barrelled gun loaded with buck-shot, secretes himself at dusk behind some convenient covert, or in a neighboring tree, and in silence awaits the approach of his unsuspecting victim.

*Crusting* is a method of destruction that is still more unfair and atrocious than that just described, and is only practised by the most worthless and depraved vagabonds. It depends, fortunately, upon a condition of the deep snows that is usually of short duration, and rarely occurs save in the months of February and March. When the snow averages four or five feet in depth on the level, a thaw, followed by a freeze, converts the surface into a stiff crust which renders the Deer very helpless. Taking advantage of this state of things, the crust-hunters sally forth. Their snow-shoes enable them to skim lightly over the surface, whilst the poor Deer

---

* The only natural deer-lick in the Adirondacks, so far as I am aware, is thus spoken of by Mr. Colvin : " I observed in a moist place a deposit of marly clay, a rare thing in this region. What was most interesting, however, was the fact that this was a natural deer-lick, many places showing where the Deer had licked the clay, possibly obtaining a trifle of potash, alumina, and iron, derived from sulphates from decomposing pyrites." (Report of the Adirondack Survey, 1880, p. 193.)

are unable to move except by the greatest effort, and are soon exhausted. They sink to their bellies at every plunge, the sharp
hoofs cutting through the frozen crust, which lacerates their
slender legs till the tracks are stained with blood. The cruel foe
is upon them, and well do they realize that the struggle is for
life. Every muscle is strained to the utmost in the frantic effort to escape, but in vain. Every leap tells bitterly on the fast-
waning strength, and they soon sink in the snow, breathless and
with heaving sides. Their large liquid eyes are turned toward
their brutal pursuers, as if to implore mercy, but none is given.
All share a like fate—they are butchered in cold blood.

### Deer Protection.

For many years an army of hardy lumbermen, wood-choppers,
and bark-peelers has been steadily at work, together with its con-
comitant devastating fires, in making progressive and disastrous
inroads upon the ill-fated forests of the Adirondacks. Much of the
proper borders of the region, long since stripped of timber, present to the eye a desolate and barren waste, whose present irregular boundaries are still contracting with ominous rapidity.

New saw-mills, pulp-mills, and numerous other manufacturing
establishments that consume vast quantities of wood, are constantly being erected; and, as if this were not enough, it is
possible that before the snows of another winter cover the earth,
a railroad will pierce the very heart of this grand Wilderness.

It augurs ill for the Deer when the footprints of the panther or
wolf are found near its winter quarters, but the cold steel tracks
of the iron horse admonish us of the presence of a tenfold more
insidious and subtle foe; for the railroad not only brings the Deer's
greatest enemy, man, into its immediate haunts, but destroys and
carries off the forests that constitute its home. Hence it naturally follows that unless the region is early converted into a State
Preserve, which, unfortunately, seems hardly probable, the laws that

heretofore sufficed to enable this animal to hold its own, will soon prove inadequate. Therefore, the subject of Deer Protection becomes one that claims earnest and thoughtful consideration from our sportsmen and hunters, and demands intelligent and judicious legislation.

The present law was a fairly good one at the time of its enactment, but it has ceased to meet existing conditions; that it will prove ineffectual against the demands of the rapidly increasing occupancy and destruction of the forests, requires no great perspicacity to foretell.

There are two weak points in the law as it now stands: 1st, the open season is too long by at least a month; and 2d, there is no limit put to the number of Deer that a party, or an individual, may kill during this period. The season begins with the month of August, and when the weather is propitious more than a hundred boats are nightly engaged in *floating*, on the various watercourses of the Adirondacks. Now it is an undisputed fact that, by this method of hunting, more than twice as many does as bucks are killed, and that a large percentage of those fired at are wounded, and escape into the woods to die. It is also a fact that, as a rule, each doe has two fawns, and that fawns deprived of their mother's milk before the first of September usually die. Hence the appalling truth becomes apparent, that for every twenty-five Deer secured by floating, at least fifty (and probably a much larger number) must be destroyed! Therefore it seems proper that the season should not open before the first of September. The second weak point in the law is also a vital one. It is notorious that during the past two years many hundreds of Deer have been slaughtered over and above the number necessary to keep the parties killing them supplied with venison. In parts of Canada, and in the State of Maine, the law sets a limit to the number of moose, caribou, and Deer that may be killed by an individual or camp during a given period, and I see no reason why a similar law might not be enacted and enforced in our own State with like good results.

## NOTES ON EXTERMINATED AND EXTINCT UNGULATES.

NOTE 1.—It is not many years since the Moose (*Alce Americanus*) was a favorite object of pursuit in the Adirondacks, from which region it was exterminated, as nearly as I can ascertain, about the year 1861.

Dr. DeKay, in his Zoology of New York, said of these animals : " They are yet numerous in the unsettled portions of the State, in the counties of Essex, Herkimer, Hamilton, Franklin, Lewis, and Warren ; and since the gradual removal of the Indians, they are now (1841) believed to be on the increase  .  .  .  .  The Moose furnishes an excellent material from its hide for moccasins and snow-shoes. The best skin is obtained from the bull Moose in October, and usually sells for four dollars. They were formerly so numerous about Raquet Lake, that the Indians and French Canadians resorted thither to obtain their hides for this purpose ; and hence we have the origin of the name of that lake, the word *raquet* meaning *snow-shoes*. They still exist in its neighborhood."

The Moose is a huge animal, the adult males often standing six feet in height at the shoulders, and exceeding a thousand pounds in weight,  Evidence of its former presence here may still be seen in various parts of the Wilderness, where the long scars of its " peelings " yet remain. These commonly consist of small soft or swamp maples (*Acer rubrum* L.) and striped maples (*A. Pennsylvanicum* L.) from which the bark has been stript, from a short distance above the ground to the height of eight or even ten feet. This bark, together with the branches of the same tree, and several kinds of browse, constitute its principal food in winter. In summer it feeds also upon marsh grasses and aquatic plants, notably upon the roots of the pond lily.

In the fall of 1853 Thoreau met an Indian, named Tahmunt Swa-sen, in the forests near Moosehead Lake, Maine, who told him that he had hunted Moose in the Adirondacks in New York, but that they were more plentiful in the Maine woods.*

Concerning the abundance of the Moose in the Adirondacks subsequent to 1850, and its final disappearance from the region, I have taken great pains to solicit information, both through private inquiry and correspondence, and publicly through the medium of *Forest and Stream.* The result of this investigation, in which I have been greatly aided by Dr. Frederick H. Hoadley, is a deluge of individual opinion and conflicting statement, together with a meagre amount of positive information of a strictly reliable character.

Early in March, 1851, Mr. John Constable and his brother Stevenson killed two Moose near the head of Independence Creek, in Herkimer County. They killed their last Moose in March, 1856, west of Charley's Pond, in Hamilton County. Mr. Constable writes me: "I never recur to those hunts with any satisfaction, for much as I enjoyed at the time the tramp of more than a hundred miles on snow-shoes, the camping in the snow, the intense excitement of the search and pursuit, I must ever regret the part I have taken unwittingly in exterminating this noble animal from our forests. Were I younger, I would assist in reinstating them, as the plan is perfectly feasible. In the early years of my still-hunting, moose were quite numerous, and I rarely, if ever, failed to see signs of their peelings or their tracks."

In the year 1852 or 1853 the well-known guides, Alonzo Wood and Ed. Arnold, killed two Moose and found a third dead, back of Seventh Lake Mountain, in Hamilton County.

Dr. J. H. Guild writes me from Rupert, Vermont, that a Moose was killed at or near Mud Lake, in the Lower Saranac region, in 1856.

---

* The Maine Woods. By Henry D. Thoreau, Boston, 1864, p. 141.

In July of the same year (1856) Ed. Arnold killed a Moose at Nick's Lake; and in the following spring a man named Baker killed another in the same vicinity.

One evening during the summer of 1858 a Moose strayed into the Wood's garden at Raquette Lake, but was not shot.

The Hon. Horatio Seymour, ex-Governor of the State of New York, killed a huge bull Moose in the forest North of Joc's Lake. Its head and horns may now be seen at his farm in Deerfield, N. Y.

The Governor writes me : " It was a very large animal and was disposed to charge upon our party ; but for our dog it might have made us trouble. The snow was very deep and covered with a crust. The dog could run upon this while the Moose sunk through it. This enabled the dog to worry the animal and turn its attention away from our party." He does not remember the year in which it was killed.

In July, 1861, the artist Mr. A. F. Tait, and Mr. James B. Blossom, both of New York, were camped on Constable Point, Raquette Lake. One night about the middle of the month, while floating on Marion River, Mr. Tait wounded a Moose, but did not kill it. On the 25th of the month, about four o'clock in the afternoon, Mr. Blossom shot and killed a dry cow Moose on South Inlet.

The measurements of this animal, taken by Mr. Blossom at the time and on the spot, are :

| | |
|---|---|
| Length, | 7 feet, 1 inch. |
| Height (at shoulder), | 6 feet, 1 inch. |
| Head, | 2 feet, 2 inches. |
| Ears, | 1 foot. |
| Girth, | 5 feet, 4 inches. |
| Fore leg, | 3 feet, 5 inches. |
| Hind leg (hip bone to hoof), | 5 feet, 5 inches. |

Early in August of the same year (1861) the hunter William Wood killed a bull calf near the place where Mr. Tait had wounded his Moose. It had a broken jaw, was very lean, and was un-questionably the animal wounded by Mr. Tait.

In *Forest and Stream* for April 2d, 1874 (p. 116), Mr. Edw. Clarence Smith states that a cow Moose was killed on Marion River (East Inlet of Raquette Lake) during the summer of 1861. He says that it was shot by a guide by the name of Palmer from Long Lake, while feeding upon lily-pads, about three o'clock in the afternoon; and that " the persons present were Isaac Gerhart, lawyer; Mr. Burgin, Rev. Augustus Smith, now settled in West Philadelphia, and the undersigned, all residents of Philadelphia." In response to interrogations, Mr. Smith writes me that this Moose was killed in the month of August. Mr. Smith had also the kind-ness to address a letter of inquiry, in my behalf, to Isaac Gerhart, Esq., a member of the party. Mr. Gerhart's reply is so full of in-teresting details that I make no apology for publishing the greater part of it *verbatim*. He writes: " I should say the Moose was shot about the end of the second week in August, 1861, at the mouth of the East Inlet of Raquette Lake, on whose shore, about four miles distant, we then had a camp. We had been up this inlet, your correspondent calls it Marion River—a name I cannot recall,—for a day's trout fishing. You and your brother [Rev. H. Augustus Smith] and guide were in one boat; Burgin, a guide, and I in another. We, as usual, 'tho' on fishing bent,' still had our trusty guns, lest some chance game should find us unprepared. At its mouth the Inlet was bordered on either hand by a thickly wooded shore, terminating on the south side in a short promontory, round the end of which a sloping shore curved off to the southwest. Off this sloping shore grew in the water a border of lily-pads, perhaps a hundred feet wide, and about half as far from the edge of the water the shore became bold and thickly wooded. We were rowing steadily down, the bottoms of our boats covered with finny spoils. I was in the bow of the foremost boat, when, as we came abreast of the end of the promontory, I caught sight of the monster up to her belly in water, cropping the tender lily-shoots.  I shall never forget the confusing impression the sight made upon me.  In my mind the Moose was always associated with imposing antlers, such as I had seen in the pictured and stuffed specimens which had all been of males ;  but this uncouth creature had only immense ears, which, though its head was below the humped shoulders, still towered above them.  I felt that it must be game because of the complete wildness of the surroundings ;  and yet it seemed so suggestive of an exaggerated caricature of a jackass, that the idea passed across my mind that there might be some clearing in the neighborhood to which it belonged.  I do not think my guide's impressions were any more coherent than mine, for, although he was a year or two past his majority and had been born and bred in the woods, he had never seen a Moose.  Meanwhile, profiting by our confusion of ideas, Madame Moose had 'slewed around' in the water, with a view to making for the friendly shelter of the woods, when your boat came within view of the creature and your guide shouted 'Moose! Moose!' which had the effect of clearing up my ideas instantaneously.  In the twinkling of an eye I had lodged in front of her shoulder the contents of my gun—not 'bird shot,' as you suggest, but 'buck-cartridge' consisting of over a dozen buck-shot enclosed in a wire frame, making a load that 'carried' very closely, and made a hole in her at that short range of not over fifty yards, that would doubtless, after one of those long runs for which these animals are famous when fatally wounded, have ended her career.  My shot lent impetus to her progress toward shore.  Then Burgin fired some shot (I think No. 6) into her and she emerged from the water.  The two guides, first ours and then yours,[*] each put a rifle ball into her, and she fell heavily to rise no more.  She doubtless had a spouse somewhere in the neighborhood, for a party who had been after her for

---

* Mr. Smith writes me: " The shot that brought her to the ground was fired by our guide, one *Palmer* of Long Lake, son of old Palmer, the original settler on Long Lake."

a week had killed a Moose-calf near by that was too young to have left its parents, and claimed to have found tracks of both the old ones. We lived on her tenderloin—after getting her to camp under great difficulties—for about a week.

"On our way out of the region, whence we made our exit at the First Saranac Lake, we stopped at Bartlett's on Round Lake, which appeared to be a famous and extensive rendezvous for hunters and guides; and on the register there we recorded conspicuously opposite our names our notable, albeit fortuitous, achievement.[*] I think we recorded it as weighing about 800 lbs. and standing about seven feet high in the hump. The derisive incredulity which this entry evoked was only silenced by the production of the hide, which we had brought with us."

No credence is to be given to the report, widely circulated by the press, that a Moose has during the past winter been seen near the Ox-bow on Moose River, in the Woodhull Lake region.

NOTE 2.—That the American Elk or Wapiti (*Cervus Canadensis*) was at one time common in the Adirondacks there is no question. A number of their antlers have been discovered, the most perfect of which that I have seen is in the possession of Mr. John Constable. It was found in a bog on Third Lake of Fulton Chain, in Herkimer County.

Dr. DeKay (Zool. N. Y., Part I, 1842, pp. 120–121) speaks of a specimen consisting of "a portion of a pair of horns attached to a fragment of skull," which was "dug up near the mouth of the Raquet River in this State, near the forty-fifth parallel of latitude. It bears a label in the handwriting of Dr. Mitchill, purporting that it

---

* Upon the receipt of the above letter, early in October, 1883, I hoped to ascertain the exact date of the killing of this Moose, and at once wrote to Mr. Bartlett, asking if he would consult his old register and send me a copy of the entry here referred to. Unfortunately, his reply has not yet been received. [Since the above went to press I have learned of Mr. Bartlett's death.]

belonged to the *C. tarandus*, or Rein-deer." * Dr. DeKay appends a table of measurements which clearly indicates that the antler in question was that of our common Elk, though he regarded it as pertaining to the fossil Elk. He mentions another antler, of a younger animal, which "was thrown out by a plow on Grand Isle," in Lake Champlain, and deposited in the Museum of the University of Vermont.

Dr. C. C. Benton, of Ogdensburg, has several specimens, more or less complete. The circumference of the largest at the burr is twelve and one half inches; immediately below the burr ten inches. These specimens were discovered at Steel's Corners in St. Lawrence County.

Mr. Calvin V. Graves, of Boonville, N. Y., has two sections of Elk horns that were "ploughed up in an old beaver meadow in Diana," Lewis County.

When the species was exterminated here is not known. Dr. DeKay, writing in 1842, states: "The stag is still found in the State of New York, but very sparingly, and will doubtless be extirpated before many years. Mr. Beach, an intelligent hunter on the Raquet, assured me that in 1836, he shot at a stag (or as he called it, an elk), on the north branch of the Saranac. He had seen many of the horns, and described this one as much larger than the biggest buck (*C. virginianus*), with immense long and rounded horns, with many short antlers. His account was confirmed by another hunter, Vaughan, who killed a stag at nearly the same place. They are found in the northwestern counties of Pennsylvania, and the adjoining counties of New York. In 1834, I am informed by Mr. Philip Church, a stag was killed at Bolivar, Allegany County. My informant saw the animal, and his description corresponds exactly with this species." †

---

* This specimen is probably the source of Professor Dana's statement . "Remains of the *Reindeer* have been found on Racket River," New York (Dana's Geology, 2d Ed., 1875, p. 568.) I have been unable to find a trustworthy record of the Reindeer or Caribou from this region.

† Zoology of New York, Part I, Mammalia, 1842, p. 119.

I do not regard the above account of Messrs. Beach and Vaughan as trustworthy, for the reason that I have never been able to find a hunter in this wilderness, however aged, who had ever heard of a living Elk in the Adirondacks.

NOTE 3.—It is also worthy of remark that wild horses, larger than our domesticated stock, once roamed the borders of this region. Dr. C. C. Benton, of Ogdensburg, has shown me several fossil molar teeth of *Equus major* that were exhumed at Keenes Station near the Oswegatchie Ox Bow in Jefferson County. I have compared them with the corresponding teeth in an immense dray-horse, and find them much larger.

NOTE 4.—It is hard for us to realize that huge Elephants, in the wild state, ever moved their ponderous bodies over this northern Wilderness; but the fact is incontestibly proved by the discovery of their remains on both sides of the Adirondacks. Dr. Zadock Thompson tells us that a fossil Elephant was found in a muck bed in the township of Mt. Holly, Vermont, (in the Green Mountains,) at an elevation of 1415 feet, in the year 1848.*

A tusk measuring five feet nine inches in length, over the curve, was found, September 20, 1877, in a marl bed about a mile west of the village of Copenhagen in Lewis County. It was purchased for the State Cabinet by Dr. Franklin B. Hough, who described it in the Lowville Times. Whether this tusk belonged to an Elephant or a Mastodon has not been determined.

---

* Appendix to Thompson's Vermont, 1853, pp. 14–15. Dr. Leidy refers this specimen to *Elephas Americanus* (Proc. Acad. Nat. Sci., Phila., VII, 392).

## Order INSECTIVORA.   Family TALPIDÆ.

## CONDYLURA CRISTATA Linnæus.

### *Star-nosed Mole.*

The Star-nosed Mole is a common animal along the outskirts of the Adirondacks, where it seems to manifest a predilection for moist situations, being usually found in low ground and in the neighborhood of streams.   Its food consists almost wholly of the earthworm, and of various insects which it discovers in its meanderings through the soil.   In general, its habits are much like those of the Shrew Mole, though it does not, apparently, make as extensive excavations, and the "mole hills" along the lines of its galleries are larger.

In gardens and ploughed ground they often work so near the surface that a ridge of loose earth is upheaved along the course of their tunnels.   In meadows and pasture lands, on the contrary, the galleries are not marked by surface ridges, for the simple reason that they cannot readily force their way through the tough sod, but excavate their burrows immediately beneath.   Late in the autumn, when the ground becomes frozen to the depth of two or three inches, the Moles sink their galleries into the soft earth below, and as winter advances they doubtless continue to deepen them sufficiently to avoid the frozen ground.   Thus both Moles and earthworms escape the severe temperature of our northern winter by withdrawing below the depth to which the frost penetrates.   It sometimes happens here that a period of severe cold sets in before much snow has fallen, in which case the ground becomes frozen to the depth of two feet or more.   But this state of things is not apt to continue, for advancing winter is almost certain to bring with it a large amount of snow, which, as is well known, keeps out the cold and dissipates the frost already in the earth.   I have known the ground to be frozen for two feet below the surface when a fall of about four feet of snow took place.   Within two weeks afterward the ground thawed and the surface became moist and mellow though the temperature remained low. Indeed, it is not uncommon for fresh green grass to spring up under the heavy covering which Dame Nature spreads over her northern possessions in winter ; and residents of cold countries often avail themselves of the protection afforded by seemingly inhospitable snow banks.

There is a low and somewhat wet piece of ground bordering a small creek near my home in Lewis County. During and after every heavy rain, and for a considerable period in spring and fall, this creek overflows its banks and a large part of the surrounding flat is converted into a swamp. Star-nosed Moles have been common here ever since I can remember, their hills dotting the surface in various directions. In the fall of 1883 a colony of them were exceedingly active in one part of this flat and their mounds could be counted by hundreds over an area a few acres in extent. For the double purpose of procuring specimens, and of ascertaining if more species than one were concerned in these excavations, I determined to trap some of the animals, and was joined in the undertaking by Dr. A. K. Fisher.

This species, as well as Brewer's and the Shrew Mole, may be trapped by taking advantage of the habit of removing obstacles from the primary galleries, which are always kept in repair. A snare of fine wire or horse hair made to surround the runway, and connected with a bit of stick that protrudes into the burrow and liberates a small springpole when moved, is the best device for their capture with which I am acquainted. The traps made by us consisted of a small strip of board with a bow or hoop set in each end, to keep the wire loops in place, and so arranged that the Mole is equally apt to be taken from whichever direction he comes. During the latter part of October and first of November we set half a dozen traps of this description, visiting them twice daily until November 13th, when a fall of six inches of snow and the freezing of the ground suspended operations for a few days. The weather moderated on the 19th and 20th, and the number of traps set was increased to fifteen. These were also visited both morning and evening and all were kept in good order. A large proportion of them were sprung almost every morning, and others were plastered up with mud in such a way that they could not spring. In fact, on an average, fully twenty traps would be sprung to every Mole secured. I think the springpoles used at first were too weak, and that a few Moles escaped by forcing themselves through the wire loops. But after stiffening the poles we still failed to secure more than a small number of Moles in comparison with the number of traps sprung. Although the traps remained set till the 28th of November, when the ground again became frozen and covered with snow, we secured but nine specimens in all. Eight were of the Star-nosed variety, while the other was a Brewer's Mole (*Scapanus Breweri*). During the same period three more Brewer's Moles were caught on a side hill near by.

Dr. Fisher is of opinion that the Moles, in repairing their galleries, often push a quantity of earth ahead of them in the direction of the mounds, and that this springs the trap before the Mole has arrived at the loop. In a large number of cases this is a very reasonable explanation of the failure to catch the animal, for the traps are frequently found packed full of earth. In other cases they dig around the trap, while occasionally a new burrow is excavated directly beneath it. Whatever else they may do, they invariably plaster over with mud any exposed part of the trap that may appear in the gallery; and they sometimes bury the whole affair by upheaving a hill directly over it.

The exact method by which the little mounds called "mole hills" are produced has long been a matter of earnest inquiry, and I am glad to be able to contribute important testimony upon this point. Repeated critical examinations of the hills themselves in different soils, and occasional observations made at the time of their upheaval, have convinced me that, when in dry earth, it is impossible to arrive at any positive knowledge of the way in which they are made. All that one sees during their formation in dry soil is the upheaval of a quantity of loose earth from a central point, which point speedily becomes indistinguishable as the mound increases in size, the only observable phenomenon consisting in a little heap of dirt every particle of which seems to be in motion, as it steadily approaches completion. The rapidity with which so much earth is thrown up is one of the most perplexing things about it; and the peculiar motion of the mass leads to the notion that it is traversed by galleries and that the Mole is at work within it and not beneath the surrounding ground. On making a section of the mound, however, it is found to contain no cavity unless it be a mere tubular extension of the gallery, and this is absent in more than half the hills examined. On opening the gallery beneath, no chamber or tortuous excavation is discovered, and the fact at once becomes apparent that so much earth as constitutes the hill could not possibly have been obtained from the excavation in its immediate vicinity, and must therefore have been brought from a distance. Just how it was conveyed to and forced through the orifice leading into the hill I have until recently been at a loss to comprehend, but the opportunity to examine some freshly made mounds in a wet pasture of rich loam or mould has cleared up the mystery.

These new mounds consisted wholly of compact cylindrical masses of damp earth, having very much the appearance of Bologna sausages, and measuring from three to five inches in length by one and a half to two in diameter. It was noticeable that the size of each was greater than that of the hole in the sod through which it had been discharged, which circumstance shows that it must have been subjected to considerable pressure during expulsion. On handling these masses they readily broke up, transversely, into a number of more or less parallel discs, or lamellæ, each of which bore evidence of having been powerfully compressed. On exposure to the air they soon lost their cylindrical form and crumbled, so that it is only under peculiarly favorable circumstances that they are to be found at all. They are never present in any but newly made mounds in wet mucky soil. Hence it is perfectly clear that the earth of which the mounds are composed is brought to and extruded through the hole intended for this purpose by being *pushed ahead* of the animal. In being thus crowded along it becomes compressed and moulded to the burrows. How the Mole always manages to force it through the hole he has prepared for it, instead of pushing it into the continuation of the gallery beyond, is by no means so evident. In a great many cases one arm of the gallery curves up into the mound so that the plugs would naturally follow this passage, but in other cases the canal leading to the mound is given off vertically and nearly at a right angle to the runway, while occasionally it commences as a horizontal offshoot, thence sloping upward to the mound.

As the main galleries from time to time require repairs, the superabundant earth is usually disposed of by crowding it up through the old mounds, which sometimes, though rarely, contain a tubular or oval cavity continuous with the holes. Thus, after a rain or frost by which the galleries have been injured, it often happens that many of the old mounds on the lines of the primary runways will be found to have been reopened and the fresh earth which has been removed in making the necessary repairs may be seen on them.

Audubon and Bachman criticise Godman's statement concerning the abundance of this species in certain localities, remarking: " We have sometimes supposed that he might have mistaken the galleries of the common Shrew Mole for those made by the Starnose, as to us it has always appeared a rare species in every part of the Union." * My experience agrees with that of Dr. Godman, for I have frequently observed this species in large colonies, and with us it is certainly one of the commonest Moles.

---

* Quadrupeds of North America, 1851, vol. II, pp. 141–142.

Audubon and Bachman observe : " In a few localities where we were in the habit, many years ago, of obtaining the Star-nosed Mole, it was always found on the banks of rich meadows near running streams. The galleries did not run so near the surface as those of the common Shrew Mole. We caused one of the galleries to be dug out, and obtained a nest containing three young, apparently a week old. The radiations on the nose were so slightly developed that until we carefully examined them we supposed they were the young of the Common Shrew Mole. The nest was spacious, composed of withered grasses, and situated in a large excavation under a stump. The old ones had made their escape, and we endeavoured to preserve the young; but the want of proper nourishment caused their death in a couple of days." * The only nest that I ever found was about two feet below the surface, in clay soil, and under a stump. It was composed of grass, and from it a passage led to a vegetable garden near by.

The same authors assert that " it avoids cultivated fields, and confines itself to meadows and low swampy places." † That this is not always the case I have positive proof, for I have caught a number of them in our garden. By following the ridge of loose earth that marks their progress, and quickly sinking a spade directly in their path, a few inches in advance of the moving earth, I have often turned them out upon the surface. They pass through the rich, soft soil of a garden bed with such rapidity that my spade has sometimes cut them in two, though aimed several inches in advance of the moving earth.

The precise function of the curious disc of tentacle-like papillæ on the snout has not as yet been positively determined, though it is highly probable that it serves as a delicate organ of touch to aid the animal in discovering the worms and insects that constitute its prey.

---

* Ibid., pp. 141–142.          † Ibid., pp. 141–142.

One March, many years ago, when sliding down hill on the crust (the snow then being over three feet in depth) Dr. C. L. Bagg and I observed at different times several dark objects which at a distance looked like little balls of fur. On coming nearer we discovered that these apparently round objects were Star-nosed Moles, trying to bore through the icy crust. They had evidently been moving about on the surface till alarmed by our approach, when, having wandered away from the holes through which they came up, they at once set to work to perforate the crust, but, owing to its unusual hardness, did not succeed in time to make good their escape. We captured two or three and brought them home.

The reason that they are not more often seen here in winter is easily explained. They do not at any time travel much upon the surface, and even when thus engaged their sense of hearing is so acute that they detect the approach of an enemy while yet at a distance, and disappear at once into the snow. All winter long one sees upon the snow many small footprints, that are designated, collectively, as mice, mole, and shrew tracks. I can distinguish, with considerable confidence, those of *Hesperomys*, *Blarina*, and *Sorex*, but who will venture to affirm that he can name the species that makes each of the others?

The tail of this species becomes enormously enlarged during the rutting season, which circumstance led Dr. Harlan to describe a specimen taken during this period as a distinct species, which he named *Condylura macroura*.* I have taken specimens as late as the middle of November whose tails measured 12mm. (.47 in.) in diameter. When in this swollen condition there is a marked constriction at the base, which causes the tail to appear as if strangulated. Two or more litters are produced each season.

The scent glands of this animal secrete a thick creamy material of a greenish yellow color that has a powerful and very disagree-

---

* Fauna Americana, 1825, p. 39.

able odor, which at certain seasons becomes exceedingly rank and nauseous.

## SCALOPS AQUATICUS (Linn.) Fischer.

### *Shrew Mole.*

This species is not common about the borders of the Adirondacks, and is seldom if ever found within the evergreen forests, though it sometimes finds the way to the frontier settler's garden.

Its specific name, *aquaticus*, like many others in Zoological nomenclature, has been unfortunately chosen and has no bearing on the habits of the animal ; for not only is the Shrew Mole not known voluntarily to swim, but in the selection of its haunts it shows no preference for the vicinity of water, but manifests rather a contrary tendency.

Its home is underground, and its entire lifetime is spent beneath the surface. Its food consists almost wholly of earth-worms, grubs, ants, and other insects that live in the earth and under logs and stones It is almost universally regarded as an enemy to the farmer, and is commonly destroyed whenever opportunity affords ; for, notwithstanding the fact that it subsists upon insects that injure the crops, it is nevertheless true that, in the procurement of these, it disfigures the garden paths and beds, by the ridges and little mounds of earth that mark the course of its subterranean galleries, and loosens and injures many choice plants in its probings for grubs amongst their roots.

The strength of the Shrew Mole is simply prodigious, for an animal of its diminutive size, and the speed with which it forces itself through the ground is marvellous. Audubon and Bachman, speaking of one they had in confinement, state : " We afterwards put the Mole into a large wire rat-trap, and to our surprise saw him insert his fore-paws or hands, between the wires, and force them apart sufficiently to give him room to pass out through them at once, and

this without any great apparent effort." * Dr. Godman also tells us
that one which he had " in a basket on the mantlepiece of a parlour
made its escape, and fell to the hearth ; apparently it sustained little
injury by the fall, but hurried on until it reached the wall, where it
began to travel round the room. Whenever its course was impeded
by the feet of the chairs, which were of large size, it would not go
round them, but wedging itself between them and the wall, pushed
them with apparent ease far enough to obtain a free passage, and it
thus continued to move several in succession. What was more
astonishing, it passed in a similar manner behind the legs of a small
mahogany breakfast-table, and pushed it aside in the same way it
had done the chairs, finally hiding itself behind a pile of quarto
volumes, more than two feet high, which it also moved out from the
wall." † Now I have made a pile, just two feet high, of quarto
volumes, and find that to move it on a smooth, painted floor requires
a force of eighteen pounds (Avoirdupois), and on a carpet, of twenty-
two pounds. In order to display a degree of strength proportionate
to the difference in weight of the two, a man would have to exert a
push pressure of twelve thousand pounds !

Its nest is commonly half a foot or more below the surface, and
from it several passages lead away in the direction of its favorite
foraging grounds. These primary passages gradually approach the
surface, and finally become continuous with, or open into, an ever
increasing multitude of tortuous galleries, which wind about in every
direction, and sometimes come so near the surface as barely to
escape opening upon it, while at other times they are several inches
deep. Along the most superficial of these horizontal burrows the
earth is actually thrown up, in the form of long ridges, by which the
animal's progress can be traced. The distance that they can thus
travel in a given time is almost incredible. Audubon and Bachman
state that they have been known, in a single night after a rain, to

---

* Quadrupeds of North America, vol. I, 1846, pp. 85–86.

† American Natural History, by John D. Godman, M. D., vol. I, 1842, p. 64.

excavate a gallery several hundred yards in length; and I have myself traced a fresh one nearly one hundred yards. The only method by which we can arrive at a just appreciation of the magnitude of this labor is by comparison; and computation shows that in order to perform equivalent work a man would have to excavate, in a single night, a tunnel thirty-seven miles long, and of sufficient size to easily admit of the passage of his body.

In following the galleries of the Shrew Mole one finds a number of little hills of loose earth, each measuring from four to six inches in height, and eight to ten in diameter. They are usually in groups, a few feet apart, but are sometimes isolated. Lawns and flower beds are often disfigured by them in a few hours, for a large number are sometimes thrown up in a surprisingly short space of time. " I have often examined these eminences," writes Dr. Godman, " and have never been able fully to understand how they are formed; a slight motion is observed at the surface, and presently this loose earth is seen to be worked up through a small orifice, whence, falling on all sides, by its accumulation the hills just mentioned are produced. It seems to be brought from some distance, for on breaking up the gallery, it was evident that more earth had been thrown out than could have been removed in excavating the immediately adjoining portions of the burrow. In one instance I have seen the shrew-mole show the extremity of its snout from the centre of one of these loose hills, where it had come at mid-day, as if for the purpose of enjoying the sunshine, without exposing its body to the full influence of the external air." *

I have many times observed small areas, several square yards in extent, particularly in meadow-land, where the ground was fairly covered with mole-hills, and so cut up with their galleries that in walking over it one was sure to break through the surface. It seems reasonable to suppose that the animal discovers, in these places, an

---

* Loc. cit., p. 62.

II

abundance of some favorite food—perhaps a colony of grubs feeding upon the roots of the grass.

When the Shrew Mole encounters a rock, or an old log or stump, in the course of his subterranean wanderings, instead of avoiding it, he takes great pains to burrow beneath, making extensive excavations in contact with its under surface. The reason is obvious, for he knows as well as we do that in such places are to be found many earth-worms, slugs, ants with their eggs, and other tender insects.

It is not probable that the remoter secondary galleries are traversed more than a few times, for the animal makes new ones every day ; but the primary passages which lead to the nest are in constant use, and are always kept in repair. In this connection Dr. Godman, whose biography of this species is the most complete and accurate we possess, observes : " It is remarkable how unwilling they are to re-linquish a long frequented burrow ; I have frequently broken down or torn off the surface of the same burrow for several days in succes-sion, but would always find it repaired at the next visit. This was especially the case with one individual whose nest I discovered, which was always repaired within a short time, as often as destroyed. It was an oval cavity, about six or seven inches in length by three in breadth, and was placed at about eight inches from the surface in a stiff clay. The entrance to it sloped obliquely downwards from the common gallery, about two inches from the surface ; three times I entirely exposed this cell by cutting out the whole superincumbent clay with a knife, and three times a similar one was made a little beyond the situation of the former, the excavation having been con-tinued from its back part. I paid a visit to the same spot two months after capturing its occupant, and breaking up the nest, all the injuries were found to be repaired, and another excavated within a few inches of the old one. Most probably numerous individuals, composing a whole family, reside together in these extensive galleries." He further says : " Shrew-moles are most active early in the morning, at mid-day, and in the evening ; after rains they are particularly busy in repairing their damaged galleries, and in long continued **wet** weather we find that they seek the high grounds for security. The precision with which they daily come to the surface at twelve o'clock is very remarkable, and is well known in the country. In many instances when we have watched them, they appeared exactly at twelve, and at this time only have we succeeded in taking them alive, which is easily done by intercepting their progress with a spade, broad blade, &c., and throwing them on the surface." *

Audubon and Bachman discourse as follows upon the feeding habits of one they had in confinement : " When this Mole was fed on earth-worms (*Lumbricus terrenus*), as we have just related, we heard the worms crushed in the strong jaws of the animal, with a noise somewhat like the grating of broken glass, which was probably caused by its strong teeth gnashing on the sand or grit contained in the bodies of the worms. These were placed singly on the ground near the animal, which after smelling around for a moment turned about in every direction with the greatest activity, until he felt a worm, when he seized it between the outer surface of his hands or fore-paws, and pushed it into his mouth with a continually repeated forward movement of the paws, cramming it downward until all was in his jaws. Small sized earth-worms were dispatched in a very short time ; the animal never failing to begin with the anterior end of the worm, and apparently cutting it as he eat, into small pieces, until the whole was devoured. On the contrary, when the earth-worm was of a large size, the Mole seemed to find some difficulty in managing it, and munched the worm sideways, moving it from one side of its mouth to the other. On these occasions the gritting of its teeth, which we have already spoken of, can be heard at a distance of several feet. . . . . Although this species, as we have seen, feeds principally on worms, grubs, &c., we have the authority of our friend Ogden Hammond, Esq., for the following example either

---

* Loc. cit., pp. 63–64, 65.

of a most singular perversity of taste, or of habits hitherto totally unknown as appertaining to animals of this genus, and meriting a
farther inquiry. While at his estate near Throg's Neck, on Long
Island Sound, his son, who is an intelligent young lad, and fond of
Natural History, observed in company with an old servant of the
family, a Shrew Mole in the act of swallowing, or devouring, a common toad—this was accomplished by the Mole, and he was then
killed, being unable to escape after such a meal, and was taken to
the house, when Mr. Hammond saw and examined the animal, with
the toad partially protruding from its throat. This gentleman also
related to us some time ago, that he once witnessed an engagement
between two Moles, that happened to encounter each other, in one
of the *noon-day* excursions, this species is so much in the habit of
making. The combatants sidled up to one another like two little
pigs, and each tried to root the other over, in attempting which,
their efforts so much resembled the manner of two boars fighting,
that the whole affair was supremely ridiculous to the beholder,
although no doubt to either of the bold warriors, the consequences
of an overthrow would have been a very serious affair; and the
conqueror, would vent his rage upon the fallen hero, and punish him
severely with his sharp teeth. We have no doubt these conflicts
generally take place in the love season, and are caused by rivalry, and
that some 'fair Mole' probably rewards the victor." *

Farther on, the same authors observe : " We had an opportunity on
two different occasions of examining the nests and young of the
Shrew Mole. The nests were about eight inches below the surface,
the excavation was rather large and contained a quantity of oak
leaves on the outer surface, lined with soft dried leaves of the crab-
grass (*Digitaria sanguinalis*). There were galleries leading to
this nest, in two or three directions. The young numbered in one
case, five, and in another, nine.

---

* Quadrupeds of North America, vol. I, 1846, pp. 85–86, 87–88.

" Our kind friend, J. S. Haines, Esq., of Germantown, near Philadelphia, informed us that he once kept several Shrew Moles in confinement for the purpose of investigating their habits, and that having
been neglected for a few days, the strongest of them killed and ate
up the others ; they also devoured raw meat, especially beef, with
great avidity." *

*Explanation of Erroneous Notions Concerning the Food of the Mole.*

It is unfortunate (for the Mole, at any rate) that the farmers and
gardeners still cling to the mistaken notion that the Mole eats the
roots of vegetables and other plants. In support of this view they
affirm that they have followed the galleries of these animals along
rows of garden plants and have found some of the roots gnawed
entirely off, and others more or less injured. Granted ; but this is
circumstantial and presumptive evidence only, and is negatived
by the facts hereinafter related. The truth of the matter is this :
The Mole follows the row of plants in order to obtain the insects
that gather in the rich soil about their roots, and doubtless occasionally injures a few by loosening the earth around them, or possibly
even by scratching them in his efforts to procure the grubs.

Presently a field mouse (*Arvicola*) comes along and discovers the
gallery of the Mole. It is just the right size, or perhaps a trifle large,
so he enters without delay and is delighted to find that it leads
directly to his favorite articles of diet, the roots of garden vegetables.
It is this abundant and destructive pest that does the mischief, while
the poor Mole gets the credit of it, and very likely loses his head in
consequence.

As bearing upon this subject I quote from the pen of Samuel
Woodruff, Esq., some evidence that may fairly be regarded as conclusive. Mr. Woodruff commences by stating that he had always
supposed the Mole to be herbivorous, and now that the contrary had
been asserted, determined to prove the matter by actual experiment,

---

* Ibid., p. 90.

as soon as he could obtain a subject. Having finally procured " a full grown, healthy, and vigorous mole " of this species, he goes on to say : " I confined him in a wooden box about two feet square, placing on the bottom six or eight inches depth of earth, and before him a potato, a beet, a carrot, a parsnip, turnip, and an apple.

" Early next morning I found him exceedingly languid, and apparently exhausted, barely able to turn himself over when placed on his back. All the vegetables remained whole—none having been bitten. I then presented him the head and whole neck of a fowl, with the feathers on ; he instantly seized it, and fed upon it with great avidity. I found him the next morning, plump, strong and active— nothing left of the head and neck of the fowl, except the beak, part of the skull, and bones of the neck, the latter being gnawed and stripped of all the flesh. I then left him with a whole chicken about the size of a quail. The next day, I found upon examination, nothing left of the chicken, with the exception of the beak, wing feathers, and a few of the larger bones. I then treated him to the head, neck, and entrails of another fowl. He first devoured the entrails, and after that, the head and neck, with the exceptions as stated in the first instance. Satisfied with this course, I changed his regimen on the evening of the 17th, from flesh to cheese, with the addition of potato boiled with meat; the animal was then full and vigorous. The next morning I found him dead—the cheese and potatoes as I had left them, none of which had been eaten. The belly and sides of the mole were much contracted and depressed.

" During the whole time of his confinement, he had been well supplied with water and ice. The whole of the vegetables put into the box remained unbitten.

" The result of this experiment has removed from my mind all doubts respecting the character and habits of this singular animal . . . . it is clearly not herbivorous, and may be truly ranked among carnivorous animals." *

---

* American Journal of Science and Arts, vol. XXVIII, No. 1, pp. 169–170.

# SCAPANUS AMERICANUS (Bartram, MS.) Coues. *

## *Hairy-tailed Mole ; Brewer's Mole.*

I have secured a number of examples of this species from the borders of the Wilderness, but have not observed it within the coniferous forests. Specimens have been taken in the garden, where it excavates long and tortuous burrows, often marked upon the surface by crumbling ridges of earth.

Its habits, so far as I am aware, resemble those of its nearest relative, the shrew mole (*Scalops aquaticus*), except that its mounds do not contain a chamber and surface opening, and its galleries are usually made a little deeper. Like this species it is most common in dry meadow lands, while the star-nose is usually found in moist or swampy places. It is much more common here than the shrew mole, and is evidently a more northern animal. It is not known to indulge in the little "noon-day excursions" which, as already related, are characteristic of the last-named species.

In a wet meadow where Dr. Fisher and I caught eight star-nosed moles in October and November, 1883, we procured but one Brewer's Mole. It was taken in the following manner : A section of stove pipe, the lower end of which had been closed with a tight-fitting board, was sunk along the line of a gallery to such a depth that its upper edge was on a level with the floor of the runway. The surface opening was covered over with a piece of rubber cloth to exclude the light. For some time the moles worked around this pitfall without tumbling in, to prevent which operation Dr. Fisher arranged a pair of wings or leads (strips of boards), placing their inner ends flush with the pipe. The Moles now adopted a new mode of procedure and filled the pipe with dirt so that they might pass over it with impunity. It was left in this condition for some days and then

---

* In the *American Naturalist* for March, 1879 (pp. 189–190), Dr. Coues refers this species, which is generally known as *S. Breweri*, to *Talpa Americana* (Bartram, MS.) Harlan. This conclusion is corroborated by Dobson in his Monograph of the Insectivora (Part II, London, June 1883, pp. 134–135).

the dirt was quietly removed.   Within twenty-four hours a large and handsome Brewer's Mole was found in the pipe.

The modification of structure that adapts this animal to its peculiar mode of life affords a most remarkable example of animal specialization.   The conical head, terminating in a flexible cartilaginous snout, and unincumbered with external ears or eyes to catch the dirt, constitutes an effective wedge in forcing its way through narrow apertures ;   the broad and powerful hands, whose fingers are united nearly to their very tips and armed with long and stout claws, supply the means by which the motive power is applied, and serve to force the earth away laterally to admit the wedge-like head ; while the apparent absence of neck, due to the enormous development of muscles in connection with the shoulder-girdle, the retention of the entire arm and forearm within the skin, the short and compact body, and the covering of soft, short, and glossy fur, tend to decrease to a minimum the frictional resistance against the solid medium through which it moves.   In fact, it presents a most extraordinary model of a machine adapted for rapid and continued progress through the earth.

The mole does not, and cannot, *dig* a hole, in the same sense as other mammals that engage in this occupation, either in the construction of burrows or in the pursuit of prey.   When a fox or a woodchuck digs into the ground, the anterior extremities are brought forward, downward, and backward, the plane of motion being almost vertical :   while the Mole, on the other hand, in making its excavations, carries its hands forward, outward, and backward, so that the plane of motion is nearly horizontal.   The movement is almost precisely like that of a man in the act of swimming, and the simile is still closer from the fact that the Mole brings the backs of his hands together in carrying them forward, always keeping the palmar surfaces outward and the thumbs below.   Indeed, when taken from the earth and placed upon a hard floor, it does not tread upon the palmar aspect of its fore-feet, as other animals do, but runs along on the sides of its thumbs, with the broad hands turned up edgewise.

Prof. Baird was the first to add the Hairy-tailed Mole to the fauna of New York State. In the Report of the Regents on the Condition of the State Cabinet of Natural History, 1862, he says: "This species of Mole, although not mentioned by DeKay in the State Natural History, is in reality very abundantly to be met with in the northern part of the State, and apparently to the exclusion of the more southern species with white naked tail, *S. aquaticus*. Its burrows are very different from those of the latter species; being at a considerable distance beneath the surface, with heaps of loose earth thrown up at intervals over the gallery, without any kind of entrance whatever." *

Dr. Harlan thus described the habits of this species, which he supposed identical with the common mole of Europe: " Subterraneous, affecting light and cultivated soils; changing locality according to atmospherical variations; seeking elevated regions during the rainy seasons; excavating long galleries which all communicate with each other, parallel to the surface of the soil, and at moderate depths; elevating the earth into what are denominated *mole-hills;* excavating with their hands, and raising the earth with their head; feeding on worms, insects, roots, bulbs of colchicum, &c.; entering in rut early in the spring, and bringing forth twice annually, four or five at a birth, between the months of March and August; raising their young with the greatest tenderness; forming their nests of leaves, in a spacious chamber, the vault of which is supported by pillars, and which is situated in a manner to be sheltered from inundations." †

But it must be remembered that Dr. Harlan confounded this animal with the European Mole (*Talpa Europæa*), and it is possible that the above is in part compiled from accounts of that species.

---

* Fifteenth Annual Report of the Regents of the University of the State of New York, on the Condition of the State Cabinet of Natural History, 1862, p. 13.

† Fauna Americana, 1825, p. 44.

## Family SORICIDÆ.

# BLARINA BREVICAUDA (Say) Baird.

## *Short-tailed Shrew.*

The Short-tailed Shrew is, I presume, the most abundant of the insectivorous mammals that occur in the Adirondack Mountains, and is found alike in the dense coniferous forests of the interior, and the cleared and settled districts of the surrounding region.

It seeks its food both by day and by night; and, although the greater part of its life is doubtless spent underground, or at least under logs and leaves, and amongst the roots of trees and stumps, it occasionally makes excursions upon the surface, and I have met and secured many specimens in broad daylight.

It subsists upon beechnuts, insects, earth-worms, slugs, sow-bugs, and mice, and can in no way be considered as other than a friend to the farmer. Its burrows are so small that their presence near the roots of plants could hardly prove injurious.

In the selection of its haunts it seems to show a preference for the neighborhood of half-decayed logs, under and within which much of its food is procured. It is also pretty sure to find and undermine old planks and boards that have been left on the ground, and I have captured it under a stone walk. While it is common on the dry ground immediately bordering swamps and streams, I have never known it either to enter the water, or to cross over wet places. It does not appear to be as abundant in those portions of the forest that are covered exclusively with coniferous evergreens, as in the vicinity of hard-wood ridges and groves. This is probably due, partly to the nature of the food supply, and partly to its fondness for travelling under the layer of dead and decomposing leaves that covers the ground in our deciduous forests.

The rigors of our northern winters seem to have no effect in diminishing its activity, for it scampers about on the snow during the severest weather, and I have known it to be out when the thermometer indicated a temperature of −20 Fahr. (−29 C.). It makes long journeys over the snow, burrowing down whenever it comes to an elevation that denotes the presence of a log or stump, and I am inclined to believe that at this season it must feed largely upon the chrysalides and larvæ of insects, that are always to be found in such places.

The eyes of the Shrew are distinctly visible in the living animal, not being covered by the integument, as is the case with some of the moles. Still, the sight is very much restricted, and is, I think, limited almost to the power of discriminating light from darkness. On the other hand, the hearing is exceedingly acute, and tactile sensibility is highly developed.

Mr. John Morden, of Hyde Park, Ontario, has recently published, in the *Canadian Sportsman and Naturalist*, an article " On the Mole." He states that in a trap set for mice he found, at one time, a Shrew and two white-footed mice (*Hesperomys leucopus*), one of the latter being dead and about half eaten. He goes on to say : " The evening of that same day, the mole was placed in an old laundry boiler and the entire dead mouse given to it, which by morning was entirely eaten, bones and all, except the hair. We then gave the mole a large rat just killed, when it at once proceeded to eat out its eyes, and by 4 o'clock next afternoon one side of the rat's head, bone, together with the brains, were eaten, and strange to say, the mole looked no larger . . . . Our curiosity was aroused to know by what means a mole or shrew could kill mice which were larger than itself ; so four large meadow mice being procured, they were placed in the boiler with the mole, which as soon as it met a mouse, showed fight, but the mouse knocked it away with its front feet and leaped as far away as it could. The mole from the first seemed not to see very plainly and started around the boiler at a lively rate, reaching and scenting in all directions with its long nose, like a pig that has broken into a back yard and smells the swill barrel. The mice seemed terror-stricken, momentarily rising on their hind legs, looking for

some place to escape, leaping about squeaking in their efforts to keep
out of the way of the mole which pursued them constantly. The
mole's mode of attack was to seize the mouse in the region of the
throat. This it did by turning its head as it sprang at the mouse, at
the same time uttering a chattering sound. The mice would strike
at, and usually knock the mole away with their front feet, but if the
latter got a hold of the mouse, it would then try to bite, and they
would both tumble about like dogs in a fight. The little chap at last
attacked one mouse and kept with it, and in about ten minutes had
it killed; but even before it was dead the mole commenced eating its
eyes and face. About ten minutes later the mole had devoured all
the head of the mouse and continued to eat. I have captured and
caged several moles this winter and they all display the same untiring
greedy nature. According to my observations the little mammal
under consideration eats about twice or three times its own weight
of food every 24 hours and when we consider that their principal
food consists of insects, it is quite bewildering to imagine the myriads
one must destroy in a year." *

Upon reading the above very interesting observations, I immediately wrote to Mr. Morden for a specimen of the " mole " in question.
It was kindly sent me and proved to be an unusually large Short-
tailed Shrew (*Blarina brevicauda*).

I had not previously known that the Shrew was a mouse-eater,
and hence determined to repeat Mr. Morden's experiments. Therefore, having caught a vigorous, though undersized Shrew, I put him
in a large wooden box and provided him with an ample supply of
beechnuts, which he ate eagerly. He was also furnished with a
saucer of water, from which he frequently drank. After he had remained two days in these quarters, I placed in the box with him an
uninjured and very active white-footed mouse. The Shrew at the
time weighed 11.20 grammes, while the mouse, which was a

---

* Canadian Sportsman and Naturalist, vol. III, Nos. XI & XII, December, 1883 [not published
till February, 1884], p. 283.

large adult male, weighed just 17 grammes. No sooner did the Shrew become aware of the presence of the mouse than he gave chase. The mouse, though much larger than the Shrew, showed no disposition to fight, and his superior agility enabled him, for a long time, easily to evade his pursuer, for at a single leap he would pass over the latter's head and to a considerable distance beyond. The Shrew labored at great disadvantage, not only from his inability to keep pace with the mouse, but also, and to a still greater extent, from his defective eyesight. He frequently passed within two inches (31 mm.) of the mouse without knowing of his whereabouts. But he was persistent, and explored over and over again every part of the box, constantly putting the mouse to flight. Indeed, it was by sheer perseverance that he so harassed the mouse, that the latter, fatigued by almost continuous exertion, and also probably weakened by fright, was no longer able to escape  He was first caught by the tail ; this proved a temporary stimulant, and he bounded several times across the box, dragging his adversary after him. The Shrew did not seem in the least disconcerted at being thus harshly jerked about his domicil, but continued the pursuit with great determination. He next seized the mouse in its side, which resulted in a rough and tumble, the two rolling over and over and biting each other with much energy. The mouse freed himself, but was so exhausted that the Shrew had no difficulty in keeping alongside, and soon had him by the ear. The mouse rolled and kicked and scratched and bit, but to no avail. The Shrew was evidently much pleased and forthwith began to devour the ear. When he had it about half eaten-off the mouse again tore himself free ; but his inveterate little foe did not suffer him to escape. This time the Shrew clambered up over his back and was soon at work consuming the remainder of the ear. This being satisfactorily accomplished, he continued to push on in the same direction till he had cut through the skull and eaten the brains, together with the whole side of the head and part of the shoulder. This completed his first meal, which occupied not quite

fifteen minutes after the death of the mouse. As soon as he had
finished eating I again placed him upon the scales and found that he
weighed exactly 12. grammes—an increase of .80 gramme.

The Shrew was half an hour in tiring the mouse, and another half
hour in killing him. But it must be remembered that he was not
fully grown, and was doubtless, on this account, longer in capturing
and killing his victim than would have been the case had he been an
adult. Still, it is clear that a Shrew could never catch mice on open
ground. His small size, however, enables him readily to enter their
holes and to follow them to their nests and the remotest ramifications
of their burrows, where, having no escape, he can slay them with
fearful certainty.

The eagerness with which my Shrew pursued the mouse placed in
his box, and the persistency and success with which he directed his
attempts to destroy the latter by eating into its head, clearly shows
that this was not his first exploit in that direction. And the fact that
Mr. Morden's Shrews, in Ontario, Canada, acted in the same manner
proves that the habit is not of local origin. Therefore, it is
reasonable to infer that the Short-tailed Shrew preys largely upon
mice, and is, consequently, of great economic value to the farmer.
Indeed, after the skunk, I am inclined to assign him the first place
amongst those of our mammals that are beneficial to the agriculturist.

The Shrews that I have had in confinement have been kept in a
large box, the bottom of which was well covered with earth and
dead leaves, fresh from the woods. Water was given them in a
saucer, which they soon discovered and drank freely. They were
exceedingly active, but always moved on a walk or trot, or by short
springs, never proceeding in a series of leaps. Whenever I approached the box they would run about with their heads thrown up,
sniffing the air in various directions, and starting spasmodically at the
slightest noise. When angry, they utter a shrill, chattering cry.

I have one alive at the present time. When first put in the box
he gathered all the leaves and rootlets into one corner, constructing

a rough nest, to which he always retires when he wants to rest. He is very fond of beechnuts and thrived when fed exclusively on them for more than a week. One evening, not long ago, I put a handful of beechnuts in his water saucer. He soon found them and carried them off. Part he buried in a hole under the saucer, part under his nest, and the rest in an excavation near one corner of the box. This certainly looks as if the animal was in the habit of hoarding for winter. In opening the nuts he invariably commences at the small end, and, after biting a little hole there, strips off one side as neatly as it can be done with a penknife. If left without food for a few hours he will eat corn from the cob, beginning at the outside of the kernel, but it is very clear that he does not relish this fare. He will also eat Indian meal and oats when other food is not at hand. Slugs and earth worms he devours with avidity, always starting at one end, and manipulating them with his fore-paws. But of the various kinds of food placed before him he shows an unmistakable preference for mice—either dead or alive.

The late Robert Kennicott, in a valuable paper upon " The Quadrupeds of Illinois Injurious and Beneficial to the Farmer," contributed the following to the life-history of this little-known mammal :—
" I have several times kept specimens in captivity for a day or two, though they always died by the end of that time, despite my care. While alive, the minute black eye is distinctly seen and always open ; but, though the sense of sight may be possessed in the dark, it certainly is not used in the full light. Upon waving different objects before one, or thrusting my finger or a stick close to its face, no notice was taken of it whatever ; but if I made any noise near by, it always started. If the floor were struck, or even the air disturbed, it would start back from that direction. I observed no indication that an acute sense of smell enabled it to recognize objects at any considerable distance ; but its hearing was remarkable. An exceedingly delicate sense of touch was exhibited by the whiskers, and if, after irritating a shrew, I placed a stick against it, in even the most

gentle manner, the animal would instantly spring at it.   I could see that, in running along the floor, it stopped the moment its whiskers touched anything ;  and often, when at full speed, it would turn aside just before reaching an object against which it seemed about to strike, and which it certainly had not seen.   Unless enraged by being teazed, it endeavored to smell every new object with which its whiskers came in contact, turning its long flexible snout with great facility for this purpose.

"My caged specimens, both male and female, exhibited great pugnacity.   When I touched one several times with a stick, it would become much enraged, snapping and crying out angrily.   When attacked by a meadow-mouse (*Arvicola scalopsoides*) confined in a cage with it one fought fiercely ;  and though it did not pursue its adversary when the latter moved off, neither did it ever retreat ;  but the instant the mouse came close, it sprang at him, apparently not guided in the least by sight.   It kept its nose and whiskers constantly moving from side to side, and often sprang forward with an angry cry, when the mouse was not near, as if deceived in thinking it had heard or felt a movement in that direction.   In fighting, it did not spring up high, nor attempt to leap upon its adversary, as the mouse, but jerked itself along, stopping firmly, with the fore-feet well forward, and the head high.   On coming in contact with the mouse, it snapped at him, and, though it sometimes rose on its hind-feet in the struggle, I did not observe that it used its fore-feet as weapons of offence, like the arvicolæ.   Its posture, when on guard, was always with the feet spread and firmly braced, and the head held with the snout pointing upwards, and the mouth and chin forward, in which position its eyes would have been of no use, could it have seen. The motions of this animal, when angry, are characterized by a peculiar firmness ;  the muscles appear to be held very rigid, while the movements are made by quick energetic jerks.   Short springs, either backward, forward, or sidewise, appear to be made with equal readiness.

" This shrew is quite active as well as strong ; the snout and head are powerful, and seem to be much used in burrowing ; the tough cartilaginous snout received no injury from the rough edge of a pane of glass, under which that of a caged specimen was forcibly thrust in endeavoring to raise it. When liberated, upon a smooth floor, it runs rapidly, without ever leaping, placing only the toes on the surface ; though in moving slowly the whole tarsi of the hind-feet are brought down. By placing an ear of corn, over 2 inches in diameter, at the edge of the room, and chasing a shrew towards it by striking the floor behind the animal, I have seen one several times spring over it, apparently without great effort ; but if not much frightened, it would always go round objects an inch high, running close along them, as it did beside the wall, invariably feeling its way. One would never leave the side of the wall to run across the room, and would always run round the side of its cage, rather than go across the middle. When hurt or irritated, it uttered a short, sharp, tremulous note, like *zee-e*, and, when it was much enraged, this note became longer, harsher, and twittering, like that of some buntings or sparrows. Sometimes, a short, clear cry was uttered, the voice calling to mind that of the common mink (*Putorius vison*), but softer and lower." *

Professor E. D. Cope published the following note " On a Habit of a Species of Blarina" in the American Naturalist for August 1873 (vol. VII, No. 8, pp. 490–491) : " I recently placed a water-snake (*Tropidonotus sipedon*) of two feet in length, in a fernery which was inhabited by a shrew, either a large *Blarina Carolinensis* or a small *B. talpoides.* The snake was vigorous when placed in the case in the afternoon and bit at everything within reach. The next morning the glass sides of his prison were streaked with dirt and other marks, to the height of the reach of the snake, bearing witness to his energetic efforts to escape. He was then lying on the earthen floor, in

---

* Report of the Commissioner of Patents for the Year 1857. Agriculture. 1858. pp. 95–96.

an exhausted state, making a few ineffectual efforts to twist his body, while the *Blarina* was busy tearing out his masseter and temporal muscles. A large part of the flesh was eaten from his tail, and the temporal and masseter muscles and eye of one side, were removed, so that the under jaw hung loose. The temporal was torn loose from the cranium on the other side, and as I watched him the *Blarina* cut the other side of the mandible loose, and began to tear the longicolli and rectus muscles. His motions were quite frantic, and he jerked and tore out considerable fragments with his long anterior teeth. He seemed especially anxious to get down the snake's throat (where some of his kin had probably ' gone before'), and revolved on his long axis, now with his belly up, now with his sides, in his energetic efforts. He had apparently not been bitten by the snake, and was uninjured. Whether the shrew killed the snake is of course uncertain, but the animus with which he devoured the reptile gives some color to the suspicion that he in some way frightened him to exhaustion."

The Shrew is rarely eaten by birds or beasts of prey, but is usually left where killed, which fact is doubtless due to the offensive odor from its scent glands. That it is sometimes eaten appears from the fact that a disgorged pellet from some bird of prey, found in the Catskills by Mr. E. P. Bicknell and Dr. A. K. Fisher, contained the recognizable remains of this species.*

The Short-tailed Shrew is readily taken in an ordinary mouse-trap, baited with meat, set near the mouth of a burrow. I have caught many in this way.

I am not aware that anything has been published relating to its breeding habits, and the only facts that I can contribute are in regard to the time when its young are produced. On the 22d of April, 1878, I found a couple of these Shrews under a plank-walk near my museum. They proved to be male and female, and the latter contained young which, from their size, would probably have been born

---

* Bicknell in Trans. Linn. Soc., vol. I, 1882, p. 122.

early in May. Another female, caught near the same place, April 21, 1884, contained five large embryos which would certainly have been born within ten days. They weighed, together, 4.20 grammes. I procured a half-grown young, February 10, 1884, which must have been born late in the fall. Hence two or three litters are probably produced each season. The young born in autumn do not breed in the spring following, as I have demonstrated by repeated dissections of both sexes.

## SOREX COOPERI Bachman.

### Cooper's Shrew.

This diminutive Shrew, the smallest known mammalian inhabitant of the Adirondacks, is quite common in most parts of the region, but much more abundant some years than others. Its food is supposed to consist wholly of insects and their larvæ, and the carcasses of animals that chance throws in its way.

Like its congeners, it manifests a predilection for the immediate vicinage of old logs and stumps, and its holes can frequently be found, both in summer and winter, in these places, and about the roots of trees.

Underground life does not appear to be as attractive to it as to its relatives, the moles, yet it avoids too much exposure and commonly moves, by night and by day, under cover of the fallen leaves, twigs, and other *debris* that always cover the ground in our northern forests.

The Naturalist well knows that, however cautiously he may walk, the stir of his footstep puts to flight many forms of life that will re-appear as soon as quiet is restored ; therefore, in his excursions through the woods, he waits and watches, frequently stopping to listen and observe. While thus occupied it sometimes happens that a slight rustling reaches his ear. There is no wind, but the eye rests upon a fallen leaf that seems to move. Presently another stirs and perhaps a third turns completely over. Then something evanescent, like the shadow of an embryonic mouse, appears and vanishes before the retina can catch its perfect image. Anon, the restless phantom flits across an open space, leaving no trace behind. But a charge of fine shot, dropped with quick aim upon the next leaf that moves, will usually solve the mystery. The author of the perplexing commotion is found to be a curious sharp-nosed creature, no bigger than one's little finger, and weighing hardly more than half a dram.* Its ceaseless activity, and the rapidity with which it darts from place to place, is truly astonishing, and rarely permits the observer a correct impression of its form.

Whenever a tree or a large limb falls to the ground, these Shrews soon find it, examining every part with great care, and if a knot-hole or crevice is detected, leading to a cavity within, they are pretty sure to enter, carry in materials for a nest, and take formal possession. Hence their homes are not infrequently discovered and destroyed by the wood-chopper.

They are sometimes found in meadows, and I remember killing eleven in one day, several years ago, under hay-cocks that had been standing a few days in the rain.

Not only are these agile and restless little Shrews voracious and almost insatiable, consuming incredible quantities of raw meat and insects with great eagerness, but they are veritable cannibals withal, and will even slay and devour their own kind I once confined three of them under an ordinary tumbler. Almost immediately they commenced fighting, and in a few minutes one was slaughtered and eaten by the other two. Before night one of these killed and ate its only surviving companion, and its abdomen was much distended by the meal. Hence in less than eight hours one of these tiny wild beasts had attacked, overcome, and ravenously consumed two of its own species, each as large and heavy as itself! The functions of digestion, assimilation, and the elimination of waste are performed with wonderful rapidity, and it seems incomprehensible that they should

* The largest specimen I have recently examined from this region weighed 2.85 grammes.

be able to procure sufficient animal food to sustain them during our long and severe winters ; indeed, I incline to believe that their diet is more comprehensive than most writers suppose, and that they feed upon beechnuts and a variety of seeds, and possibly roots as well, though I confess that I have no direct evidence to adduce in support of this supposition.

## SOREX PLATYRHINUS (DeKay) Linsley.

### *Broad-nosed Shrew.*

This species, which was first described by Dr. DeKay, from a specimen taken in this State, is not rare in the Adirondacks, though I do not think it is as plentiful here as *Sorex Cooperi*, which it much resembles in habits.

Its diminutive size does not exempt it from the attacks of predatory birds, for, in April, 1882, I shot, at Morse Lake, a Canada Jay whose stomach contained the remains, including the under jaw, of a Shrew which seemed to be of the present species. I have also taken it at Big Moose Lake.

The individual from which Dr. DeKay's description was drawn, was captured " at Tappan, Rockland county, in the cellar of a dwelling-house, having taken up its abode between the stones of the foundation. It was exceedingly agile ; and when excited, emitted a shrill, twittering squeak. It ate greedily of fresh meat, but died in the course of a few days. Through the politeness of my friend, the Rev. J. H. Linsley of Elmwood Place, Connecticut, I had an opportunity of examining another specimen, which was obtained from a log in the forest in winter, near Stratford. According to Mr. Linsley, it weighed 47 grains." * Prof. Baird mentions a specimen that weighed but 37 grains. †

---

* Zoology of New York. Part I, 1842, p. 23.
† Pacific Rail Road Reports, vol. VIII, 1857, p. 26.

Order CHIROPTERA.  Family VESPERTILIONIDÆ.

## ATALAPHA CINEREA  (Beauvois) Peters.

### *Hoary Bat.*

This species, which differs from the red bat in its much larger size, as well as in coloration, is not rare in the Adirondacks, and I have taken it both in the interior and along the western border of the region.

The Hoary Bat can be recognized, even in the dusk of evening, by its great size, its long and pointed wings, and the swiftness and irregularity of its flight.  It does not start out so early as our other bats, and is consequently much more difficult to shoot.   The borders of woods, water courses, and roadways through the forest are among its favorite resorts, and its nightly range is vastly greater than that of any of its associates.   While the other species are extremely local, moving to and fro over a very restricted area, this traverses a comparatively large extent of territory in its evening excursions, which fact is probably attributable to its superior power of flight.

Imagine for the moment, sympathetic reader, that you are an enthusiastic bat hunter, and have chanced to visit some northern forest where this handsome species occurs.   The early evening finds you, gun in hand, near the border of a lonely wood.   The small bats soon begin to fly, and in the course of fifteen or twenty minutes you may have killed several, all of which prove to be the silver-haired species (*Vesperugo noctivagans*).   The twilight is fast fading into night, and your eyes fairly ache from the constant effort of searching its obscurity, when suddenly a large bat is seen approaching, perhaps high above the tree-tops, and has scarcely entered the limited field of vision when, in swooping for a passing insect, he cuts the line of the distant horizon and disappears in the darkness below.   In breathless suspense you wait for him to rise, crouching low that his form may be sooner outlined against the dim light that still lingers in the northwest, when he suddenly shoots by, seemingly as big as an owl, within a few feet of your very eyes. Turning quickly you fire, but too late! He has vanished in the darkness. For more than a week each evening is thus spent, and you almost despair of seeing another Hoary Bat, when, perhaps, on a clear cold night, just as the darkness is becoming too intense to permit you to shoot with accuracy and you are on the point of turning away, something appears above the horizon that sends a thrill of excitement through your whole frame. There is no mistaking the species—the size, the sharp, narrow wings, and the swift flight serve instantly to distinguish it from its nocturnal comrades. On he comes, but just before arriving within gunshot he makes one of his characteristic zig-zag side-shoots and you tremble as he momentarily vanishes from view. Suddenly he reappears, his flight becomes more steady, and now he sweeps swiftly toward you. No time is to be lost, and it is already too dark to aim, so you bring the gun quickly to your shoulder and fire. With a piercing, stridulous cry, he falls to the earth. In an instant you are stooping to pick him up, but the sharp grating screams, uttered with a tone of intense anger, admonish you to observe discretion. With delight you cautiously take him in your hand and hurry to the light to feast your eyes upon his rich and handsome markings. He who can gaze upon a freshly killed example without feelings of admiration is not worthy to be called a naturalist. From its almost boreal distribution, and extreme rarity in collections, the capture of a specimen of the Hoary Bat must, for some time to come, be regarded as an event worthy of congratulation and record. Although I have been fortunate enough to shoot fourteen, I would rather kill another to-day than slay a dozen deer. During the past season Dr. A. K. Fisher, Walter H. Merriam, and myself shot nineteen specimens of this elegant species in and near the western border of the Adirondacks. It is not to be imagined, however, that the procurement of this extensive series (extensive for so rare an animal) was an easy task. Scarcely a suitable evening passed, throughout the entire season, that was not devoted to bat hunting. From the middle of June to the middle of July, when there is nearly an hour of twilight, the silver-haired and little brown bats begin to fly shortly after eight o'clock, but the present species is seldom seen till half an hour later, and those we killed were common- ly shot about 9 P. M. As the season advances and the evenings be- come shorter, all bats, of course, appear proportionately earlier. On the 3d of August I shot *Atalapha cinerea* at eight o'clock, and on the 8th of October at precisely 6 o'clock—three hours earlier than the same species was killed during the first part of July.

In warm evenings it was not to be seen at all, and I have never observed it when the temperature was above 15° C. (59° F.). It was most often seen when the thermometer ranged from 10° to 12° C. (50° to 53.6° F.). Assuming that the species does not leave its hiding-place when the temperature is above 15° or 16° C. it might be supposed that it would suffer for food if there were several suc- cessive warm evenings. But it must be remembered that the coolest part of the twenty-four hours is just before daylight, and throughout the northern regions inhabited by this species there are few days when the temperature does not fall to 15° C. in the early morn- ing. Moreover, it is well known that most bats are as active just before daylight as in the evening. Hence, if the evenings are too warm for its comfort, it would almost always be enabled, by the falling temperature, to sally forth at some later hour of the night.

The Hoary Bat occurs about the Red River settlement in British America, and Dr. Richardson obtained it at Cumberland House on the Saskatchewan, in lat. 54° N. * Robert Kennicott procured it in the Hudson's Bay Company's territory, farther north than any other species of bat has been taken. It is a summer resident of high latitudes, its southern limit in the east coinciding, apparently, with that of the Canadian Fauna. In the west it has been taken in Arizona and New Mexico, but only, so far as I am aware, at considerable altitudes. In the fall and early winter isolated indi-

---

* Fauna Boreali Americana, vol. I, 1829, p. 1.

viduals have been procured from localities so far to the southward
of its usual habitat that I am constrained to believe it a migratory
species.   William Cooper mentions a specimen that was killed, " in
the month of November, near the hights of Weehawken, in New
Jersey ;" *   DeKay says that he " noticed two flying about quite
actively shortly before noon " on the 12th of December, 1841
(locality not mentioned, but presumably Long Island, N. Y.) ; †
Zadock Thompson secured one that was taken alive at Colchester,
Vermont, about the last of October, 1841 ; ‡ and Mr. E. P. Bicknell took one from an overhanging branch at Riverdale-on-the-
Hudson, New York, September 30th, 1878.§   Dr. A. K. Fisher
has never taken it at Sing Sing, New York, where he has shot
several hundred bats in summer, though he is confident that he
saw a single individual there on the evening of October 1st, 1883.

Nothing whatever appears to be known of the breeding habits
of the Hoary Bat.   On the evening of the 30th of June last (1883)
Dr. A. K. Fisher shot a large female (measuring 422mm. in spread
of wings) at my home in Lewis County.   It had already given
birth to its young, and each of its four mammæ bore evidence of
having recently been nursed.   That the species ruts about the first
of August there can be no reasonable doubt, for I saw more of
them from the 30th of July till the 6th of August than I have seen
in all before and since, and twelve adult specimens killed during
that brief period were all males.   They were not feeding, but were
rushing wildly about, evidently in search of the females.   Many
flew so high as to be entirely out of range though directly overhead.   The only young I have ever seen was shot here, August
6th, 1883, by Walter H. Merriam.   It was nearly full grown

---

* Researches on the Cheiroptera of the United States, Annals Lyceum Natural History, N. Y.,
1837, p. 56.

† Zoology of New York.   Part 1, 1842, p. 8.

‡ Natural and Civil History of Vermont, 1842, p. 25.

§ Mr. Bicknell writes me that "it was met with about sunrise, hanging at a height of about six
feet, in a young tree in an opening near the border of a wood."

(measuring 400mm. in extent) and differed from the adults chiefly in being a little lighter colored.

Zadock Thompson, in his paper upon the mammals of Vermont, speaks thus of this species : " The only Vermont specimen, which I have examined, and that from which the preceding description was drawn, was sent me alive by my friend, David Reed, Esq., of Colchester.   It was taken at his place in Colchester, the latter part of October, 1841, and was kept alive for some time in a large willow basket with a flat cover of the same material.   On opening the basket, he was almost invariably found suspended by his hind claws from the central part of the cover.   When the basket was open, he manifested little fear, or disposition to fly, or get away, during the day time, but in the evening would readily mount on the wing and fly about the room, and on lighting always suspended himself by his hind claws with his head downward.   He ate fearlessly and voraciously of fresh meat when offered to him, but could not be made to eat the common house fly." *

The hour at which bats leave their retreats to begin their nocturnal excursions is governed, first, by the latitude, longitude, and altitude of the locality, and the time of the year ; and, second, by the character of the sky (whether clear or overcast), and the exposure—those living along the southern and eastern borders of woodlands, and in dark ravines, appearing earlier than those whose hiding-places face the setting sun.   In other words, the time at which bats appear depends solely upon the *degree* of darkness.

Hence it follows that their nightly exodus, in a given locality, does not take place at a fixed period after the disappearance of the sun ; for, during the first part of October, in this latitude, the darkness is as great half an hour after sunset as it is an hour after three months earlier.   Therefore, in estimating the exact hour at which bats are to be expected at any stated date, it is necessary not only to consider the time the sun sets, but also to take into account the

* Natural and Civil History of Vermont, 1842, p. 25.

duration of the twilight. Moreover, in the same locality, the several species do not commence to fly at the same hour, for each seems to await a particular and different degree of darkness. The Hoary Bat is one of the last to appear, and for this reason its capture is the most difficult. In Lewis County, during the latter part of June, it does not start out (excepting in deep forests and dark valleys) till about 8.45 P. M., or a full hour after sunset; while in the early part of October I have killed it at 6 P. M., or just half an hour after sundown. The following table is calculated to illustrate the above remarks :—

*Times of evening appearances of Atalapha cinerea at Locust Grove, New York, at different dates in 1883.*

| Date. | Sunset. | First Bat Seen. | Time after Sunset. |
|---|---|---|---|
| June 30, | 7.42 o'clock, | 8.45 o'clock, | 63 minutes. |
| July 9, | 7.38 " | 8.30 " | 52 " |
| July 31, | 7.21 " | 8.10 " | 49 " |
| Aug. 3, | 7.17 " | 8.00 " | 43 " |
| Aug. 21, | 6.52 " | 7.30 " | 38 " |
| Oct. 8, | 5.30 " | 6.00 " | 30 " |

## ATALAPHA NOVEBORACENSIS (Erxleben) Peters.

### *Red Bat ; New York Bat.*

This species ranks among the least common bats of the area under consideration. I have shot it here as late as October 12th (1883).

Excepting the hoary bat it is the most beautiful of its tribe, being clad in a thick coat of soft, glossy fur of a bright golden-red color, varying somewhat in shade, and tipped to a greater or less extent with silvery white. This coloration serves, at a glance, to distinguish it from all its associates.

The Red Bat generally makes its appearance earlier in the evening than the other species, evidently fancying the dusk of

twilight more than the increased darkness of advancing night; and
I have killed it even on a cloudy afternoon, while flying to and fro
in pursuit of insects, near the border of a hard-wood grove. I have
found several of them asleep, in the day-time, hanging by their
thumb-nails to small twigs or leaf-stems within easy reach. When
thus suspended they are, at a little distance, easily mistaken for
dead leaves, or the cocoons of some large moth.

"In most portions of the United States, the Red Bat is one of
the most abundant, characteristic, and familiar species, being rivalled
in these respects by the little Brown Bat alone. It would be safe
to say that, in any given instance of a bat entering our rooms in
the evening, the chances are a hundred to one of its being either
one or the other of these two species. The perfect noiselessness
and swiftness of its flight, the extraordinary agility with which it
evades obstacles—even the most dexterous strokes designed for its
capture—and the unwonted shape, associated in popular superstition
with the demons of the shades, conspire to revulsive feelings that
need little fancy to render weird and uncanny."*

As illustrating the devoted attachment of the mother for her
young, Dr. Godman quotes the following circumstance from Mr.
Titian Peale: "In June, 1823, the son of Mr. Gillespie, keeper of
the city square, caught a young red Bat, (*Vespertilio Nov-Ebora-
censis*, L.) which he took home with him. Three hours afterwards,
in the evening, as he was conveying it to the Museum in his hand,
while passing near the place where it was caught, the mother made
her appearance, followed the boy for two squares, flying around
him, and finally alighted on his breast, such was her anxiety to save
her offspring. Both were brought to the Museum, the young one
firmly adhering to its mother's teat. This faithful creature lived
two days in the Museum, and then died of injuries received from

---

* Drs. Coues and Yarrow in their "Monographic Essay" on North American Chiroptera, published in chap. II, vol. V, Report upon Explorations and Surveys West of the One Hundredth
Meridian, in charge of Lieut. G. M. Wheeler, 1875, p. 89.

her captor. The young one, being but half grown, was still too young to take care of itself, and died shortly after." *

Like our other bats, this species frequently hibernates in vast assemblages; and in regions remote from civilization each colony usually occupies a rocky cavern or hollow tree; in inhabited districts they often take up quarters in the ruin of some deserted building, particularly of structures composed of stone and brick. Dr. Godman publishes a letter from Prof. Jacob Green, of Princeton, containing an account of the presence and actions of a host of this species in a cave that he visited November 1st, 1816. The letter runs as follows: " I this day visited an extensive cavern about twelve miles south of Albany, N. Y. I did not measure its extent into the mountain, but it was at least three or four hundred feet. There was nothing remarkable in this cave, except the vast multitudes of Bats which had selected this unfrequented place, to pass the winter. They did not appear to be much disturbed by the light of the torches carried by our party, but, upon being touched with sticks, they instantly recovered animation and activity, and flew into the dark passages of the cavern. As the cave was, for the most part, not more than six or seven feet in height, they could very easily be removed from the places to which they were suspended, and some of the party, who were behind me, disturbed some hundreds of them at once, when they swept by me in swarms to more remote, darker, and safer places of retreat. In flying through the caves they made little or no noise; sometimes upon being disturbed in one place they flew but a few yards and then instantly settled in another, in a state of torpor apparently as profound as before. These Bats, in hibernating, suspend themselves by the hinder claws, from the roof or upper part of the cave; in no instance did I observe one along the sides. They were not promiscuously scattered, but were collected into groups or clusters, of some hundreds, all in close contact. On holding a candle within a

---

* American Natural History. By John D. Godman. Vol. I, 1842, p. 42.

few inches of one of these groups, they were not in the least
troubled by it : their eyes continued closed, and I could perceive
no signs of respiration.   On opening the stomach of one of these
Bats, it was found entirely empty ; the species, I believe, was the
*V. Noveboracensis.*" *

The young of this species continue to nurse till at least a month
old.   I shot a female on the 31st of July (1883) whose udders still
contained milk, and whose long nipples were much drawn out.   A
week later (Aug. 7th), I killed a full grown young flying over the
same meadow.

## VESPERUGO SEROTINUS FUSCUS (Schreber) Dobson.

### *Dusky Bat ; Carolina Bat.*

Professor Baird has taken this species at Westport, in Essex
County, on the eastern border of the Adirondacks, and I have
procured a single specimen in Lewis County, on the western side
of the district ; but it is unquestionably the rarest bat found within
the limits of this region.   It pertains to a more southern fauna.

In writing of the habits of the Carolina Bat, Dr. A. K. Fisher
observes : " They are the last to make their appearance in the
evening.   In fact, when it gets so dark that objects are blended in
one uncertain mass, and the bat hunter finds that he is unable to
shoot with any precision, the Carolina Bats make their appearance
as mere dark shadows flitting here and there while busily engaged
in catching insects.   We have to make a snap shot as they dodge
in and out from behind the dark tree-tops, and are left in doubt as
to the result until in the gloom we may perchance see our little
black and tan, seemingly as interested in the result as we are,
pointing the dead animal.   This species is particularly fond of
fields well surrounded by trees." †

---

* Ibid., pp. 48–49.
† Forest and Stream, vol. XVI, No. 25, July 21, 1881, p. 490.

The large membranous wings of the bat serve a double function : not only do they sustain the animal in a strong and rapid flight, enabling it to make quick and abrupt turns in the noiseless pursuit of its insect prey ; but they are also sensitive to an extreme degree, constituting organs of touch of unusual delicacy. They thus enable the bat with a certainty that is little short of marvellous, to avoid the most inconspicuous objects that may lie in its way. On this point Dr. Godman remarks : " We have already glanced at the singular fact, that Bats have the power of directing their flight with perfect correctness, even when deprived of their sight. In 1793, Spallanzani put out the eyes of a Bat, and observed that it appeared to fly with as much ease as before, and without striking against objects in its way, following the curve of a ceiling, and avoiding, with accuracy, everything against which it was expected to strike. Not only were blinded Bats capable of avoiding such objects as parts of a building, but they shunned, with equal address, the most delicate obstacles, even silken threads, stretched in such a manner as to leave just space enough for them to pass with their wings expanded. When these threads were placed nearer together, the Bats contracted their wings, in order to pass between them without touching. They also passed with the same security between branches of trees placed to intercept them, and suspended themselves by the wall, &c., with as much ease as if they could see distinctly." (American Natural History, vol. I, pp. 42–43.)

Dr. Joseph Schöbl, of Prague, repeated these experiments, but instead of putting out the eyes he covered them with adhesive plaster.

" He has kept bats, thus treated, for a year alive in his room, and has entirely confirmed Spallanzani's results. To account for these phenomena, the wings of bats have been examined for peculiar nerve-endings, by Cuvier, Leydig, and Krause, but without any success. The author's discoveries are therefore quite new to science. The following is a short abstract of his results. The

bat's wing membrane consists of two sheets of skin, the upper derived from that of the back, the lower from that of the belly.    The
epidermic and Malpighian layers in each sheet remain separate,
whilst the true skin is inseparably fused.    In this fused medium
layer are imbedded the muscles, nerves, vessels, etc., of the wing.
.  .  .  .   The whole wing is covered, both on the upper and
under surface, with extremely fine, sparsely scattered hairs.  .  .  .
Each hair sac has from two to seven sebaceous glands, according
to the species, and one sweat gland opening into its sac.   The two
outer fibrous layers of the hair sac have no sharp line of demarca-
tion to separate them from the surrounding connective tissue, but
the inner or hyaline coat is highly developed, and, after being con-
stricted beneath the hair bulb, widens out and encloses the sense-
bodies (Tastkörperchen), one of which organs is connected with
each hair.

" The nerves of the wings may be considered to consist of five
layers, i. e., there is one occupying the centre of a transverse section of the wing, which gives off on each side of it four others, and
these are successively finer and finer as they approach the opposite
surfaces.   The inner layer and the one immediately on each side
of it, consist of nerve fibres with dark borders, the other layers of
pale fibres only.   The tastkörperchen are connected with the second
layer.   The fifth layer of finest fibres ends as a network between
the innermost layer of cells of the Malpighian layer of the epidermis.
The tastkörperchen are shaped like a fir-cone with a rounded apex
turned inwards.   They lie immediately below the root of the hair ;
and their core or central substance is formed of a prolongation of
the cells forming the two root sheaths of the hair.   Their length
is 0.0259 and their breadth 0.0175mm.   A nerve containing about
six dark-edged fibres is distributed to each körperchen.   Just
before the nerve reaches this organ it splits into two, and three
fibres pass to one side of it, three to the other.   The fibres are
then wound round the body so as to sheathe its cellular core.   Dr.

Schöbl thinks it probable that the fibres on one side are continuous with those on the opposite side, and that there is thus a bipolar arrangement here. He attributes to the fine network of pale nerve fibres belonging to the fifth layer the appreciation of temperature, pain, &c.; to the tastkörperchen the highly exalted sense of touch. It is curious that both kinds of nerve endings are connected with the Malpighian layer of the skin." *

Rafinesque, that eccentric, irascible, and not over liberal naturalist, whose inaccurate and ambiguous descriptions of species have created so much confusion in many departments of Natural History, was once the guest of the illustrious Audubon. The event was the occasion of a somewhat ludicrous adventure, which Mr. Audubon thus graphically narrates : " When it was waxed late I showed him to the apartment intended for him during his stay, and endeavored to render him comfortable, leaving him writing material in abundance. I was indeed heartily glad to have a naturalist under my roof. We had all retired to rest. Every person I imagined was in deep slumber, save myself, when of a sudden I heard a great uproar in the naturalist's room. I got up, reached the place in a few moments, and opened the door, when, to my astonishment, I saw my guest running about the room naked, holding the handle of my favorite violin, the body of which he had battered to pieces against the walls in attempting to kill the bats, which had entered by the open window, probably attracted by the insects flying around his candle. I stood amazed, but he continued running round and round, until he was fairly exhausted; when he begged me to procure one of the animals for him, as he felt convinced they belonged to a new species." †

---

* American Naturalist, Vol. V, No. 3, May, 1871, pp. 174–175.
† Quoted in Allen's Monograph, pp. xvi–xvii.

## VESPERUGO NOCTIVAGANS (LeConte) Dobson.

### *Silver-haired Bat ; Silver-Black Bat.*

This is our commonest bat, far outnumbering all the other species together. I have killed it in various parts of the Wilderness, and during the past summer Dr. A. K. Fisher, Walter H. Merriam, and myself shot over one hundred and twenty-five in Lewis County, along the western border of the region.

Like many other bats, it has a decided liking for water ways, coursing up and down streams and rivers, and circling around lakes and ponds. In some places its habit of keeping directly over the water is very marked. At Lyon's Falls it is exceedingly abundant, particularly just below the falls. I have stood, gun in hand, on a point on the east bank of the river, and have seen hundreds passing and repassing, flying over the water, while during the entire evening not more than two or three strayed so far that if shot they would fall on the land. Several that were wounded and fell into the water, at a distance of fifteen or twenty feet from the bank, swam ashore. They swam powerfully and swiftly, for the current is here quite strong and would otherwise have carried them some distance down stream.

Next to water courses, the borders of hard-wood groves are the favorite haunts of the Silver-haired Bat. By standing close under the edge of the trees one sees many that at a little distance would pass unobserved. While searching for their insect prey they may be seen to dart in and out among the branches and to penetrate, in various directions, the dense mat of foliage overhead. They often pass within a few inches of one's face, and yet it is rare that a sound is heard from their delicate wings.* In the early dusk

---

\* In localities where we had hunted bats for some time, Dr. Fisher and I have on several occasions heard a bat, when swooping overhead, produce a sound which was distinctly audible at a distance of several paces. But in each instance, if the bat rose against the clear western horizon, we saw the light shine through numerous perforations in its wings, and the noise was unquestionably produced by the whistling of the air through these shot holes.

the Silver-haired Bat emerges from its hiding-place.* After a few turns about the immediate neighborhood it generally takes a pretty direct course for water. I have seen it start from the summit of a high, densely-wooded hill, circle around for a few minutes, and then, keeping far above the tree-tops, sail leisurely toward a distant river till lost from sight in the valley below. And, standing on the banks of the large stream that winds along the foot of this hill, I have seen the bats flying over at a height of several hundred feet, all moving in the same direction—toward a more distant river.

Whether it remains abroad all night, or limits itself to comparatively brief excursions in evening and early morning, can only be conjectured. I am inclined to favor the latter view, for the reason that the greater number always disappear before the darkness becomes sufficiently intense to hide them from sight. Against this opinion it may be argued that, as night advances, the bats move on to other parts of the neighborhood ; to which I can only reply, that it has never been my good fortune to discover their midnight haunts, though I have visited various sections of the country at all hours of the night, and frequently under the light of the full-moon. It is true that solitary individuals are occasionally met with later, but never in anything like the numbers that are to be seen in the early evening. The flight of this species is neither so rapid nor so irregular as that of the red or the hoary bat.

In Lewis County, the best locality for bats that I am acquainted with is near the junction of Sugar and Black Rivers. The numerous caves in the lime rock at this point afford them a multitude of hiding-places just suited to their liking, and they here have the additional advantage of close proximity to running water. The disproportionate abundance of the Silver-haired Bat to other

---

* Leaving out of consideration the red bat, which is not sufficiently common in the region under consideration to afford satisfactory data, the present species is the first to appear. When the evenings begin to shorten, after the end of June, it may be looked for about one minute earlier each night.

species is shown by the fact that of seventy specimens procured here, sixty-three were of this species, six were the little brown bat (*V. subulatus*), and amongst them all there was only a single red bat (*Atalapha Noveboracensis*).

The dissociation of the sexes is sometimes most remarkable. Out of eighty-five adult specimens killed in Lewis County during the past summer (1883) there was but a single male. Two other males were killed in the early autumn. Of thirty-two young killed during the same period there were nineteen males and thirteen females, showing that the disproportion does not exist at birth. I am at a complete loss to explain this enormous preponderance of females among the adults. At first, I was inclined to think that the sexes separated during the period of bringing forth and caring for the young, but, although we visited a number of different localities, we were never able to find the males. Thinking that they might not fly until early morning, I several times went out before daylight, but females only were killed.

Mr. Frank Hough tells me that when looking for young crows, some years ago, in the deep ravine that runs through the village of Lowville, in Lewis County, he espied a crow's nest in a large and densely-foliaged hemlock. On climbing the tree he found the nest to be an old one, and commenced tearing it in pieces, when, to his astonishment, he discovered thirteen young bats embedded in the sticks and litter of which it was composed. These bats were taken home and shown to several members of the family. Their eyes were not yet open. They were, of course, the progeny of a number of females, and *presumably* were of the species now under consideration, because it is by far the most common in the region. The young, generally two in number, are born about the first of July, and commence to fly when three weeks old.* Those

---

* Females killed during the latter part of June were heavy with young, but up to July 1st not one had given birth to its offspring. All that were killed after July 4th had already been in labor and were then suckling their young. Of three females shot June 30th, 1883, one contained but a single embryo, and the others, two each. All were nearly ready for extrusion and would doubtless

killed on the first evening of their appearance averaged 90mm. in length by 261mm. in stretch, but weighed only half as much as their parents. The adults average about 104mm. in length by 302mm. in stretch. When on the wing the young may be distinguished from the old by the weakness and hesitancy of their flight, rather than by the difference in size. The young are much more beautiful than the adults, and they alone possess the perfect silvery tips to the hairs from which the species derives its name. Even before going into winter quarters their soft silvery backs have given place to the grizzly coats that characterize the adults.

My esteemed friend, Mr. William Brewster, has kindly favored me with the following very interesting account of a colony of bats that he discovered during an ornithological excursion into the extensive coniferous forests of western Maine :—

" On June 18, 1880, I was searching for woodpecker's nests among the stubs that line the shores of Lake Umbagog, when I noticed a small ragged-looking hole about two feet above the water in a trunk that stood well out on the flooded meadows. I should hardly have turned aside to examine it had I not fancied that I saw something move at its entrance ; accordingly, paddling to the spot, I struck the tree sharply with the butt of an axe. The blow was followed, not by the appearance of a woodpecker's or nuthatch's head, as I had expected, but by an outbreak of shrill squeaking sounds that seemed to come from every part of the interior. As

---

have been born within forty-eight hours. The single one, a male, weighed 1100 milligrammes, and measured 43mm. in length by 79mm. in extent ; the cord measured 20mm., and the placenta 10x14mm. One of the other females contained twins, both of which were females ; one of them weighed 1380 milligrammes, measuring 41mm. in length by 72mm. in stretch ; cord 18mm.; placenta 9x14mm. The other weighed 1100 milligrammes, and measured 39x68mm.; cord 17mm.; placenta 8x13mm. That the young are brought forth in the southern part of the State at about the same date as with us is evidenced from the following. Dr. A. K. Fisher states that a female which he killed at Sing Sing, in Westchester County, June 24, 1881, "contained two young, well developed, and probably would have been delivered in a few days. The young each weighed 1,450 milligrammes. On removing the amnion the ears of one of the young bats became erect. The placenta of this species is different from that of the Little Brown Bat ; instead of being circular it is elliptical, measuring 10 by 15 millimetres. The placentæ were attached to the posterior wall of the uterus near the summit of each cornu. The umbilical cord measured twenty millimetres in length." (Forest and Stream, Vol. XVI, No. 25, July 21, 1881. p. 490.)

nothing could be seen at the hole, I drove the blade of the axe
through the thin shell a little below and pried off a large piece.
The result was fairly startling, for in a twinkling the opening was
filled with swarms of Bats which, for the space of several minutes,
poured forth uninterruptedly in a solid, dusky stream. The majority
took flight at once, making off over the Lake or in the direction
of the nearest wooded shore, but dozens, in their haste, fell into
the water or sought refuge in the boat where they scrambled about
under the seats or attempted to climb my legs.

" After the rush was over I was astonished to find that the tree
had been by no means emptied. Indeed, the squeaking sounds
within continued almost unabated. Investigating further I discovered that although the trunk was hollow for nearly its entire
length, there was a central core which touched the walls in places,
thus dividing the interior into separate spaces or chambers connected with one another by numerous passages. The side that I
had opened had been promptly vacated, but many of the occupants
had probably crawled around into the other chamber instead of
following their more impulsive companions. At least when this,
their last refuge, was laid bare by another application of the axe,
the torrent that rushed forth rendered the first exodus insignificant
by comparison. In fact, as my guide remarked at the time, it
seemed as if all the Bats of New England had congregated in that
one tree. Of their total numbers I should not care to attempt any
definite estimate, but there were certainly hundreds· and probably
thousands. All were adults, and all apparently of the same species,
a small dark-colored one which, as you suggest, was probably
*Vesperugo noctivagans* although as I preserved no specimens (a
piece of negligence that I now deeply regret) I cannot be positive
on this point.

" None of the guides or lumbermen to whom I told this experience had ever met with a similar colony, although it is not unusual
for them to find single Bats, or small families, hibernating in the

hollow trees which are cut for firewood during winter. I may add that the season of 1880 was very backward in Maine, cold rains and occasional flurries of snow occurring with disagreeable frequency well into June."

The bat hunter has many difficulties to contend with. Night creeps upon him so insidiously that he is only made aware of its presence by the number of shots missed (which multiply with painful rapidity with the increasing darkness), and by the great trouble and loss of time experienced in finding the bats that fall to the ground. The temptation to linger as long as the bats can be distinctly seen is very great, but should be resisted if the hunter has any regard for his reputation as a wing shot. When two shots out of three are missed, it is time to go home. Moonlight evenings are also very misleading, but the novice soon learns to avoid such illusions. I believe that I could not average one bat for every dozen shots by the brightest moonlight. The greatest obstacle in bat shooting is the inability to calculate distance after early night-fall, objects invariably appearing much farther off than they really are. Thus, a bat is frequently fired at when supposed to be at proper range, when in reality it is so near that the shot have not time to scatter, and it is consequently either missed altogether or so blown to pieces as to be worthless. I have sometimes, after missing a bat with the first barrel, brought it down with the second, when it seemed so far away that I was surprised to find that my gun carried to so great a distance. On going to pick it up I have been still more astonished to find it within short range, rarely over seventy-five feet (22.86 metres) from the spot where I had stood. This deceptiveness in distance manifests itself in another embarrassing way, for in searching for the bat in this dim light one is almost certain to overestimate the distance at which it fell. Hence a well-trained dog, with a good nose, is of the greatest assistance.

The length of time that the fading light will permit of bat shooting in any single evening varies from a little over half an hour, to less than ten minutes, according to the season. The loss of time, therefore, occasioned by searching for fallen bats is of the most serious consequence, and can only be overcome by the aid of a dog, or of an associate. In fact, the value of a willing assistant can scarcely be exaggerated. He stands a little to one side of the hunter and carefully notes the line in which a bat falls. The hunter likewise marks the direction, and as both advance simultaneously, the point of intersection of the two lines shows the exact position of the bat. A lantern with a good reflector is of some service, but too much reliance must not be placed upon it, and it should always be carried by the assistant, who, where bats are fairly abundant, may double the number of specimens secured.

The earliest date at which I have observed the Silver-haired Bat in the Black River Valley is the 26th of April (1884). It commenced to fly at about 7.20 P. M.

## VESPERTILIO SUBULATUS Say.

### *Little Brown Bat.*

Next to the silver-haired bat, this is the commonest and most universally distributed species in the Adirondacks, so far as my observations extend. Professor Baird has taken the typical animal at Elizabethtown, and the form known as *lucifugus* at Westport. Dr. A. K. Fisher and Mr. Oliver B. Lockhart have killed it at Lake George, and Walter H. Merriam in Keene Valley, these localities being all upon the eastern slope of the mountains ; and I have a specimen from Big Moose Lake in the interior, and have found it in considerable numbers at several places on the western side of the Wilderness.

In coloration, the young of the Little Brown Bat differs from its parents even more than does the young of the silver-haired species. An immature male which I shot August 15th, 1883, had attained the full dimensions of the adult, but was of an entirely different color, its whole body being of a very pale yellowish-brown, almost inclining to gray on the belly.*

Mr. Figanierre E´ Morao, Minister Plenipotentiary from Portugal to the United States, published, some years ago, an account of a colony of bats that caused him great annoyance. This paper contains so much of interest that a few pertinent extracts from it are here introduced :—

"In the winter of 1859, having purchased the property known as Seneca Point, in the margin of the Northeast River, near Charlestown, in Cecil County, Maryland, we took possession of it in May of the next year. . . . Having been uninhabited for several years, it exhibited the appearance, with the exception of one or two rooms, of desolation and neglect. . . . The weather, which was beautiful, balmy and warm, invited us towards evening to out-door enjoyment and rest, after a fatiguing day of travel and active labor ; but chairs, settees, and benches were scarcely occupied by us on the piazza and lawn, when, to our amazement, and the horror of the female portion of, our party, small black bats made their appearance in immense numbers, flickering around the premises, rushing in and out of doors and through open windows. . . . . Evening after evening did we patiently though not complacently watch this periodical exodus of dusky wings into light from their lurking-places. . . . Their excursions invariably commenced with the cry of the 'whippoorwill,' both at coming evening and at early dawn, and it was observed that they always

---

* Concerning the number of young produced at a birth, *et cetera*, by *Vespertilio subulatus*, Dr. A. K. Fisher writes. "Of ten pregnant females which we examined last June, 1880, each contained two young. Prof. Burt. G. Wilder (Pop. Sci. Mo., No. 42, p. 651) examined twenty females in June, 1874. Each contained two little bats, though Dr. C. C. Abbott states (Geology of New Jersey, Appendix, p. 752), that they bring forth a litter of three to five. We consider this number unusual, as all the specimens examined by us never contained more nor less than two. The abdomen of the female is not so prominent, but very much broadened, a fœtus developing in each horn of the uterus. The uterine walls at term are very thin, the entire organ weighing only about a centigramme. The placenta of this species is circular, measuring nine millimetres in diameter, the umbilical cord being twelve millimetres long. A young one taken from a female whose mammæ contained milk, weighed 1,350 milligrammes " (Forest and Stream, Vol. XVI, No. 25, July 21, 1880, p. 490.)

first directed their flight towards the river, undoubtedly to damp
their mouse-like snouts, but not their spirits, for it was likewise
observed that they returned to play hide-and-seek and indulge in
all other imaginable gambols ; when, after gratifying their love
of sport and satisfying their voracious appetites (as the absence of
mosquitoes and gnats testified) they would re-enter their habitation, again to emerge at the first signal of their feathered trumpet-
er.   I thus ascertained one very important fact, namely, that the
bat, or the species which annoyed us, ate and drank twice in twenty-
four hours."   After resorting to many ineffectual expedients in the
vain attempt to rid his home of these multitudinous pests, he
caused " all the holes, fissures in the wood-work, and apertures in
the slating to be hermetically sealed with cement.   This put a stop
to their egress, but to avoid their dying by starvation and depriva-
tion of water, which would much increase the annoyance by
adding their dead to their living stench, I ordered apertures of
about two feet square to be opened in the lathed and plastered
partition on each side of the garret windows and also in the ceiling
of every garret room ; lastly, when the bat's reveille was sounded
by the bugle of the whippoorwill, all the hands of our establishment, men and boys, each armed with a wooden implement (shaped
like a cricket-bat), marched to the third floor ' on murderous deeds
with thoughts intent ' ; a lighted lantern was placed in the middle
of one of the rooms, divested of all furniture, to allure the hidden
foe from their strongholds.   After closing the window to prevent
all escape into the open air, the assailants distributed themselves
at regular distances to avoid clubbing each other, awaited the
appearance of the bats, enticed into the room by the artificial light
and impelled by their own natural craving.   The slaughter commenced and progressed with sanguinary vigor for several hours, or
until brought to a close by the weariness of dealing the blows that
made the enemy bite the dust, and overpowered by the heat and
closeness of the apartment.   This plan succeeded perfectly.   After

a few evenings of similar exercise, in which the *batteurs* became quite expert in the use of their weapon, every wielding of the wooden bat bringing down an expiring namesake, the war terminated by the extermination of every individual of the enemy in the main building. However there still was the cock-loft of the laundry, which gave evidence of a large population. In this case I had re-course to a plan which had been recommended, but was not carried out in regard to the dwelling-house. I employed a slater to re-move a portion of the slating which required repairing. This pro-cess discovered some fifteen hundred or two thousand bats, of which the larger number were killed, and the surviving sought the barn, trees, and other places of concealment in the neighborhood.

" In the main building nine thousand six hundred and forty bats, from actual counting, were destroyed. . . . At the end of five years the odor has now nearly disappeared, being barely percepti-ble during a continuance of very damp weather." *

## Order GLIRES. Family SCIURIDÆ.

# SCIUROPTERUS VOLUCELLA (Pallas) Geoffroy.

### *Flying Squirrel.*

Two varieties of Flying Squirrel occur in the Adirondacks : the present form, confined mainly to the borders of the region, and a northern race, commonest in the elevated portions of the interior.

The subject of this sketch feeds upon a variety of nuts, seeds, and buds, and upon beetles and perhaps other insects, not hesita-ting to eat flesh when occasion offers. I have caught many in box-traps baited with beef, and have frequently known them to devour dead birds, the heads of which they particularly relish. Whether they prey upon the smaller species that roost in the forest I am unable to say, but their agility and their noiseless movements

* An Account of a Remarkable Accumulation of Bats. Smithsonian Annual Report for 1863 1864, pp. 407–409.

would enable them to capture the most wary with ease. Moreover the eagerness and avidity with which they seize and feast upon a dead bird placed within reach would indicate that they were not strangers to such a repast.* In confinement they will eat bird's eggs, not discarding the shells.

A more gentle, docile, and graceful animal than the Flying Squirrel does not exist, and though without anything striking in the way of color or markings, it is nevertheless one of the most beautiful of our mammals. The dense silky fur of an ashen-brown above and creamy white beneath, rivalling that of the chinchilla in glossy softness, and the large, prominent, and expressive eyes, together with its pretty ways, render it an attractive and justly esteemed pet.

Prof. F. H. King mentions the interesting circumstance that when an assortment of nuts was placed within reach of a Flying Squirrel which he had in confinement, it carried off all the acorns and hazel-nuts, but did not touch any of the others. These two kinds of nuts were the only ones that grew in the immediate neighborhood of the place where this squirrel was captured, but it was taken so young that it could never have seen any nuts prior to its confinement. Hence the case seems clearly one of inherited habit.†

Whether, in the region under consideration, this variety of the Flying Squirrel hibernates, I am unable to state with positiveness, though strongly of opinion that it does. It certainly remains in its nest during the severer weather of our winters.

Next to the bats, it is the most strictly nocturnal of our mammals, very rarely being seen abroad till after nightfall. He who quietly wanders through our groves and forests during the warm, still

---

* Prof. F. H. King, in his admirable and comprehensive treatise upon the Economic Relations of Wisconsin Birds, says : " In the spring of 1879, I placed the young of the Chipping Sparrow in the cage with a young pet flying squirrel (*Sciuropterus volucella*). The bird was seized with energy and killed but not eaten." (Geology of Wisconsin, Vol. I, 1883, p. 444.) The reason the bird was not eaten is hard to explain unless the squirrel was surfeited with food.

† Mr. E. P. Bicknell suggests that the squirrel may have selected the acorns and hazel-nuts because they were thinner-shelled than the others.

nights of summer and early autumn cannot but mark the myriads of sounds that betoken the presence and activity of animal life. The faint rustling of leaves, the pattering of light footsteps on the ground, the constant dropping of something from the trees, the springing back of a branch relieved from the weight of some animal, the sharp squeaking of unseen creatures, the lonesome note of a wakeful bird, the occasional low grating of teeth overhead, the bustle and chipper of something chasing something else up the trunk of a neighboring tree, the cry of distress as some bird or beast of prey seizes its unhappy victim;—these and numberless other noises, mostly vague and indescribable,—fill the air and bear evidence to the profusion of life. And yet the very multiplicity of sounds is confusing, and prevents the perception of those that are distinctive. To the ear accustomed to the whisperings of Nature many of these noises are recognized as easily as the voices of familiar friends. The shrew, the mouse, the bat, the chickaree, and the Flying Squirrel are almost sure to be present, and the latter is generally responsible for no small share of the perplexing sounds. His activity is intense, his sailing leaps frequent, his gambolings almost ceaseless, his sly chuckle and saucy scold are occasionally heard, and his dropping of beechnut shucks is sometimes well nigh continuous.

Audubon and Bachman narrate an interesting experience that no other naturalists seem to have been fortunate enough to witness. They say : " We recollect a locality not many miles from Philadelphia, where, in order to study the habits of this interesting species, we occasionally strayed into a meadow containing here and there immense oak and beech trees. One afternoon we took our seat on a log in the vicinity to watch their lively motions. It was during the calm warm weather peculiar to the beginning of autumn. During the half hour before sunset nature seemed to be in a state of silence and repose. The birds had retired to the shelter of the forest. The night-hawk had already commenced its low evening flight, and here and there the common red bat was on the wing; still for some time not a Flying Squirrel made its appearance. Suddenly, however, one emerged from its hole and ran up to the top of a tree; another soon followed, and ere long dozens came forth, and commenced their graceful flights from some upper branch to a lower bough. At times one would be seen darting from the topmost branches of a tall oak, and with wide-extended membranes and outspread tail gliding diagonally through the air, till it reached the foot of a tree about fifty yards off, when at the moment we expected to see it strike the earth, it suddenly turned upwards and alighted on the body of the tree. It would then run to the top and once more precipitate itself from the upper branches, and sail back again to the tree it had just left. Crowds of these little creatures joined in these sportive gambols; there could not have been less than two hundred. Scores of them would leave each tree at the same moment, and cross each other, gliding like spirits through the air, seeming to have no other object in view than to indulge a playful propensity." *

The Flying Squirrel is the most highly specialized of the family to which it pertains, its whole structure pre-eminently fitting it for arboreal life. The peculiar tegumentary expansion along the sides enables it to make flying leaps that far exceed those of other squirrels; and the ease, grace, and rapidity with which it glides from tree to tree inspires the merest passer-by with wonder and admiration. Its ordinary mode of progression is by a series of alternate climbs and leaps. Upon reaching a tree the first act is to ascend, for, being unable to sail horizontally, it must attain a considerable elevation before venturing to leap to the next. Instead of moving off in this way when disturbed, it sometimes runs up into the topmost branches of the nearest tree, and, coiling itself into surprisingly small compass, remains motionless till the intruder has taken his departure.

---

* Quadrupeds of North America, Vol. I, 1846, p. 218.

The modifications of structure that adapt it to its habit of life are by no means so great as in the case of the mole or bat, and yet it is not less inseparably associated with an almost exclusively arboreal existence than are these others with the special conditions of their environment.

Flying Squirrels make their nests in the hollows of trees, frequently taking possession of deserted woodpecker's holes. They are easily aroused and driven out by hammering against the trunk. I have thus expelled the occupants of as many as half a dozen nests in a single day's hunt. Their progeny must be brought forth early in April, for on the 30th of April, 1878, Dr. C. L. Bagg and myself took three half-grown young from a woodpecker's hole, about fifteen feet above the ground, in a decayed stub. They did not seem at all frightened, but were tame and gentle from the beginning, and my sister and I kept two of them alive. At night they were excessively active and playful, but, unless disturbed, would sleep during the greater part of the day. They preferred to remain upon our persons, and one used to sleep in my pocket. At first it could jump but a short distance, and if placed upon a chair or table became very unhappy and would come to the edge nearest the place where I was standing and cry to be taken. If I extended my arm and approached it, the little creature, trembling with delight, would stand on its hind legs and leap upon my hand ; thence, either running up my sleeve or down my neck, it would nestle in my bosom and sleep for hours, or until forcibly removed. Prof. F. H. King, in a recent communication, records an experience with the young of this species that calls to mind many of the actions and peculiarities of those that I have had. He says : " I have never known wild animals that became so perfectly familiar and confiding as these young squirrels did ; and they seemed to get far more enjoyment from playing upon my person than in any other place, running in and out of pockets, and between my coat and vest. After the frolic was over they always esteemed it a great favor if

I would allow them to crawl into my vest in front and go to sleep there, where they felt the warmth of my body, and it was very rare indeed, during the first six months, that they failed to ask the privilege ; indeed they came to consider themselves abused if turned out. When forced to go to sleep by themselves, the attitude taken was amusing, the nose was placed upon the table or other object it happened to be upon, and then it would walk forward over it, rolling itself up until the nose almost protruded from between the hind legs ; the tail was then wrapped in a horizontal coil about the feet, and the result was an exquisite little ball of life in soft fur which it seemed almost sacrilegious to touch. If they escaped from the cage during the night, I was sure to be warned of the fact by their coming into the bed to roll themselves up close to my face or neck." *

The most extended account which I have seen of this animal's habits in confinement, is from the pen of Prof. Geo. H. Perkins, of the University of Vermont. He describes his interesting pets in the following language : " At dusk they begin to stir. Not all at once it would seem do they awake, for the material of the nest quivers and shakes for some time before the squirrel appears. When, however, they conclude that they are all ready, out pop their heads, each to be followed by the rest of the body, after a glance on all sides with the glistening black eyes ; and now all drowsiness has disappeared and an activity more incessant and more intense than can be described takes its place. All night long, often with only the briefest rest now and then, these little animals are in vigorous motion, jumping, bounding, capering, running with ever-varying movement and astonishing energy. Everything they do is done with all their might. It would seem to any one watching them that the exercise of the first few minutes must wholly exhaust their powers, but, on the contrary, the more their muscles are used, the more capable of use they seem, and great as is the

---

* American Naturalist, Vol. XVII, No. 1, Jan. 1883, p. 39.

energy of their movements at first, they usually increase in vigor
and speed until after midnight and scarcely grow less before morning. Nothing affords them so much gratification as a large wheel
which is placed inside the cage. Into this wheel they jump whenever aught disturbs or pleases them, and even when quite hungry
they often find it necessary to take a few turns before commencing
their meal, after which exercise they draw themselves into a bunch
with the tail over the back. after the manner of squirrels, and set
briskly to work on the nut or other food they may have
received. They are almost as fond of riding as of running, and
work their passage by running till the wheel is in rapid motion and
then clinging to its wires, and so are carried around and around,
the pure white of the under side of the body contrasting prettily
with the soft brownish-gray of the back and sides as each comes
into view. When both are in the wheel one often rides while the
other turns the wheel, the latter bounding over the other as each
turn brings him around, and, no matter how rapidly the wheel
turns, these movements are executed with perfect exactness and
gracefulness. Being desirous of knowing with some degree of
accuracy how rapidly the wheel moved, I made some experiments
for that purpose and found that the usual rate of revolution was
from sixty to over a hundred and twenty times a minute, and, as
the wheel is forty-four inches in circumference, when its rate is the
latter of the two numbers named, the squirrel turning it must
travel four hundred and forty feet a minute, or about five miles an
hour, a distance requiring a great many steps when they are
so short as squirrels must take. The sides of the wheels are formed
of spokes radiating as in any wheel, these spokes are only five
inches apart at the circumference and of course constantly grow
less toward the centre ; yet through this narrow space which passes,
when the wheel is at full speed, in the sixteenth of a second, they
dart in and out with perfect ease. So quickly do they move that
the eye can scarcely follow them ; one instant a squirrel is in the

14

wheel running with all his might, and the next he is seated on a
shelf at the opposite end of the cage, the wheel whirling behind
him  .   .   .   .   Though usually very quiet they are not always
displeased with noise, if it be a lively one ; for instance, they drop
a nut in the wheel and then as it rattles when the wheel moves
they are highly delighted, sometimes more so than some of the
other listeners.   Once when a butternut thus became quite a trouble
to me I removed it, but no sooner had I left the cage than they put
it back and set it rattling louder than ever, leaping over it as it came
near them and jumping about as if performing a war dance, and this
they repeated over and over again till, finally, the nut was removed
from the cage.   Now and then the freak takes one or the other to
leave the wheel altogether for several days, and in the meantime
they relieve their over-buoyant feelings by executing a brilliant
series of somersets with an agility and daring that would excite the
envy of the most skilful acrobat.   They always turn backward, going
completely over and alighting almost exactly upon the spot from
which they started.   Now they run a few steps before going over
and now stop and turn around as if a spit ran through the centre of
the body on which it turned.   These gyrations are often extremely
ludicrous, especially, when turning side by side, they seem to be
racing   .   .   .   .   They are exceedingly inquisitive, prying into
everything that comes in their way ; and, if watched and fearful lest
they are to be interrupted, they assume a most impudent and reckless air, glancing out of one eye, and shaking their heads and sniffing
every now and then for an instant, and then returning to their investigations with renewed energy, pulling away desperately at anything that can be laid hold of, and if anyone starts toward them to
drive them away, they wait till the very last minute, when, with a
twinkle of the eye, a toss of the head, and a jerk of the tail, they are
off and across the room in a trice, perhaps stopping to chatter their
disapproval of the whole proceeding as soon as safely out of reach
.   .   .   .   When the actions of an animal are so suddenly varied, so

constantly changing and of such interest in all their phases as are those of the Flying Squirrel, a complete account can scarcely be given. Certainly it is not easy for words to represent the merry, rollicking, don't-care manner in which they do everything. Such a combination of earnestness and carelessness is seldom seen. For they are earnest about their work, and in emptying a box of nuts they seem to feel the great importance of their undertaking and the necessity of soberness and dignity in its execution, but yet one cannot help seeing that all this is but assumed for the occasion, for their eyes, and indeed their whole body, are all the time expressive of mischief, and the little rogues are never so sedate that they do not seem to be bubbling over with fun and to be ready at a moment's notice to engage in any mischief that may occur to their scheming little heads." *

An adult that I once had in captivity used to make a practice of leaping from the floor, or from some object in the room, to the top of my head, where it would scratch and dig as if searching for beech-nuts.

The late Dr. Gideon B. Smith, of Baltimore, in a letter to Audubon and Bachman, speaks thus of these squirrels : " They are gregarious, living together in considerable communities, and do not object to the company of other and even quite different animals. For example, I once assisted in taking down an old martin-box, which had been for a great number of years on the top of a venerable locust tree near my house, and which had some eight or ten apartments. As the box fell to the ground we were surprised to see the great numbers of Flying Squirrels, screech-owls, and leather-winged bats running from it. We caught several of each, and one of the Flying Squirrels was kept as a pet in a cage for six months. The various apartments of the box were stored with hickorynuts, chestnuts, acorns, corn, &c., intended for the winter supply of food. There must have been as many as twenty Flying Squirrels in the box, as many bats, and we

---

* American Naturalist, Vol. VII, No. 3, March, 1873, pp. 133–139.

know there were six screech-owls. The crevices of the house were always inhabited by the squirrels. The docility of the one we kept as a pet was remarkable ; although he was never lively and playful in the day-time, he would permit himself to be handled and spread out at the pleasure of any one. We frequently took him from the cage, laid him on the table or on one hand, and exposed the extension of his skin, smoothed his fur, put him in our pocket or bosom, &c., he pretending all the time to be asleep." *

# SCIUROPTERUS VOLUCELLA HUDSONIUS (Gmelin) Allen.

## Northern Flying Squirrel.

The Northern Flying Squirrel is a common inhabitant of the elevated central area of the Adirondacks and is not particularly rare about the outskirts of the region, where I have found both varieties nesting in adjoining trees. Although this is much the larger of the two, and may also be distinguished by some peculiarities of coloration, individuals are sometimes met with that are more or less intermediate ; still, I have yet to see the specimen that cannot at once be referred either to the one or the other.

The Northern Flying Squirrel is a hardier animal than its smaller relative, and remains awake and active during the whole of our long and severe winters. The mercury may indicate a temperature many degrees below zero, or snow may be falling in quantities sufficient to obstruct the vision, without seeming in any way to dishearten this merry adventurer. The last rays of the departing sun have scarcely disappeared from the western horizon before the sombre shades that mark the approach of winter night commence to gather about the snow-clad forest. Whether bright stars sparkle and shine through a frosty atmosphere, or heavy, leaden clouds overhang the scene, makes little difference to the Northern Flying Squirrel. He emerges from his warm nest, takes a hasty survey of the surroundings lest some wily

---

* Quadrupeds of North America, Vol. I, 1846, p. 220.

owl should lurk hard by, glides silently to a neighboring tree, and starts forthwith upon his nightly tour in quest of food and sport. Prompted either by hunger or curiosity, or by a combination of the two, he examines every unusual object with scrupulous care, and as one result is always getting into traps set for valuable fur—and this whether they are baited with mammal, bird, or fish. Indeed, the nature of the bait seems to be a matter of the most trivial consequence, as it often consists of red and Flying Squirrels that have previously been taken in the trap. Even in this case another Flying Squirrel is as likely to be the next thing caught as any animal in the Wilderness. Hence it happens that the trapper comes to look upon him as an unmitigated nuisance.

These handsome Squirrels are very fond of beechnuts, and during "nut years" feed largely upon them. They are thirsty creatures and in the early spring, when certain of the woodsmen are engaged in making maple sugar, many are found dead in the sap buckets— drowned in their efforts to obtain the sweet fluid.

They breed about a month later than their smaller relative. June 18th, 1883, Dr. A. K. Fisher and the writer found the nest of a Northern Flying Squirrel at West Pond, near Big Moose Lake. It was in the last year's nest of a three-toed woodpecker (*Picoides arcticus*) in a tamarack (*Larix Americana*) and the entrance hole faced the east, about ten feet above the ground. On cutting down the tree the nest was found to contain three nursing young, not yet one-third grown ; they were estimated to be about a month old. They were fed on condensed milk diluted with water until we left the woods, and afterwards on fresh milk and vegetables. One of them grew very rapidly, attaining nearly two-thirds the size of its parent by the 10th of July, when it was accidentally killed. They all were perfectly tame and acted much like the young of the common Flying Squirrel (*S. volucella*) already described.

In searching the scanty literature relating to this animal, which has not previously been recorded from the State of New York, I have been unable to find anything upon its habits excepting the following account of a female and young, narrated by Audubon and Bachman :

" A brood of young of this species, along with the mother was kept in confinement by an acquaintance of ours, for about four months, and the little ones, five in number, were suckled in the following manner : the younglings stood on the ground floor of the cage, whilst the mother hung her body downwards, and secured herself from falling by clinging to the perch immediately above her head by her forefeet. This was observed every day, and some days as frequently as eight or ten times.

" The brood was procured as follows : a piece of partially cleared wood having been set on fire, the labourers saw a Flying Squirrel start from a hollow stump with a young one in her mouth, and watched the place where she deposited it, in another stump at a little distance. The mother returned to her nest, and took away another and another in succession, until all were removed, when the wood-cutters went to the abode now occupied by the affectionate animal, and caught her already singed by the fire, and her five young unscathed.

" After some time a pair of the young were given away to a friend. The three remaining ones, as well as the mother, were killed in the following manner :

" The cage containing them was hung near the window, and one night during the darkness, a rat, or rats (*Mus decumanus*), caught hold of the three young through the bars, and ate off all their flesh, leaving the skins almost entire, and the heads remaining inside the bars. The mother had had her thigh broken and her flesh eaten from the bone, and yet this good parent was so affectionately attached to her brood that when she was found in this pitiable condition in the morning, she was clinging to her offspring, and trying to nurse them as if they had still been alive." *

* Quadrupeds of North America, Vol. III, 1854, pp. 203–204.

## SCIURUS HUDSONIUS Pallas.

### *Red Squirrel; Chickaree.*

The Red Squirrel is one of the commonest and best known of the mammalian inhabitants of the Adirondacks, being found in all parts of the Wilderness at all seasons of the year.

His diet is more varied than that of our other squirrels. In addition to nuts and acorns he feeds upon a variety of seeds and roots, the buds and leaf-stems of certain trees, several species of " toad-stools" and other fungi, seeds from the cones of pines and spruces, fruits and berries of many kinds, beetles, birds' eggs, and even young birds. And in winter he does not look with disdain upon scraps of meat or fish that may have been left within his reach.

He is the most hilarious of the pre-eminently merry and frolicsome family to which he belongs, and his joyous and jubilant nature enables him to triumph over the sense of gloom that pervades the sombre coniferous forests of the North, rendering him cheerful and contented in the darkest and most impenetrable of our evergreen thickets. Indeed, it is this happy faculty of adapting himself and his modes of life to a diversity of surroundings that has permitted his wide dispersion, the present boundaries of his habitat being co-extensive with those of the wooded portions of the northern part of our continent.*

The Chickaree combines qualities so wholly at variance, so unique, so incomprehensible, and so characteristic withal, that one scarcely knows in what light to regard him. His inquisitiveness, audacity, inordinate assurance, and exasperating insolence, together with his insatiable love of mischief and shameless disregard of all the ordinary customs and civilities of life, would lead one to suppose that he was little entitled to respect; and yet his intelligence, his untiring perseverance, and genuine industry, the cunning cleverness displayed in many of his actions, and the irresistible humor with which he does

---

* The species and its several geographical races are here spoken of collectively.

everything, command for him a certain degree of admiration. He is arrogant, impetuous, and conceited to an extreme degree, his confidence in his own superior capabilities not infrequently costing him his life. In fact, these contradictions in character and idiosyncrasies in disposition render him a psychological problem of no easy solution.

From earliest dawn till the setting sun has disappeared behind the distant hills, the Red Squirrel enlivens the silent solitude of the forest with his merry ways and saucy chatterings ; and he may sometimes be discovered in the darkest hours of the night, stealing softly over the ground—bent, doubtless, on some errand of dubious propriety. Moonlight evenings he is often as active, though not so noisy, as during the day, and in early autumn he vies with the flying squirrel in nocturnal nut-husking exploits. Though an expert climber, delighting in long leaps from bough to bough, which he executes with grace and precision, he spends far more time on the ground than the other arboreal squirrels, sometimes even making his home in holes in the earth. Old logs, stumps, wood-piles, and brush-heaps are favorite places of resort, and, by excavating burrows beneath, he converts them into the securest of retreats. Our fences serve as highways upon which he travels from wood to wood, and the zig-zag rail fence in particular is one of the boons of his existence. It is his most frequented path, his playground, his race-course, and when pursued, his readiest means of escape. It is the step-ladder from which he leaps into the branches of neighboring trees, and the place where he meets his friends at all hours of the day. He frequently follows it to the farm-house and takes up his abode in the woodshed or other outbuilding, placing his nest between the ceiling and roof, or in some other equally out-of-the-way spot, whence he is with great difficulty dislodged.

He is the least wary of the squirrels, rarely taking the trouble to hide himself at the approach of man. In fact, on such occasions he usually assumes an aggressive attitude, chippers, shakes his tail in an impudent and wholly uncalled-for manner, but takes care to keep just out of reach. This daring fearlessness is clearly the result of the fact that he is not worth the powder necessary for his destruction, and he is therefore tolerated, though an acknowledged nuisance. But there are times when his conduct becomes so scandalous that the shot-gun is brought out for his suppression. He is soon deeply impressed with the range and effect of this weapon, and, though many of his brothers may have perished before the warning was heeded, he now becomes, in this particular locality, the most circumspect of brutes. He scorns the thought of running away, but grows so vigilant, sly, and crafty that the farmer is put to his wit's end to devise means for his riddance.

His curiosity is almost as striking as his impudence, and more than once when I have been standing or sitting motionless in the forest he has approached nearer and nearer, eyeing me inquisitively, chippering, and shaking his tail, till finally he has jumped upon my person, to be off again in a trice. When sleeping on the ground in July, 1878, I was awakened, just at daybreak, by a noisy and excited chippering close at hand, but before my eyes were fairly open one of these mischievous imps alighted in my face. The surprise was common, and I must have started rather unceremoniously, for he sprang so suddenly to the nearest tree that the prints of his claws were visible for sometime after upon my forehead and nose.

Of all the annoyances that beset the trapper in this region, none compare with the Red Squirrel. Not only is he the most vexatious of all the animals that roam the Adirondack wilds, but he often proves a source of disaster to the fur dealer. From an overhanging limb he looks on with unfeigned interest while the trapper arranges the bait for the martin or fisher; but a moment later he has sprung the trap and is chippering with exulting derision at the result. He is often caught, it is true, but half a dozen others are always ready to take his place, and it affords little satisfaction to the hunter, on his lonely rounds through the snow-clad forest, to find a worthless

Squirrel in his trap, instead of the valuable fur for which it was set. But if, instead of consulting the hunter's interests, we take another view of the case, it is easy to see that the Chickaree is a good friend to the martin. He furnishes the latter with food of an exceptionally agreeable kind, and though it cost him his life, takes great pains to discover and spring the traps set for the martin's destruction.

He is not always to be found in equal numbers, but is influenced in a marked degree by the beechnut crop. In seasons when mast is plentiful there seems to be a Squirrel for every tree, bush, stump, and log in the entire Wilderness, besides a number left over to fill possible vacancies. When, on the other hand, the nut crop has been a failure, a corresponding diminution in the numbers of Squirrels is observable, and they are sometimes actually scarce.* Hence it is clear that while the diet of the Red Squirrel is varied, his staple commodity is the beechnut, the yield of which in any year determines his abundance in the succeeding winter and spring. That he migrates, on a small scale at least, is a fact concerning which there can be no reasonable doubt : on any other hypothesis we are at a loss to account for the suddenness of his increase and decrease over certain areas of large extent, and find it difficult to explain why he is sometimes met with in numbers swimming our lakes and rivers, always in one direction.

As might be inferred from the boreal distribution of this animal, he is the hardiest of our squirrels. Not only does he inhabit regions where the rigors of Arctic winter are keenly felt, but, refusing to hibernate, he remains active throughout the continuance of excessive

---

* To be more explicit : The yield of beechnuts was good in the fall of 1881. In October and November of that year I found Red Squirrels abounding in all parts of the region traversed—from the Black River Valley to the Saranacs and Tupper's Lakes. Dr. F. H. Hoadley, who spent the winter at Big Moose Lake, informs me that they continued in undiminished numbers throughout the months of January, February, and March, proving a serious grievance to the trapper. The next fall, that of 1882, the nut crop failed (as it always does here on the alternate years), and I found but few Red Squirrels in the Adirondacks in October and November. As the winter advanced they became less and less common, and in January I did not see a single one, and but two of their tracks, while on a snow-shoe tramp from Big Otter to Big Moose Lake.

cold. When fierce storms sweep over the land he retires to his nest, to appear again with the first lull of the wind, be the temperature never so low. I have many times observed him when the thermometer ranged from thirty to forty degrees below zero Centigrade (−22 to −40 F.), but could never see that he was inconvenienced by the cold. When running upon the snow he often plunges down out of sight, tunnels a little distance, and, reappearing, shakes the snow from his head and body, whisks his tail, and skips along as lightly and with as much apparent pleasure as if returning from a bath in some rippling brook during the heat of a summer's afternoon.

He possesses the rare and philosophical accomplishment of combining work with recreation, and sets about the performance of his self-imposed tasks with such roguish humor that it is a pleasure to watch him. In marked contrast to these free and happy habits is the stealth and sullenness that characterize the actions of some of the Carnivores, notably of the family Mustelidæ.

The Red Squirrel enjoys a game of "tag" even 'more than the average schoolboy, and one is often startled by a couple of them as they rush madly through the leaves, chasing each other hither and thither over the ground, up and down and around the trunks of trees, and in and out of hollow logs and stumps with a degree of recklessness that is astonishing to behold.

However frivolous the Red Squirrel may appear to the casual observer, he is, nevertheless, a most industrious animal. Unlike most of his associates, and many of our own species, he is not content with the enjoyment of present plenty, but takes pains to provide against a time of future need. When the summer has grown old, and the mellow days of early autumn cast a glow of color over the sumac and woodbine, the prudent Squirrel has commenced to gather the provision for his winter's use. Impatient to make sure his store, he does not wait for the nuts to ripen and fall, but cuts the stems by which they hang, till many lie scattered on the ground below. He then descends and collects them in a heap between, or near, the roots of the trees; or, if he thinks them here too exposed, carries them directly to some hollow log or stump.    Later in the season, when the mast is fully ripe, and the danger from mould is past, he fills the hollows of the limbs and trees about his nest, and often secretes reserve hoards in his burrows in the earth.    In the evergreen forests he lays up large supplies of cones.    I have seen him, even before the middle of September, engaged in gathering those of the white pine (*Pinus strobus*).    At this early date he cuts the yet green cones from the branches, and, when a sufficient number have fallen, takes them to some hiding-place to ripen for his winter's fare.    He eats the little buds that may be found scattered sparingly along the small branches of the spruce, and, in order to obtain them easily, bites off the terminal twigs and drags them back where the limb is large enough to allow him to sit comfortably on his haunches while feeding.    Under single trees, both in the great forest and on our own lawn, I have found enough twigs to fill a bushel basket.    The injury thus done is sometimes very extensive.

He is fond of a variety of fruits, and sometimes commits great havoc in the apple orchard.    From his liking for mushrooms some would consider him an epicure, but in whatever light we regard this taste, it is a droll spectacle to see him drag a large " toadstool " to one of his storehouses.    If the " umbrella " happens to catch on some stick or log and is broken from the stem, as is frequently the case, he is pretty sure to scold and sputter for a while, and then take the pieces separately to their destination.

Throughout the first half of June I have often observed a family of Red Squirrels feeding upon the winged seeds of a red or swamp maple (*Acer rubrum*), directly in front of my office window. They rarely came during the day, but in the evening both parents and five young were frequently seen on the tree at one time, and they commonly remained till it was so dark that I could no longer discern their outlines.    In reaching down from the slender twigs to the drooping clusters of fruit they sometimes slipped and seemed about to fall, but I never knew even one of the youngsters to lose his hold. On these occasions they were always silent. I have also seen them, in June, in the act of eating the leaf-stems of the sugar maple (*Acer saccharinum*), to which habit my attention was directed by observing the frequent dropping of green leaves to the ground.*

The propensity to suck the eggs and destroy the young of our smaller birds is the worst trait of the Red Squirrel, and is in itself sufficient reason for his extermination, at least about the habitations of man. I have myself known him to rob the nests of the red-eyed vireo, chipping sparrow, robin, Wilson's thrush, and ruffed grouse, and doubt not that thousands of eggs are annually sacrificed, in the Adirondack region alone, to gratify this appetite. Therefore, when abundant, as he always is during the springs that follow good nut years, his influence in checking the increase of our insectivorous birds can hardly be overestimated.

Dr. A. K. Fisher informs me that on three occasions he has known these Squirrels to destroy young robins. In the first instance he heard the old birds making a great outcry near his home at Sing Sing, and on going to ascertain the reason found a Red Squirrel in the act of devouring a young robin. A well-directed stone caused him to drop the bird, which was found with its head cut into and the brains eaten. One wing and both feet had also been eaten. The details of the other cases are much the same. In one instance the Squirrel returned several times to the nest and carried off all the young.†

---

* Mr. E. P. Bicknell writes me from his home at Riverdale, New York: "On our place they feed through the winter and early spring on the flower-buds of the white maple (*Acer dasycarpum*). Often several are to be seen perched among the leafless and bud-besprinkled branches about the top of one of these trees, scattering the snow below with fragments of the red buds and even entire twigs which later would have become sprays of blossoms and fruit."

† Dr. Edgar A. Mearns, in his valuable paper upon the Birds of the Hudson Highlands, states: "Among the Robin's worst enemies may be ranked the Red Squirrels (*Sciurus Hudsonius*), for, though their young are subject to the attacks of Crows, Jays, and particularly to the ravages of the Black Snake (*Bascanion constrictor*), yet none of these enemies inflict as much injury as the Squirrels, because, not only do they seek out and devour the eggs, but the young are also eaten."

I have long been aware that this animal was an occasional depredator of the poultry yard, and find, in a journal written twelve years ago, a note to the effect that a case had then come to my knowledge where one was caught in the act of killing both chickens and young ducks.

The Red Squirrel is a good swimmer, swimming rapidly and with much of the head, back, and tail out of water, On the 18th of August, 1874, I was paddling silently down a sluggish stream in the heart of the Adirondacks when a slight noise on the shore arrested my attention. A Squirrel soon appeared at the water's edge, but turned back upon perceiving the boat. The stream, which was about twenty feet (approximately 6 metres) in width, here flowed through an extensive marsh, the nearest tree being more than a hundred yards (nearly 100 metres) away. Surprised at seeing a Squirrel in such a place, I stopped the boat, holding fast to a few bushes on the opposite bank, and after remaining motionless a few moments had the satisfaction of seeing him return, climb out on a little bush, and swim across. Again, June 28th, 1878, while rowing on Brantingham Lake, in Lewis County, I saw a Red Squirrel swimming about midway between "the Point" and the main shore opposite. He was moving toward the Point, and, as I reached him, climbed up on the oar, ran over my back and legs, then along the gunwale, jumping ahead from the bow in the direction toward which he was swimming when first seen. On overtaking him he again came aboard and jumped ahead as before. This was

---

etc. (Bull. Essex Inst., X, 1878, p. 9.) Mr. John Burroughs says : "Nearly all the birds look upon it as their enemy and attack and annoy it when it appears near their breeding haunts. Thus, I have seen the pewee, the cuckoo, the robin, and the wood thrush pursuing it with angry voice and gestures. If you wish the birds to breed and thrive in your orchards and groves, kill every red squirrel that infests the place." (The Tragedies of the Nests, in The Century Magazine, Vol. XXVI, No. 5, Sept., 1883, p. 686.) Prof. F. H. King tells us that at Ithaca, New York, his attention was attracted by a pair of robins dashing wildly about the branches of an evergreen: "On examining the tree the nest of the birds was discovered, and just below it sat a Chickaree eating one of the Robin's eggs." (Geol. Wis., 1883, p. 443.) In *Forest and Stream* for November 17, and December 29, 1881, Mr. Bainbridge Bishop contributes much valuable testimony of a similar nature. Examples might be multiplied almost indefinitely, but enough has already been said to demonstrate that the Red Squirrel must be ranked among the worst enemies of our small birds.

done a number of times, the Squirrel gaining each time two or three boat's lengths, till finally he succeeded in reaching the shore. I have repeatedly been told by hunters and guides that they occasionally meet these Squirrels swimming various lakes and rivers in the Wilderness, and James Higby tells me that in June, 1877 he saw as many as fifty crossing Big Moose Lake, and that they were all headed the same way—to the north.

I am informed by Dr. A. K. Fisher that at the southern end of Lake George, in early autumn, it is sometimes an every-day occurrence to see Red Squirrels swimming across the lake, from west to east—never in the opposite direction. The chestnut grows abundantly on the eastern side of the lake, but it is comparatively scarce on the western, and these extensive migrations always take place in years when the yield of chestnuts is large.* Mr. Winslow C. Watson, in his History of Essex County, says: "The autumn of 1851 afforded one of these periodical invasions of Essex county. It is well authenticated, that the red squirrel was constantly seen in the widest parts of the lake [Lake Champlain], far out from land, swimming towards the shore, as if familiar with the service; their heads above water, and their bushy tails erect and expanded, and apparently spread to the breeze. Reaching land, they stopped for a moment, and relieving their active and vigorous little bodies from the water, by an energetic shake or two, they bounded into the woods, as light and free as if they had made no extraordinary effort."

Hawks and owls are the Squirrel's mortal enemies, often seizing him unawares; but his movements are so well timed that if he sees them coming he is almost certain to escape. When either

---

* A few Squirrels are occasionally seen crossing the lake when the nut-crop is only moderate In September, 1882, Mrs. Fisher was angling between Diamond Island and the west shore when a Red Squirrel swam to the boat and was lifted in by the tail. After resting a few minutes it ran out on an oar, jumped into the water and swam to the island (which is half a mile from the west shore), and thence, doubtless, to the chestnut groves on the eastern side of the lake.

of these birds is discovered perching on a limb near his home he invariably pesters it till it is glad to fly to some more congenial place.

He is sometimes caged and makes an intelligent but unruly and destructive pet.

In the choice of a site for his nest he does not limit himself to any fixed conditions, usually placing it in a hollow limb, sometimes in a hole in the ground, and occasionally in a hollow log. The young are generally born about the first of April, four to six constituting an average litter.

Where the climate is milder than it is in the Adirondack region the Red Squirrel often builds outside nests. Dr. A. K. Fisher writes me that he has found them about the southern end of Lake George, in Warren County; and that they are so common in Westchester County, New York, that "half a dozen may be in sight at one time in favorable localities. The nest is usually situated near the top of some evergreen, in the midst of a tangled grape-vine. Preference is given to the red cedar (*Juniperus Virginiana*), for the reason, probably, that this tree furnishes most of the material for the nest. It may occasionally be found in a deciduous tree. The nest, which is globular in shape, varies from two to three hundred millimetres in diameter. As a rule, the cavity is situated nearer the top than the bottom, thus making the roof thinner than the floor. At a little distance the entrance cannot be seen, for its borders fall together after the entrance or exit of the animal. The material generally used for the nest is the soft, silky bark of the red cedar. Sometimes that of the grape-vine, or the inner bark of the chestnut, is intermixed." Mr. W. L. Scott, of Ottawa, Canada, tells me that outside nests of the Red Squirrel are common as far north as that place; but it must be borne in mind that lower Ontario is Alleghanian in fauna, while the Adirondacks is Canadian.

# SCIURUS CAROLINENSIS LEUCOTIS (Gmelin) Allen.

### Gray Squirrel ; Black Squirrel.

The Gray Squirrel has no liking for forests of coniferous ever-greens, and is, consequently, of extremely rare occurrence in the central area of the Adirondacks. He is common enough, however, in the hardwood groves along the borders of the region, varying in numbers from year to year according to the abundance or scarcity of the nut supply.*

The immortal Humboldt, in his *Ansichten der Natur*, asks : " Who is there that does not feel himself differently affected beneath the embowering shade of the beechen grove, or on hills crowned with a few scattering pines, or in the flowering meadow where the breeze murmurs through the trembling foliage of the birch ? A feeling of melancholy, or of solemnity, or of light buoyant animation is in turn awakened by the contemplation of our native trees. This influence of the physical on the moral world—this mysterious reaction of the sensuous on the ideal, gives to the study of nature, when considered from a higher point of view, a peculiar charm which has not hitherto been sufficiently recognized." †

This meditation of Humboldt's leads me to suggest that causes which have exerted so marked an influence upon the dispersion, mental culture, and disposition of the various races of mankind have

---

* For more than forty miles the valley of the Black River extends along, and parallel to, the western border of the Adirondack region, and the fact is of local interest that this river valley con-stitutes, throughout a great part of its course, the dividing line between the area inhabited and that uninhabited by the Gray Squirrel. While this animal is abundant in the hardwood groves west of the river, it is of rare or casual occurrence on the eastern side. Many hunters and guides who have spent almost their whole lives in the Wilderness tell me that they have never seen a Gray Squirrel in the interior of the Adirondacks. In the course of their irregular migrations, however, isolated stragglers do sometimes occur there. James Higby informs me that he saw one near Copper Lake many years ago, and another near the old Arnold clearing. In September and early October, 1882, they invaded the region in unusual numbers. About the middle of September, of that year, E. L. Sheppard caught one that was swimming across 2d Lake, Fulton Chain, and a few days later one was seen in the water near the head of Big Moose Lake. Garrie Riggs caught one swimming in 4th Lake, Fulton Chain, about Sept. 25th ; C. Wood saw one on the outlet of this lake, Wayne Bissell another on 2d Lake, and Ned. Ball killed one between Moose River and the Forge.

† Bohn's translation, 1850, p. 219.

15

not been inoperative in determining the distribution of many of our lower animals. Indeed, when nearly related species, having similar habits, and subsisting in the main upon the same kinds of food, are found inhabiting contiguous areas,—areas of equal altitude and subject to identical climatic conditions,—and we learn that these species are limited, so far as we can ascertain, solely by the character of the arboreous vegetation, we are forced to admit that influences other than those which have to do merely with the necessities of existence have played an important part in fixing the arbitrary and irregular boundaries of the places occupied by each. In the case of the present species it seems probable that the dark and sombre hues, the oppressive silence, and the imposing solitude of our evergreen forests impress it with a pervading sense of gloom and sadness against which its cheerful nature revolts. The red squirrel teems with such a superabundance of hilarity that he easily overcomes this feeling of oppression which his larger cousin is powerless to combat.

In sparsely populated districts that have long been settled, one sometimes finds, half-hidden among the trees, a neglected but time-honored mansion, near which a row of stately elms, extending from some neighboring wood to distant fields, leads the eye past clumps of scattered butternuts, beneath whose gnarled and spreading branches groups of grazing cattle seek shelter from the noonday sun. Here, in early autumn, a few joyous Squirrels gather at break of day to feast upon the yet green nuts. Following the line of elms they leap from tree to tree or run upon the zig-zag fence beneath, fairly revelling with delight; and long before the savory nuts are ripe, indeed when they have scarce attained their growth, the eager Squirrels haste to pluck them as they hang in heavy clusters from the boughs. While biting through the adhesive, staining velvet of the outer coat they sit perched upon their haunches, with a merry twinkle in the eye, but, not forgetting their exposed position, maintain a prudent silence.

Should some farmer's boy chance to pass near by, not a Squirrel

is to be seen from where he walks, for each one, clinging to a vertical branch or limb, constantly shifts its position so that it always
keeps out of sight on the opposite side. Everything about this
breakfast is thoroughly enjoyed—the early journey to the butternuts, the flying leaps from bough to bough amongst the summits of
the lofty elms, the meal itself, and the bit of excitement attending the
alarm and escape; each contributes its part toward the pleasure of
the occasion. The repast over, the Squirrels do not linger here but
hurry to their homes within the grove. The slanting sunbeam has
pierced but not dispelled the drop of pearly dew upon the waving
grass, when they are already well upon the way. One auda-
cious adventurer, more courageous than the rest, steals down yonder
tottering cross-fence to the orchard, quickly picks an apple from an
overhanging branch, and rejoins his comrades ere they reach the
wood. This haven once attained all constraint is cast aside and the
cautious, silent, and circumspect Squirrels of a moment ago become
the heedless, noisy, rollicking fellows that they really are. While
chasing one another about the tree-tops they sometimes clear a distance of more than twenty feet (about 6 metres) in a single horizontal
leap. And when at full speed they often stop short, clinging head
downward to a smooth-barked beech, and utter their saucy, scolding
cry—qua-qua-qua-qua-a, qua-qua-qua-qua-a-a, qua-qua-qua-qua-qua-
a-a, qua-a-a-a, qua-a-a-a-a,—in an exasperating, impudent tone,
keeping time, the while, with spasmodic contortions of the body and
impertinent jerks and flourishes of the large and bushy tail. To
observe their utter recklessness during these gambols one would
suppose that nothing could be easier than to approach and shoot the
entire troop. Never was man more mistaken. Despite their bois-
terous manners their eyes are always open and they are ever on the
alert. Let some one try to get within gunshot and observe the
result. His very approach seems to render them invisible. Those
that were near their holes have disappeared within, and the others
are hiding behind the trees upon which they were sporting when the

enemy appeared. As he advances they rotate slowly about the trunk, always keeping on the farther side, so that the body of the tree remains between them. Even if he knows that a Squirrel is on a certain tree it is doubtful if he gets a shot. A momentary glimpse of its ears or a part of its tail constitutes all he is likely to discover as he walks round the tree.

While watching a bird I once noticed what seemed to be a little tuft of hair protruding from the side of an ash sapling near by. On going nearer, I perceived the object to be the tip of a Gray Squirrel's tail. The animal was clinging vertically to the trunk, hugging it so closely that this bit of hair was the only part visible from the ground beneath, though where he lay the trunk was not four inches in diameter. Not wanting the Squirrel, I fired at the bird, and to my astonishment the former came tumbling headlong to the ground, almost at my very feet—an illustration of the effect of terror upon a sensitive animal. He did not tarry long, however, but in a twinkling was off and up another tree. One summer, several years ago, I surprised a Gray Squirrel on the ground in the edge of an open field, and chased him up a large hemlock that stood by itself in the clearing. Imagine my surprise to see him run out on a limb, fully eighty feet high, and leap to the ground, striking more than fifty feet from the base of the tree. Before I could reach the spot he had disappeared in the adjacent forest.

In winter, when the trees and branches are coated with ice, I have several times seen these Squirrels fall nearly a hundred feet, landing in the snow, but never knew one to be injured by the accident. But at such times they usually proceed with great caution and do not attempt to make leaps of any great length. In fact, during the continuance of extreme cold they do not venture out at all. My observations on this point are very full, and extend over a period of years. In winters that follow good yields of nuts they are usually well-conditioned, and seldom appear, in any numbers, when the temperature is below $-8°$ C. ($17.6°$ F.). It must be remembered, however, that mild and open winters are likely to succeed "nut years" in this region, and that during these winters it is not common to have a continuance of very low temperature. The alternate winters, on the other hand, are generally severe. There are few if any nuts, and the Squirrels are none too fat when the heavy snows set in. They have laid up little or no provision in their holes in the trees, and consequently, since they do not hibernate for any great length of time, must often roam about in search of food when they would much prefer to remain coiled snugly in their nests. Under such circumstances they frequently come out, during continued cold, when the thermometer stands at ten degrees below zero C. (14° F.), but not during storms. They are occasionally met with when it is still colder, and I have seen a few individuals come to a place where corn was kept for them when the temperature was −19° C. (−2.2° F.), but only on mild days during protracted periods of low temperature. In this respect they differ markedly from their cousins, the red squirrels.

During the winters of deep snows and scarcity of food, my father has, for many years, kept a stock of corn and nuts within easy reach of the Squirrels, and but a short distance from the house. Knowing that they are always sure of finding a bountiful supply here, they repair to it with great regularity, coming daily except during stormy or very cold weather, often visiting it at times when their neighbors, in more remote portions of the wood, do not venture out at all. Sometimes as many as a dozen Grays and six or eight Blacks have been seen there at one time, running on the snow and feeding at the boxes and barrels within twenty feet (about 6 metres) from the dining-room window. While part of them remained on the boxes, others carried their nuts to a tree near by, eating one at a time and then returning for another. Some winters they became very tame, and while we were at breakfast inside, a few used to bring their nuts to the window and eat them there, perched on their haunches on the sill, with their handsome bushy tails cocked over their backs. When anyone went out of doors they commonly scampered off or ran up a tree, yet several often remained and would allow a near approach without manifesting alarm. They were extremely fond of music (in the most comprehensive sense of the term), and it affected them in a peculiar manner. Some were not only fascinated, but actually spell-bound, by the music-box or guitar. And one particularly weak-minded individual was so unrefined in his taste that if I advanced slowly, whistling "*Just before the Battle, Mother*," in as pathetic a tone as I could muster for the occasion, he would permit me even to stroke his back, sometimes expressing his pleasure by making a low purring sound. This was a Gray, and I several times approached and stroked him as above described. I once succeeded in getting near enough to a Black to touch him, whereupon he instantly came to his senses and fled. When listening to music they all acted in very much the same way. They always sat bolt upright, inclining a little forward (and if eating a nut were sure to drop it), letting the fore-paws hang listlessly over the breast, and, turning the head to one side in a bewildered sort of a way, assumed a most idiotic expression.

Those who have observed the habits of this species in summer must have noticed their propensity for burying nuts just beneath the surface, in various parts of the woods. They do not, so far as I am aware, make a great accumulation in any one place, but dig a thousand little holes, plant a nut or two in each, scrape a few leaves over the spot and hurry off, as if afraid some one would discover the treasure. In winter this habit is almost equally marked, and the first thing a Squirrel thinks of after his hunger is satisfied is to secrete a portion of the food remaining at his disposal. In accomplishing this he tunnels into the snow in various directions, hiding some of the surplus provision in each excavation. Many persons who have observed this habit in summer regard it as an idle pastime, and ques-tion if the Squirrel ever finds the nuts again, knowing that he could never remember the exact positions of so many. But those who have kept tame Squirrels must have been struck with the remarkable certainty and quickness with which they detect the whereabouts of nuts that are hidden from sight. A Squirrel will often scratch and gnaw at a tight box or drawer that he has never seen before, if a few nuts happen to be in the bottom of it. His sense of smell is very acute, enabling him to detect the presence of a nut at some little distance; hence, though he does not, of course, remember the exact spot where each one is buried under the leaves, he can, by moving carefully over the ground, discover a great many of them.

In summer, and in winter when the temperature is above the freezing point, Gray Squirrels are out in greatest numbers early in the morning and in the latter part of the afternoon; throughout the winter, except during thaws, they only appear for an hour or two in the warmest part of the day; and in very cold or stormy weather, as previously stated, they do not venture abroad at all.

This species is not nearly so plentiful along the outskirts of the Adirondacks as it was twelve or fifteen years ago, and it varies in abundance from year to year according to the condition of the nut crop. Beechnuts and butternuts are alone alluded to here because they are the prevailing nuts. All others are of such limited distribution in the area under consideration that they are unworthy of mention. The nut yield is bountiful here, with great regularity, on alternate years. This has been the case, without a single exception, for the past twelve years at least. My notes show that the beechnut crop was good in the autumns of 1871, 1873, 1875, 1877, 1879, 1881, 1883,—always on the odd years,—while on the alternate seasons it failed. And strange as it may at first sight appear, Squirrels are usually most numerous during the summer and early autumn of those years when there are few or no nuts. The reason is this: when the yield is large there is a noticeable influx of Squirrels from distant parts, and they, together with those that were here at the time, winter well, having an abundance of food, and breed here the following spring. During the summer and early autumn a multitude of young, now nearly full grown, mingle with the parent stock. Hence the species attains, at this time, its maximum in numbers·

But this is the year when the nut crop is a failure. Therefore, as the fall advances and they find that there is a scarcity of provision for the winter, many of them migrate—we know not where. Then come the October " Squirrel hunts "—a disgrace to the State as well as to the thoughtless men and boys who participate in them—and the number left to winter is deplorably small.

As the abundance of the Gray Squirrel in winter is governed by the supply of beechnuts, so is the presence, at this season, of its assailant, the red-headed woodpecker (*Melanerpes erythrocephalus*), determined by the same cause. I have elsewhere called attention to this fact, remarking that " with us a good Squirrel year is synonymous with a good year for *Melanerpes*, and *vice versa*." * Gray Squirrels, red-headed woodpeckers, and beechnuts were numerous during the winters of 1871–72, 1873–74, 1875–76, 1877–78, 1879–80, 1881–82, 1883–84, while during the alternate years the Squirrels and nuts were scarce, and the woodpeckers altogether absent.

Several years ago I published the following account of the way that these handsome birds sometimes harass the Squirrels : "In midwinter (January, 1876) my attention was called, by the noise they made, to a pair of red-headed woodpeckers who were diving at something on one of the highest limbs of a large elm. A near approach showed the object of their malice to be a handsome Black Squirrel who had been unfortunate enough to excite their ire by climbing a tree in broad daylight. The Squirrel at first evaded their attacks from above by clinging to the under surface of the limb, and dodged their lateral shoots by a quick side shift, but this was temporary. The woodpeckers, realizing that they were not tormenting the Squirrel to their full satisfaction, alighted for a brief council, during which the Squirrel took occasion to commence a hasty retreat. But the birds were at him in an instant, this time changing their tactics; both dove together, the one following closely behind the other, so that as the Squirrel dodged the first he was sure to be struck by the

---

* Forest and Stream, Vol. XVII, No. 18, Dec. 1, 1881, p. 347.

second. The blows from their hard bills were so severe and so painful that the poor Squirrel had not been struck half a dozen times when he let go his hold and fell to the ground, but was off and up another tree before I could reach the spot. I witnessed a similar attack upon a Gray Squirrel (color-variety of the same species) last August, but this time the Squirrel succeeded in getting into a hollow limb. The time of year at which the above instances occurred precludes the possibility that the cause of the difficulty arose from an intrusion on the nesting-ground of the woodpeckers, for the first took place in midwinter, and the second after the young were fully fledged and had left the nest. Neither is it at all likely that the trouble was due to an old grudge which might have arisen from a habit, on the part of the Squirrel, of robbing the woodpeckers of their eggs, for the size of the animal is such as to prevent his ready entrance into the woodpecker's hole, and should he even succeed in getting in, he would doubtless pay the penalty with his eyes, if not his life." * At this time I was in ignorance of the cause of enmity between them, but was soon after enlightened on this point. While much the larger part of the beechnut crop falls to the ground after the first hard frosts, a few nuts remain on the trees throughout the winter. These the woodpeckers consider as their exclusive property, assailing and punishing all rivals with a valor, persistence, and severity, astonishing to behold. Now the Squirrels find it much more convenient to procure the nuts that still cling to the branches than to dig down through the snow in search of those that lie buried beneath. Therefore, it often happens that the woodpeckers, on coming to the grove to feed, discover that the Squirrels are there before them, stealing the scattered nuts. Their wrath knows no bounds, and they attack the intruders with such unmistakable earnestness and efficiency that the latter, unable to defend themselves, are glad of any haven to which they may escape. During the last five years I have witnessed these encounters over and over again, and am convinced

---

* Bull. Nutt. Ornith. Club, Vol. III, No. 3, July, 1878, pp. 125–126.

that the misunderstanding is wholly in regard to the possession of the nuts. The red-headed is the only species of woodpecker that I have seen quarrel with the Gray Squirrel.

On the 7th of November, 1879, I witnessed an exciting skirmish between a goshawk and a Gray Squirrel. The hawk dove repeatedly for the Squirrel, and as often did the latter evade him by quickly sliding around the trunk. He then chippered and scolded and shook his tail in the most aggravating manner imaginable. The hawk was much enraged, but finding himself unable to capture the object of his pursuit, finally alighted to wait till the Squirrel should venture on a limb—a proceeding which the latter wisely showed no inclination to attempt. I put an end to the affair by shooting the hawk. Audubon and Bachman state that the red-tailed hawks hunt them in pairs, thus rendering the capture of the helpless animal certain and easy.

The minor migratory movements of this species occur with more or less regularity from year to year, but on so small a scale as to escape general notice. They must not be confounded with the great migrations, not rare in former times, when these animals, actuated by some unknown influence, congregated in vast armies and moved over the land, crossing open prairies, climbing rugged mountains, and swimming lakes and rivers that lay in their path. Though hundreds, and sometimes thousands, perished by the way, the multitude moved on, devouring the nuts that grew in the forests through which they passed, and devastating the grain fields of the farmer along the route. Though these remarkable expeditions have been known and commented upon for many years, yet our knowledge of them is limited almost to the recognition of the fact of their existence. Scarcity of food very probably gives rise to the disquieting impulse that prompts them to leave their homes, but the true motives that operate in drawing them together, and in determining the direction and distance of their journeys, are as little understood to-day as they were before the discovery of the continent on which they dwell.

In the year 1749 they invaded Pennsylvania in such vast hosts as to endanger the crops of the entire inhabited portion of the State, and a reward of three pence a head was offered for their destruction. This necessitated the payment of eight thousand pounds sterling (six hundred and forty thousand individuals having been killed), which so depleted the treasury that the premium was decreased one-half. Commenting upon this statement Pennant observed: "How improved must the state of the *Americans* then be, in thirty-five years, to wage an expensive and successful war against its parent country, which before could not bear the charges of clearing the provinces from the ravages of these insignificant animals!"*

Since nearly all parts of our great country have become populated, since thousands of square miles of forests have been hewn down, and the lands tilled and made to yield to the wants of man, there has been such a vast decrease in the numbers of these animals that it is doubtful if another great migration will ever be recorded. It was their enormous abundance in former times, and the extensive depredations which they committed in the autumn, that caused the inhabitants to organize for their destruction. Robert Munro, in "A Description of the Genesee Country," published in 1804, states that in the western part of New York, "Squirrels are so numerous in some years as considerably to injure corn; and upwards of 2000 of them have sometimes been killed in a day, which is occasionally appointed for that purpose by the inhabitants; the most common kinds of them are the black, and the red; the grey coloured being very scarce." † Aside from the constant warfare which every man waged against those upon his own premises, there came to be established a much more effective system of extermination. Certain days were set apart, and every male person capable of carrying a gun, and who owned or could borrow one to carry, was supposed to join in the chase. Captains were appointed, sides

---

* Pennant's Arctic Zoology, Vol. I, 1792, p. 136.

† Documentary History of New York, Vol. II, p. 1175.

chosen, and everything was in readiness the night before. At daybreak the hunt commenced, and it ended only with the setting of the sun. Then the participants gathered at some rendezvous previously agreed upon, where a bountiful supper was in waiting. So many Squirrels had been killed that the hunters could not possibly carry them, hence the tails alone were preserved. These were then counted in order to ascertain which side had killed the greater number, the defeated party meeting the expense of the banquet. This was the "Squirrel hunt" of our forefathers. But the time when these animals could be ranked among the enemies of the farmer has long since passed away, probably never to return. And yet, for some unaccountable reason, the "Squirrel hunts" still continue—in name at least—but they have degenerated into the most despicable of "pot-hunts." Not only are the Squirrels slain wherever found, though innocent of the deeds for which they were originally persecuted, but large numbers of our insectivorous birds are likewise destroyed, and for no other reason than because each counts a certain tally in the reckoning that determines the victorious party !

The Gray Squirrel is easily tamed, if captured early enough, and being one of the most intelligent of our native mammals, makes a desirable pet, and may be allowed entire freedom of movement. The main objection to it is its tendency to gnaw objects about the premises.

In the Adirondack region its nest is invariably concealed within the hollow of some tree or limb, while in more temperate quarters it is commonly built on the outside, like that of the crow, which it closely resembles, and is placed either in a fork or at the point where a large branch leaves the trunk. Audubon and Bachman, and other writers, speak of these latter as "summer nests," affirming that the Squirrels spend the winter and bring forth their young in the hollows of trees. My experience proves the incorrectness of this statement, in certain localities at least ; for, in southern Connecticut, in the southern part of New York State (Westchester County), and in northern New Jersey, I have myself taken more than a hundred young from these outside nests.

A number found at Elizabeth, New Jersey, during March and the early part of April, 1872, contained young. They were, according to my note book, " composed of sticks, lined with the inner bark of trees and vines, mixed with other soft substances. They are entirely covered over above, the entrance being on one side. From the ground below they cannot be distinguished from crows' nests." In many instances dead leaves enter largely into their composition.

The number of young produced at a birth varies from three to five, exceptional litters containing six  They are born in a very diminutive and helpless condition, wholly devoid of hair, and with the eyes not yet open. They usually remain in the nest fully two months, and do not shift for themselves till some time later. On the 19th of May, 1877, Mr. Walter R. Nichols and I took three half-grown young from a nest at Brandford, Connecticut. It so happened at the time that Mr. Nichols had a cat which had recently given birth to a kitten. The kitten we destroyed, and in its stead placed one of the Squirrels. Presently the cat returned to the barn, eyed the stranger suspiciously for a moment, and then entered the nest. The young Squirrel, who had now been several hours away from his mother and was evidently quite hungry, approached the cat in the most familiar manner possible. After a little hesitation the latter lay down beside the new comer, who lost no time in discovering the object of his desire, and forthwith commenced to nurse, keeping it up with an energy and perseverance that must have proved as satisfactory to the cat as a whole litter of kittens. From this time on the two were the most inseparable of friends ; in fact, the cat seemed quite pleased with the change and no doubt considered the personal appearance of her new charge, who was now well formed and possessed a most extraordinary tail, a great improvement on that of her own ill-shaped offspring. The Squirrel grew and thrived under the devoted attention of its foster mother, and the pair soon became the centre of attraction in the neighborhood.

It is stated by Audubon and Bachman that the young are brought forth in May and June, which statement is at least two months out of the way. Even in this northern region the period when the important event takes place is rarely later than the first of April, and is frequently in March. The cause of their error, however, is not hard to explain ; for if they were unacquainted with the very immature condition of the young at birth, and were ignorant of the time required to attain full growth, they might easily have made the mistake of considering young found in the nest in June to be only a few weeks from birth, when in reality they were two or three months old. In many localities south and west of the Adirondacks the Gray Squirrel commonly has two litters in a season, the second usually being born in September or October.

In closing the biography of this interesting species it seems hardly necessary to remark that the Black and Gray Squirrels are identical, both color varieties being sometimes found in the same litter.* Fifteen years ago the two forms were about equally abundant along the western border of the region under consideration ; but the Black has gradually become less and less common, till now it may almost be regarded as one of our rarer mammals. However, it is still abundant in a number of places bordering Lake Ontario, both in this State and in Canada.

## SCIURUS NIGER CINEREUS (Linn.) Allen.

### Fox Squirrel.

The Fox Squirrel cannot at present be regarded as other than a rare or accidental straggler in the Adirondack region. So far as I am aware, the only specimen taken here of late was killed by

---

* The case has a well-known parallel in our common mottled owl, in which species both red and gray plumages are occasionally met with in the same nest.

Oliver B. Lockhart at Lake George, Warren County, in 1872 or 1873. Mr. W. W. Lockhart saw another near the same place at about the same time.*

Formerly, the species was found in many parts of the State. In the year 1853 a specimen was presented to the State Cabinet of Natural History by Isaac B. Lottridge, who shot it at Hoosic, in Rensselaer County.† Two other specimens (male and female) were afterwards presented to the State Cabinet by Mr. Lottridge. Both "were taken in Rensselaer County, New York, in the spring of 1854." ‡

Dr. J. Bachman, writing in 1839, speaks thus of this animal: "In the northern part of New York it is exceedingly rare, as I only saw two pair during fifteen years of close observation. In the lower part of that State, however, it appears to be more common, as I recently received several specimens procured in the County of Orange." §

## TAMIAS STRIATUS (Linn.) Baird.

*Chipmunk; Ground Squirrel; Striped Squirrel; Chipping Squirrel.*

The Chipmunk or Ground Squirrel is always present in greater or less numbers in some parts of the Adirondacks. It is a migratory animal and is exceedingly abundant some years, while during others it is scarcely seen at all, the difference being dependent upon the quantity of the food-supply.

The Striped Squirrel feeds upon a variety of nuts and roots,

---

* Since the above was written I have learned, through Dr. A. K. Fisher, that a caged Fox Squirrel escaped, near the southern end of Lake George, previous to the date of killing of Mr. Lockhart's specimen. Hence it is possible, though I think hardly probable, that the specimen in question was imported.

† Seventh Annual Report of the Regents of the University on the Condition of the State Cabinet of Natural History, 1854, p. 15.

‡ Eighth Annual Report on the Condition of the State Cabinet, 1855, p. 15.

§ Monograph of the Genus Sciurus. Charlesworth's Magazine of Natural History, Vol. III, 1839, p. 161.

and is fond of corn and several kinds of grain. It also eats the
larvæ of certain insects. In this region the beechnut constitutes
its staple commodity, as it does that of all our squirrels, and
since this nut is produced in large quantity each alternate year,
we are able to predict with considerable certainty the periods
when the Chipmunk will be abundant. For wherever, in autumn,
this animal finds a sufficient supply of nuts he is sure to remain
until the following summer. Here, in beechnut years, the fore-
runners of the great migration arrive in September, and by the
first week in October the woods literally swarm with them. Finding an abundance of food they immediately establish themselves
for the winter, and begin at once to hoard up large stores. They
are the least hardy of our squirrels, commonly going into winter
quarters before the middle of November, and rarely appearing
again in any numbers till the warm sun, in March or April, has
caused plots of bare ground to appear between the snow-banks.
Early thaws sometimes bring them out in February; and after
having once emerged, they often make little excursions over the
snow during pleasant days, though the temperature may be several
degrees below freezing. In running from tree to tree, even when
not pursued, the length of their bound varies from twenty-five to
thirty-four inches (635 to 863 mm.), a long leap for so small an
animal. The season of spring is occupied with the duties of rear-
ing the young, which, before June, are old enough to leave the nest.
At this time the species attains its maximum in numbers, the
young and old together inhabiting all parts of the woodland. Foreseeing that the nut crop will fail (this being the even year), they
commonly emigrate in July and do not again appear till September
or October of the ensuing year.

Briefly, then (leaving out of consideration the small number
of resident individuals, and the migrants that sometimes pass
through on their way to distant parts), we find that Chipmunks
reach the Adirondack region during September or October of the

odd years (nut years), remaining till the following July. They then depart and are not seen again till the autumn of the next year. Hence they are here about ten months and absent about fourteen months, the period of greatest abundance being in June of the even years (when there are no nuts).

They are most industrious creatures, and, though small, lay up an astonishingly large supply of food. Audubon and Bachman, who once dug out a nest occupied by four Chipmunks, speak thus of the larder : " There was about a gill of wheat and buckwheat in the nest ; but in the galleries we afterwards dug out, we obtained about a quart of the beaked hazel nuts (*Corylus rostratus*), nearly a peck of acorns, some grains of Indian corn, about two quarts of buckwheat, and a very small quantity of grass seeds." *

In addition to their store-houses, they frequently, like the gray squirrel, make little caches, burying here and there beneath the leaves the contents of their cheek-pouches. Mr. Ira Sayles thus graphically describes this habit :—

" I lately noticed in my garden a bright-eyed Chipmunk, *Sciurus striatus*, advancing along a line directly towards me. He came briskly forward, without deviating a hair's breadth to the right or the left, until within two feet of me ; then turned square towards my left—his right—and went about three feet or less. Here he paused a moment and gave a sharp look all around him, as if to detect any lurking spy on his movements. (His distended cheeks revealed his business : he had been out foraging.) He now put his nose to the ground, and, aiding this member with both forepaws, thrust his head and shoulders down through the dry leaves and soft muck, half burying himself in an instant.

" At first, I thought him after the bulb of an *Erythronium*, that grew directly in front of his face and about three inches from it. I was the more confirmed in this supposition, by the shaking of the plant.

---

* Quadrupeds of North America, Vol. I, 1846, p. 70.

" Presently, however, he became comparatively quiet. In this state he remained, possibly, half a minute. He then commenced a vigorous action, as if digging deeper; but I noticed that he did not get deeper; on the contrary, he was gradually backing out. I was surprised that, in all his apparent hard work (he worked like a man on a wager) he threw back no dirt. But this vigorous labor could not last long. He was very soon completely above ground; and then became manifest the object of his earnest work: he was refilling the hole he had made, and repacking the dirt and leaves he had disturbed. Nor was he content with simply refilling and repacking the hole. With his two little hand-like feet he patted the surface, and so exactly *replaced the leaves* that, when he had completed his task, my eye could detect not the slightest difference between the surface he had so cunningly manipulated, and that surrounding it. Having completed his task, he raised himself into a sitting posture, looked with a very satisfied air, and then silently dodged off into a bush-heap, some ten feet distant. Here he ventured to stop, and set up a triumphant 'chip! chip! chip!'

" It was now my turn to dig, in order to discover the little miser's treasures. I gently removed enough of the leaves and fine muck to expose his hoard—half a pint of buttercup seeds, *Ranunculus acris.*" *

On the western side of the Adirondack region the Chipmunk feeds largely upon the tuberous roots of the dwarf ginseng or ground-nut (*Aralia trifolia*), and the yellow grain-like tubers of the unspurred dicentra or squirrel corn (*Dicentra Canadensis*). The winged seeds of the maple can also be ranked among his staple articles of diet. In June of the present year (1884), Mr. W. E. Bryant shot a Chipmunk, in Lewis County, whose cheek-pouches contained a number of larvæ and pupæ of insects.

Of the six species of squirrels known to occur in the Adirondacks, the present is the only one belonging to the group of ground

---

* American Naturalist, Vol. IV, No. 4, June, 1870, p. 249.

squirrels, a group that is largely represented in our western States and Territories. The Chipmunk establishes his head-quarters in some log or stump, or in a hole excavated by himself in the earth, generally among the roots of a tree. He is partial to brush-heaps, wood-piles, stone walls, rail fences, accumulations of old rubbish, and other places that afford him a pretty certain escape, and at the same time enable him to see what is transpiring outside. For, though by no means wary, he delights in these loosely sheltered hiding-places where he can whisk in and out at will, peep unobserved at passers-by, and dart back when prudence demands. If suddenly surprised he utters a sharp *chip'-per'*, *r*, *r*, *r*, and makes a quick dash for his retreat, which is no sooner reached than, simultaneously with the disappearance of his tail, out pops his head, his keen dark eyes gazing intently at the source of alarm. If not pursued farther he is very apt to advance toward the supposed enemy, betraying his excitement by a series of nervous starts and precipitous retreats, till finally, making a bold rush, he dashes by the object of his dread and in another instant is peering out from a hole beneath the roots of a neighboring tree.

Though a very inquisitive creature, this habit does not seem to be attributable to curiosity alone, but rather to the same reckless foolhardiness that prompts the small boy to cross and recross the road in front of a swiftly advancing carriage or locomotive.

With us the Chipmunk is not ordinarily given to climbing trees. But when at play he often runs part way up the trunks, and when pursued by man or dog and unable to reach his hole, he does not hesitate to take refuge in the topmost branches. Still, he is ill at ease there, apparently becoming giddy on attaining a little height, and often commences the descent while his pursuers are yet watching him from the ground beneath. This unfortunate habit has cost many a Chipmunk his life, and gave origin, in my younger days, to an effective method of hunting them. · With the aid of a small dog the poor animal was readily "treed," and the dog soon learned to watch one side of the tree while the boy guarded the other. Presently the affrighted and giddy Chipmunk, head downward, would commence to descend, circling around the trunk. Harassed on whichever side of the tree he appeared he usually lost his head and soon came rushing toward the ground, when he was either knocked over with a stick, or seized by the dog.

It occasionally happens that Chipmunks are met with that do not show this aversion to tree climbing, particularly when collecting food for their hoards. The trail from Big Moose Lake to West Pond crosses a low beech ridge whose northern exposure slopes gradually to the lake. Here, during the latter part of October and early November, 1881 (beechnut year), Chipmunks abounded. Here also Dr. A. K. Fisher and the writer, seated upon a half-decayed log, observed their actions unheeded. They were very busy. Some were gathering the nuts and crowding them into their over-distended cheek-pouches; others were carrying their loads to the store-houses in the ridge; whilst others still, returning for more, were bounding lightly over the fallen leaves and playfully chasing one another among the logs and brushwood that lay upon the ground. A few, more venturesome than the rest, were not content to gather the nuts that frost and wind had strewn upon the earth, but essayed to climb and pick them from the boughs. Two were seen at one time high up in the trees, and one in particular was observed making regular journeys from his hole in the side-hill to the uppermost branches of a beech fully sixty feet (over 18 metres) in height. He seemed as much at ease here as would any of our arboreal squirrels, but we noticed that he never tried to leap from limb to limb.

The Chipmunk is such a beautiful, graceful, active, and seemingly confiding animal in the wild state, that he would naturally be expected to become one of the most charming of pets. Experience, however, has not confirmed this supposition. Most writers, as well as myself, have found him morose and uninteresting in confinement, and altogether too fond of biting his captor's fingers on insufficient provocation. It is proper to state, however, that the very young have not, to my knowledge, been caged, and I incline to the belief that they would well repay one for the care bestowed upon them.

In the *American Naturalist* for March, 1870 (p. 58), Mr. A. J. Cook, of Lansing, Michigan, states that a Chipmunk was observed "busily nibbling at a snake that had been recently killed. He could hardly be driven away, and soon returned to his feast when his tormentors had withdrawn a short distance."

Thomas Pennant says of this species : " During the *mayz* harvest, these squirrels are very busy in biting off the ears, and filling their mouths so full with the corn that their cheeks are quite distended. It is observable, that they give great preference to certain food ; for if, after filling their mouths with rye, they happen to meet with wheat, they fling away the first, that they may indulge in the last." *

John Josselyn, writing in 1675 of the animals of New England, called the Chipmunk "mouse-squirril", and said of it : "The mouse-squirril is hardly so big as a Rat, streak'd on both sides with black and red streaks, they are mischievous vermine destroying abundance of Corn both in the field and in the house, where they will gnaw holes into Chests, and tear clothes both linnen and wollen, and are notable nut-gathers in *August ;* when hasel and filbert nuts are ripe you may see upon every Nut-tree as many mouse-squirrils as leaves ; So that the nuts are gone in a trice, which they convey to their Drays or Nests." †

* Synopsis of Quadrupeds. 1771, p. 289.
† Two Voyages to New England. Boston reprint, p. 69.

## ARCTOMYS MONAX (Linn.) Schreber.

### *Woodchuck ; Marmot.*

The Woodchuck delights in the open meadows and rocky hill-sides that mark the possessions of the farmer, but has no love for the extensive evergreen forests that exist in districts remote from civilization. He is, therefore, of rare occurrence within the proper limits of the Adirondacks, though he has been found, sparingly, in the remotest parts of the Wilderness.* In the cultivated area surrounding the Adirondacks he is very abundant, and often proves a serious annoyance to the farmer.

He is a strict vegetarian, feeding chiefly upon clover and grass. Only in rare instances does he enter the garden, and were it not for the size of his holes he could hardly be regarded as an enemy to the agriculturist.

With us, the Woodchuck commonly lives in extensive burrows, excavated by himself, though he sometimes takes up his abode in rocky ledges, and in the hollow roots of large trees. During the summer season the greater number live in the open fields, gener-ally selecting good meadows where they are sure to be surrounded with a luxuriant growth of rich grass or clover, so that they can procure an abundance of the best of food without exposing them-selves to the danger of wandering far from their holes. As the season for going into winter-quarters draws near, many of them retire to the groves and borders of woods near by and take posses-sion of other burrows which they occupy till late in the following spring. Some, indeed, leave the meadows immediately after the

---

* To cite a few cases : June 12th, 1883, I saw a large Woodchuck in the Brown's Tract road near the Hellgate Lakes ; and later, on the same day, saw another between Third and Fourth Lakes of the Fulton Chain. I have also seen their holes between Upper and Lower Saranac Lakes, and in the side of a knoll between Morse Lake and Second Lake of North Branch, in which latter place E. L. Sheppard caught one in February or March, 1880. James Higby tells me that in the early part of July, 1878, he almost stepped on a full-grown and very fat Woodchuck on the portage between Seventh and Eighth Lakes, Fulton Chain.

hay is cut in July, while there are a few that never abandon their forest homes. But few reside permanently in the open fields.*

The Woodchuck is our most remarkable example of a hibernating mammal. He lays up no store of provision, but remains dormant throughout the winter. Neither temperature nor quantity of food at hand has to do with the beginning of his voluntary seclusion.

The first copious rains that fall after haying is over cause fresh green grass to spring up anew upon the meadows. This second crop, termed rowen or aftermath, usually attains a luxuriant growth by the latter part of August. In many places it consists largely of red clover (*Trifolium pratense*), the favorite food of the Wood-chuck. And this animal eats so much during the month previous to his withdrawal into the earth that he becomes exceedingly fat, and proportionally inert, and is therefore in excellent condition for hibernating. Along the western border of the Adirondacks he usually goes into winter-quarters between the 18th and 25th of September, not to reappear till the middle or latter part of March. It is indeed a curious coincidence that the limits of the dormant state should so closely correspond with the periods of the equinoxes. In nine cases out of ten he disappears, with astonishing precision, within a few days of the autumnal equinox, and remains under ground till about the time the sun cuts the plane of the equator at the vernal equinox.†

---

* It may not be amiss to acquaint my readers with the reasons that lead me to believe that the majority of our Woodchucks desert the meadows in autumn and hibernate in burrows in the woods. There are two principal facts, either of which is sufficient, in my opinion, to establish the existence of this habit. First: As will be hereafter shown, Woodchucks, in this region, come out from their burrows in early spring two or three weeks before the disappearance of the snow, and may easily be tracked to their holes. Now it has been my experience (an experience covering at least fifteen years) that fully 99 per cent. of those that appear before the snow goes in spring, come from holes in the woods. Second: In the fall of the year I have opened a number of meadow burrows, which I knew were inhabited up to a week of the time when the animals went into winter-quarters in September, and almost without exception such burrows have been found to be tenantless.

† To this rule there are, of course, exceptions, but they are not sufficiently frequent to in any way invalidate the accuracy of the above general statement. During very warm weather it some-times happens that a Woodchuck may be seen sunning himself at the mouth of his hole for an hour or two in the hottest part of the afternoon as late as the first of October, but such instances are

The remarkable circumstance has already been noticed that the Woodchuck often retires to winter-quarters when surrounded by an abundance of food, and during the continuance of fine warm weather; but still more surprising is the fact that he generally emerges from his hole and tunnels to the surface while the ground is buried in snow to the depth of several feet, and when no green thing is to be found upon which he can feed. He not only comes to the surface, but makes long journeys in various directions over the snow-covered land, and is apt to continue these apparently aimless pilgrimages night after night until the fast-melting snow enables him to reach the much-coveted grass, which has been kept fresh and green in places by its heavy covering.

The Hon. Daniel Wadsworth, of Hartford, Connecticut, once kept a Woodchuck alive for upwards of two years, and furnished Audubon and Bachman with the following interesting account of its hibernation : " Winter coming on, the box was placed in a warm corner, and the Woodchuck went into it, arranged its bed with care, and became torpid. Some six weeks having passed without its appearing, or having received any food ; I had it taken out of the box, and brought into the parlour ;—it was inanimate, and as round as a ball, its nose being buried as it were in the lower part of its abdomen, and covered by its tail—it was rolled over the carpet many times, but without effecting any apparent change in its lethargic condition, and being desirous to push the experiment as far as is in my power, I laid it close to the fire, and having ordered my dog to lie down by it, placed the Wood-Chuck in the dog's lap. In about half an hour my pet slowly unrolled itself, raised its nose from the carpet, looked around for a few minutes, and then slowly crawled away from the dog, moving about the room as if in search of its own bed ! I took it up, and had it carried down stairs and

rare. In the early springs that sometimes follow exceptionally mild winters, Woodchucks occasionally appear in February, but re-enter their burrows and again become dormant if the temperature suddenly falls. In Southern New England they commonly remain out till late in October, and I have seen them in the Connecticut Valley even in November.

placed again in its box, where it went to sleep, as soundly as ever, until spring made its appearance. That season advancing, and the trees showing their leaves, the Wood-Chuck became as brisk and gentle as could be desired, and was frequently brought into the parlour. The succeeding winter this animal evinced the same dispositions, and never appeared to suffer by its long sleep." *

In Rensselaer County in this State, during the summer of 1814, Dr. Bachman marked a burrow that he knew to be inhabited by a pair of Woodchucks. Early in November he had it opened and found the animals lying close together in a nest of dry grass about twenty-five feet (7.62 metres) from the entrance. " They were each rolled up," he writes, " and looked somewhat like two misshapen balls of hair, and were perfectly dormant." †

In hibernation the temperature of the animal approximates that of the surrounding atmosphere, the heart's action slackens, and respiration can only be detected by means of delicate instruments devised for the purpose. This latter fact was known to Spallanzani nearly a hundred years ago, for he wrote to Senebier : " You will remember about my Marmot which was so exceedingly lethargic in the severe winter of 1795 ; during that time I held him in carbonic acid gas for four hours, the thermometer marking $-12°$, he continued to live in this gas which is the most deadly of all . . . at least a rat and a bird that I placed with him perished in an instant."

It is well to observe that different animals exhibit in different degrees the physiological process of hibernation ; and that this fact is amply illustrated by the representatives of the family to which the present species belongs. Animals that are able to procure subsistence in the winter season, and those that lay up large stores in their nests, do not sleep so continuously, and their lethargy is not so profound as in the case of those species that are

---

* Quadrupeds of North America, Vol. I, 1846, pp. 20–21.
† Ibid., p. 22.

wholly cut off from food during this period.   Thus the gray squirrel, being able to find a certain amount of sustenance when the
ground is covered with snow, remains dormant during severe cold
only ; and the chipmunk, which lays up a great store of provision,
frequently awakes to eat, and is at all times easily aroused ; while
the Woodchuck, whose food is of such a nature that he can neither
gather a supply for winter's use, nor find any were he to go in
search of it, must needs sleep long and soundly or starve.

The Woodchuck and the flying squirrel occupy the two extremes
of the family to which both belong, while the ground squirrels and
spermophiles hold intermediate positions.   The flying squirrel is
the most highly specialized form, showing the most perfect adapta-
tion of structure to habit ; while the Woodchuck must at present
be regarded as the most generalized type of the living members of
the group.   These animals are so widely different that, taken
alone, they would naturally be regarded as pertaining to separate
families ; but a careful study of the numerous intermediate forms
not only proves this view to be incorrect, but also shows that the
gradation of connecting species is so complete that it is even difficult, in many cases, to draw the line between genera.

The Woodchuck lacks the grace and agility of the arboreal
squirrels, but his heavy body and powerful paws are well adapted
to his terrestrial mode of life.   Both animals are modified, but to
widely different ends.

Woodchucks are both nocturnal and diurnal, the periods of feeding being determined, in a general way, by the time of the year,
the weather, and the proximity and nature of enemies.   In summer,
throughout the farming districts, they commonly leave their burrows early in the morning, late in the afternoon, and during moonlight nights ; but may sometimes be found abroad at all hours.   As
autumn approaches, and they become more and more fat and sleepy,
they usually appear only in fine weather, and then but for a few
hours in the hottest part of the afternoon.

In localities where they are much hunted they become wary and difficult of approach. Their hearing is so acute that they take alarm at sounds which escape our observation altogether. When feeding or otherwise occupied they frequently stop to listen, sitting bolt upright with the head inclined forward and the fore legs hanging down over the breast. If a suspicious noise is heard and a man or dog can be discerned in the distance, they are apt to precipitate themselves into their holes, not to emerge again till sufficient time has elapsed to discourage the most enthusiastic and patient of hunters who may be waiting for a shot. However, when seen in an open field they may generally be stalked by a very simple artifice. They seem to be wholly unacquainted with man except in the erect or semi-erect posture. Taking advantage of this fact, the hunter has merely to prostrate himself at full length upon the ground and crawl slowly till within easy rifle range of the astonished beast, which, seeing little save the top of the man's hat, and curious to see more, often stands erect at the mouth of his burrow, converting himself into a target that no marksman could fail to hit. When a Woodchuck, seeing a man approach, withdraws into his hole, he does not always retreat immediately to its innermost recesses, but sometimes tarries near the mouth to await developments. The hunter, availing himself of the knowledge of this fact, proceeds deliberately till within range, throws himself upon the ground and utters a sharp whistle, when, not infrequently, the animal's head will be seen to pop up inquiringly from its hole.

Woodchucks live singly or in pairs, the young as a rule remaining with their parents only through the first few months. In the latter part of the summer they usually begin to shift for themselves, and in early autumn they may often be met with in the fields and forests far from their holes. They now take refuge in stone walls, hollow logs, and even in hollow trees when there is a sufficiently large opening near the ground. It is not long before each has fixed upon a spot agreeable to his individual fancy, where he at

once commences to establish a home. The diversity of taste
exercised in this selection is hardly outdone by our own idiosyncrasies in the same field.

Some evince a love for home and take up their abodes in the
very door-yards of their parents ; while others, impelled by a desire
to see more of the world, wander far and wide before settling down
to the sober task of excavating their holes. Some, indeed, never
give themselves this trouble, but merely take possession of the deserted burrows of their ancestors, where a small amount of labor
is all that is necessary to render the easily acquired, though somewhat musty apartments habitable. Woodchucks' holes are not all
alike. There are two principal types: the first slopes at a moderate angle from the surface and has a mound of dirt near its
entrance ; * the other is more or less vertical for several feet
(often a metre or more) immediately below the surface, and no
loose earth can be found in its neighborhood. The latter are usually smaller than the others and several are often clustered about
one of the large family burrows, though they are occasionally
isolated. If the surface opening is in a meadow, the hole through
the sod is apt to be sharp cut and more or less circular in outline.
Intermediate forms are sometimes met with, and many of these
are in time converted into primary burrows.

The galleries do not conform to any definite or uniform pattern,
but vary in length, depth, and direction, and in the number of
branches, nests, and surface openings, according to the location,
character of soil, number of inhabitants, and individual idiosyncrasy.
However, they resemble one another sufficiently in some respects
to admit of general description. As a rule they slant abruptly
downward from the entrance to a depth of from three to four feet
(.914 to 1.219 metres), whence, inclining slightly upward and
usually curving to one side, they extend horizontally for a varying

---

* The mounds in front of the large holes frequently, if not generally, contain accumulations of
the animal's excrement, and in one case I removed fully half a bushel from a single mound.

distance (commonly from 10 to 25 feet, or 3.048 to 7.620 metres). Two or more short lateral branches are generally given off from the main gallery, and lead, sloping upward and then downward, to the more or less circular chambers that contain the animal's nests.    It has been my invariable experience to find these chambers above the level of the bottom of the entrance incline, and I have seen one that was within a foot and a half (.457 metres) of the surface. The nest itself is usually composed of dry grasses and leaves, and rarely exceeds a foot in diameter.*

It not infrequently happens, where there are two surface openings, that the main gallery takes the form of a more or less irregular semicircle, with one or more lateral branches of considerable length, both ends of the main gallery coming to the surface.

During the last week of April or first of May, the Woodchuck commonly gives birth to from four to six young.    A nest which was dug out May 11th, 1884, contained two young, whose eyes and ears were not yet open, though the animals were well haired.    Each measured two hundred and five millimetres in length, and weighed one hundred and sixty-seven grammes.    The nest was one metre below the surface, and was connected with the main burrow by a steeply sloping branch.

When unexpectedly surprised at close quarters the Woodchuck utters a loud, shrill, and tremulous whistle that pierces the ear and evokes from the intruder an involuntary movement or exclamation, even though he may have been similarly startled many times before.†

The Woodchuck is pre-eminently a terrestrial animal, usually spending the whole of his life in or upon the ground, yet some ambitious individuals, prompted either by choice or necessity,

---

* The main gallery or one of its branches commonly terminates in a slight excavation which is found to contain the animal's excrement.    No other of the lower animals with which I am acquainted constructs a special receptacle for the deposit and accumulation of its dejections.

† Dr. Coues speaks of this note as "The merry whistle of the woodchuck at the mouth of its burrow" (Familiar Science, Vol. V, No. 12, Dec., 1878, p. 230.), but I am unable to conceive how a sudden cry of alarm can be construed into a "merry whistle."

occasionally take a more elevated view of the earth. Concerning these "tree-climbing Woodchucks" I quote from an article on the subject that I once wrote for *Forest and Stream :* —
"Woodchucks, when unmolested, and particularly during their youthful days, often climb up ten or twelve feet in shrubbery and young trees that abound in low branches, and not infrequently scramble up the trunks of large trees which have partially fallen or slant sufficiently to insure them against slipping. Occasionally, especially when hard pressed by a fast approaching enemy, they ascend large erect trees whose lowest branches are some distance from the ground. But, in order to do this, they must take advantage of the impetus of a rush, for they cannot start slowly upon the trunk of an upright tree and climb more than a few feet without falling. Neither can they stop and go on again before reaching a branch or other resting place." *

In the *American Naturalist* for September, 1881 (pp. 737-738), the Hon. Charles Aldrich, of Webster City, Iowa, writes : "About two years ago a young man who was living with me, came in one day saying that he had just seen a small animal, possibly a raccoon, ascending a tree in the woods some sixty rods away. Taking my shot-gun, I went to the place, where I soon saw the creature in the top of a black oak tree, almost forty feet from the ground. The animal seemed very cunning, and managed for some time to keep on the opposite side of some of the larger limbs, but I finally got a shot at him. He came to the ground with a bounce, when I found it was a woodchuck. It was but slightly wounded in one of the fore legs, and I captured it and took it home. I put it in a hollow tree near my residence, and it remained there a couple of weeks, freely eating the corn which I regularly fed it."

As a rule the Woodchuck manifests great antipathy for water. In confinement he rarely partakes of it, and in the wild state his burrows are frequently so remote from it as to preclude the idea

---

* Forest and Stream, Vol. XVI, No. 23, July 7, 1881, p. 453.

of his journeying there to drink. Hence it seems probable that the moisture which his system requires is derived from the juices of the plants on which he feeds, together with the dew or rain that may have lodged upon them.

Having searched in vain for the record of an instance where a Woodchuck has been known to swim, voluntarily, I take great pleasure in being able to contribute an account of a case that recently fell under my personal observation. On the 12th of June, 1883, while rowing up the Fulton Chain of Lakes, in company with Dr. A. K. Fisher and Walter H. Merriam, a Woodchuck was observed in the water directly ahead of the boat swimming across the channel between Second and Third Lakes. He swam deep, at times the top of his head and the tip of his tail alone appearing above the surface. He crossed from the north to the south shore and was evidently very much fatigued and somewhat confused, for, although I pushed the boat close after·him as he was about to emerge, he only partly climbed out upon a small log that extended into the water, and showed no inclination to move off, or even to change his position. He was poked several times with a stick, and finally Dr. Fisher actually stroked him with his hand before he became sufficiently aroused to show that he was aware of our presence. We left him standing partly upon the log, with one leg still in the water, shivering, and apparently in a very unhappy state of mind. This animal was young, and was evidently travelling about in search of a suitable place in which to establish his home.

The Woodchuck can always be taken in a steel trap set with proper care, and concealed from view. By this means it is generally easy to rid our fields of his presence. Dr. C. L. Bagg and I once caught thirty-three Woodchucks in a large meadow during a single season.

In a recent number of the *American Field* (Vol. XX, No. 10, Sept. 8, 1883, p. 225) I recorded the following very unusual occurrence : On the 28th of July last, hearing a commotion among some

half-grown chickens that had taken up their abode in the underbrush back of my office, Dr. A. K. Fisher, who was with me at the
time, betook himself thither and much to his surprise found a
Woodchuck to be the cause of the disturbance.   The animal was
chasing the fowls with much earnestness, and evidently meant to
catch one ;  while the poor chickens, already well-nigh exhausted,
were straining every nerve to escape.    Fearing that the beast
(which was a young and ambitious female) might propagate a race
of Woodchucks that would rank among the depredators of the
poultry yard, the Doctor brought the chase to an abrupt termination and added the rodent's skeleton to my osteological cabinet.
This is the only example that has thus far come to my knowledge
where a Woodchuck has pursued either bird or beast, and the
question may be fairly asked whether in this instance it purposed
to seize and devour the fowl, or, being of a jocose turn of mind,
was merely chasing it to see it run, just as a puppy would do under
similar circumstances.

Dr. Godman, who once had a tame Woodchuck, speaks thus of
its habit of lugging various articles into its burrow : " Every thing
fit to make a bed of, that he could get at, was sure to be carried
under ground, and when clothes were missed, which had been hung
out to dry, it was only necessary to fasten a hook to a long stick
and draw them out of his burrow.   When this was to be effected,
it was necessary to tie the Marmot up short, as he appeared to
understand perfectly what was to be done, and was by no means
willing that his bed should be rendered less comfortable.   Although
he would not attempt to bite the person engaged in removing his
plunder, he would rush to the entrance and endeavor to make his
way in, as if to secure his prize, or remove it to a still greater distance.   On one occasion he carried off and stowed at a distance of
six feet from the entrance, eight pairs of stockings, a towel, and a
girl's frock, and had he not been discovered in the act, would have

made a still larger transfer of materials to form a more luxurious bed." *

The power of song is not often attributed to mammals lower in the scale than ourselves, and yet it is a fact that several species are capable of producing musical notes which are pleasing to the ear.   In the *American Naturalist* for June, 1872 (Vol. VI, No. 6, pp. 365–366), is an article from the pen of Dr. A. Kellogg, entitled "*Singing Maryland Marmot.*"   The writer states : " For the last forty years the fact of the common Maryland Marmot, or Wood-chuck, being able to sing like a canary bird, but in a softer, sweeter note, has been quite familiar to myself, and others who could be brought forward as witnesses."   He then speaks of a very young Woodchuck which he raised, and goes on to say : " It had a seat in the little high chair at the children's table full oft.   Its earnest and restless concupiscent purr as it scented sweet cake and fragrant viands was wonderful.   At length it became as familiar as the family cat and finally burrowed under the doorstep.   My impres-sion is now, and has always been, that it was a female.   I used to watch the pet very closely to see how it sang, as children are apt to do.   There was a slight moving of the nostrils and lips and consequently whiskers with an air of unmistakable happy or serene enjoyment.   I question much if this is altogether unknown to others, *always excepting naturalists.*"

Woodchucks are so abundant in some parts of New Hampshire that the farmers have long demanded legislative aid for their riddance.   At length the clamors from this source became so loud and continuous that the Legislature was forced to recognize the

---

* American Natural History. Vol. I, 1842, p. 329.   In treating of the habits of this species, Dr. Godman makes some very astonishing statements, statements that are wholly incorrect as applied to it in this region, though possibly true in some parts of its extensive habitat.   His figure bears as close a resemblance to the wolverine as it does to the Woodchuck, and yet, strangely enough, he speaks thus of those of his predecessors : " All the figures which have been heretofore pub-lished of this animal (with the exception of one given in the English translation of Cuvier, borrowed from a drawing by Le Sueur) have been copied from Edward's, which is altogether unlike the animal " (pp. 330–331).

17

postulations of its rural constituency, and a committee was appointed, of which the Hon. Charles R. Corning was made chairman. In due course of time the committee prepared a report which was submitted to the House, accompanied by a bill providing for a bounty of ten cents for each Woodchuck killed within the limits of the State. This act was approved Sept. 11, 1883.*

---

* From the " Report of the Woodchuck Committee " I beg leave to reproduce the following extracts : " Your committee finds that the Woodchuck is absolutely destitute of any interesting qualities, that is, such qualities as would recommend it to the average inhabitant of New Hampshire. . . . Its body is thick and squatty, and its legs so short that its belly seems almost to touch the ground. This is not a pleasing picture. Its size varies all the way from those reared in Strafford County to the huge fellows that claim a homestead among the fertile farms of Grafton. Woodchucks have been known to attain a large size, even fifteen pounds. This, however, would not be an average Woodchuck. The casual observer is not attracted by the brilliancy of a Woodchuck's color. When one thinks it over, it certainly would seem that the family of Woodchucks was designed and brought forth under conditions of severe simplicity. While the usual color cannot be said to be a decided red, it is not Auburn, but more like Derry, which is next to Auburn. Your committee has now in mind the under side of the creature. The body even in very young Woodchucks, is inclined to be gray—a very significant circumstance in the mind of your committee, when the total depravity of the animal is considered. Besides Derry and gray, there are other hues blended about the Woodchuck ; but these are merely details, and of no practical account. . . . . Like thieves in all climes, the Woodchuck remains securely concealed in its hole for a great part of the day. Its only purpose in venturing forth during the daytime is to get a good lay of the land. . . . Like the bear, the gait of the thing under consideration is plantigrade, but in order to occasionally exercise its toes it climbs small trees and shrubs ; then, perfectly satisfied that its pedal extremities are in good working trim, it descends to the ground and again resumes its monotonous waddle. The Woodchuck, despite its deformities both of mind and of body, possesses some of the amenities of a higher civilization. It cleans its face after the manner of the squirrels and licks its fur after the manner of a cat. Your committee is too wise, however, to be deceived by this purely superficial observance of better habits. Contemporaneous with the ark, the Woodchuck has not made any material progress in social science, and it is now too late to attempt to reform the wayward sinner. The average age of the Woodchuck is too long to please your committee, but the estimate of Woodchuck population can only be approximated. . . . The Woodchuck is not only a nuisance, but also a bore. It burrows beneath the soil, and then chuckles to see a mowing machine, man and all, slump into one of these holes and disappear. . . . Your committee is confident that a small bounty will prove of incalculable good ; at all events, even as an experiment, it is certainly worth trying ; therefore your committee would respectfully recommend that the accompanying bill be passed. CHARLES R. CORNING, for the Committee.

" AN ACT PROVIDING FOR A BOUNTY ON WOODCHUCKS.

" Be it enacted by the Senate and House of Representatives in general Court convened :

" Section 1. If any person shall kill any Woodchuck within this State, and shall produce the tail thereof to any one of the selectmen of the town within which said woodchuck was killed, or if there be no selectmen in said town, then to any one of the selectmen of the nearest town having such selectmen, said selectmen shall take the said tail and so dispose of it that it shall not again be used for the purposes of bounty, and shall pay to the person so producing it the sum of ten cents : Provided, that no bounty shall be paid for any woodchuck killed on Sunday.

" Section 2. The selectmen of every such town shall keep a true account of the moneys so paid as bounty on woodchucks, and upon presentation of such amount, certified by a majority of such

## Family CASTORIDÆ.

# CASTOR FIBER CANADENSIS (Linn.) Allen.

### *American Beaver.*

That the Beaver was once abundant in all parts of the Adirondacks is attested by the numerous remains and effects of their dams; but at present they are so exceedingly rare that few people know that they still exist here.

Samuel de Champlain found them abundant in the Richelieu River in the early part of July, 1609. He said of them: "There is also quite a number of Beavers, as well in the river as in several other streams which fall into it." (Documentary History of New York, Vol. III, p. 5.)

Dr. DeKay says that, in 1815, "a party of St. Regis Indians from Canada ascended the Oswegatchie river in the county of St. Lawrence in pursuit of Beaver. In consequence of the previous hostilities between this country and England, this district had not been hunted in some years, and the Beaver had consequently been undisturbed. The party, after an absence of a few weeks, returned with three hundred Beaver skins. These were seen by my informant [Mr. T. O. Fowler], who adds that since that time very few have been observed." * They were not immediately exterminated, however, for Mr. Calvin V. Graves writes me that in 1834 a trapper named Hume caught six Beavers in Silverdog Pond, in the northeastern part of the town of Diana, in Lewis County; and that a few years later Norman and Hume caught three Beavers on the middle branch of the Oswegatchie, near Harrisville. These are believed to have been the last Beavers which inhabited that part of the Wilderness.

---

selectmen to be just and true, to the treasurer of the state, in the month of June, the same shall be paid from the state treasury either to the representative of such town or to the selectmen thereof, upon their written order.

"Section 3. This act shall take effect from and after its passage.

"Approved September 11, 1883."

* Zoology of New York, Part I, 1842, p. 73.

I am informed by William Clowbridge, an old hunter and trapper, that during his boyhood Beavers were common along the western border of the Adirondacks. In the year 1819 he caught two in one of their huts on the outlet of Brantingham Lake, in Lewis County, on which stream they had then two dams. In March, 1837, he caught, at Little Otter Lake, also in Lewis County, the last Beaver observed on this side of the Adirondacks. The veteran hunter, Asa Puffer, was at the time trapping for the same animal. Mr. Clowbridge tells me that the spring was unusually forward, and that there was some open water along the north shore of the lake, and about its outlet. He made a small opening in the dam, and in the gap thus formed set his trap, a few inches below the surface of the water. On returning to the lake, a week afterward, an eagle was seen to rise and fly away from the vicinity of the outlet. Proceeding to the dam he could find neither the trap nor the weight to which it had been attached. He then went to the spot from which the eagle rose and there found the Beaver in the trap.

Mr. John Constable has kindly presented me with the skull of a very large Beaver which was " trapped by William Wood, in the fall of 1837, in a pond northwest of Indian Point on the Raquette." Mr. Constable writes me that an old Indian who had been unsuccessful in his attempts to capture this same Beaver, and who was then about to leave this part of the Wilderness, told Wood where the animal was to be found. Wood carried his boat to the pond and paddled twice around it, searching carefully for signs, without going ashore. At last he discovered fur upon the root of an old birch that projected into the water. Here he placed the trap, attached to a float, and on the second day found the Beaver in it.

Dr. DeKay, writing in 1841, says : " In the summer of 1840, we traversed those almost interminable forests on the highlands separating the sources of the Hudson and St. Lawrence, and included in Hamilton, Herkimer, and a part of Essex counties. In the course of our journey we saw several *beaver signs*, as they are termed by the hunters. The Beaver has been so much harassed in this State, that it has ceased making dams, and contents itself with making large excavations in the banks of streams. Within the past year, (1841,) they have been seen on Indian and Cedar rivers, and at Paskungameh or Tupper's lake; and although they are not numerous, yet they are still found in scattered families in the northern part of Hamilton, the southern part of St. Lawrence and the western part of Essex counties. Through the considerate attention of Mr. A. McIntyre, those yet existing in the southern part of Franklin county are carefully preserved from the avidity of the hunter, and there probably the last of the species in the Atlantic States will be found. We noticed the remains of an old and large beaver dam at the outlet of Lake Fourth in Herkimer county, but it is now nearly covered up by the drift sand from the lake" (loc. cit., p. 74).

Watson, in his History of Essex County, published in 1869, says: "The Beaver was found in great abundance throughout the region, by the first occupants. They no longer exist, it is believed, in the territory of Essex County" (p. 348).

During the fall of 1880, a Beaver was caught on Raquette River, between the Upper Saranac and Big Tupper's Lake, and about a mile below the "Sweeney carry." The skin was stuffed and preserved by the hunter who captured the animal. Subsequent to this date, saplings were cut in the neighborhood, showing that another was at work there. I have myself examined the locality and brought away a number of cuttings. They consist of young poplars (*Populus tremuloides*) averaging from two to four inches (50 to 100 mm.) in diameter; the largest measured fourteen inches (355 mm.) in circumference.

At present there is a small colony of Beavers on a stream that empties into the West Branch of the St. Regis River. It is probably the colony referred to by DeKay, in 1842, as "yet existing in the southern part of Franklin county." It is to be earnestly hoped that the hunters who frequent that part of the Wilderness will spare no pains to protect these animals from molestation.

No animal has figured more prominently in the affairs of any nation than has the Beaver in the early history of the "New World." Its influence on the exploration, colonization, and settlement of this country was very great. The trade in its peltries proved a source of competition and strife, not only among the local merchants, but also between the several colonies, disputes over the boundaries having frequently arisen from this cause alone. Indeed, on more than one occasion, jealousy of the Beaver trade led to serious difficulties in the struggle for supremacy between the three rival powers—the Dutch, English, and French.

The Provincial Seal of New Netherland was a Beaver resting on a shield, encircled by the words "*Sigillum Novi Belgii.*"

In the year 1671, there appeared in Amsterdam a paper entitled, "De Nieuwe en Onbekende Weereld: of Beschryving van America en't Zuidland: door Arnoldus Montanus." Much of this account is devoted to the natural history of the country, and it contains some extraordinary tales concerning the animals found there. The author's remarks upon the Beaver run as follows: " But in addition to other wild animals *New Netherland* furnishes, according to the occular evidence of *Adriaen van der Donk*, full eighty thousand beavers a year. *Pliny* relates how these animals castrate themselves, and leave these parts to the hunters, inasmuch as they are much sought after, being an effectual remedy for mania, retention of the afterbirth, amenorrhœa, dizziness, gout, lameness, belly and tooth aches, dullness of vision, poisoning and rheumatism. But *Pliny* commits a grave error; for the Beavers have very small testicles fastened in such a manner to the back bone that they cannot remove them except with life. Moreover, they live in the water and on land together in troops, in houses built of timber over a running stream. The houses excite no common ad-

miration; they are thus constructed—the Beavers first collect together all the drift wood which they find along the river, and
whenever this falls short, they gnaw away, in the next adjoining
wood, the sweetest bark all around with the front teeth, of which
they have two in the upper, and two in the lower gum, they then
cut right around the trunk until the tree falls; when they also
shorten the pieces in like manner, to adapt them to the proposed
building.  The females carry the pieces on the back, the males
support it behind so that it may not fall off.  The houses rise ingeniously to the height of five stories; they are smeared above
with clay to protect them from the rain; in the middle is a convenient aperture through which to dive into the water as soon as
they perceive any person.  Wherefore, one of the troop keeps
watch by turns, and in the winter a second keeps the water open
by constant beating of the tail.  The tail is flattish without hair,
and most dainty food which in some places is served up as a rare
delicacy.  The beavers go with young sixteen weeks; they bear
once a year four young, which cry and suck like young children;
for the mother rises on her hind paws and gives each two a breast
as she has only two breasts between the fore legs; these legs resemble somewhat those of the dog; the hindmost, like those of
geese, lap in some measure over each other.  On both sides of the
privy parts lie two swellings enclosed in separate membranes.
From the privy parts oozes an oleaginous humor, with which they
smear all the accessible parts of the body in order to keep dry.
Inwardly they resemble a cut up hog; they live on leaves and
bark; are excessively attached to their young; the wind-hairs
which rise glittering above the back, fall off in the summer, and
grow again by the fall; they are short necked; have strong sinews
and muscles; move rapidly in the water and on land; attacked by
men or dogs, they bite fiercely.  The pure *Castor*, so highly prised
by physicians, consists of oblong follicles, resembling a wrinkled
pear which are firmly attached to the *os pubis* of the female beaver;

the Indians cut up the little balls of the males with their tobacco as they afford no castor." *

In the year 1732 the immortal Linnæus was sent, by the Royal Academy of Upsal, on a tour through Lapland. In his personal journal he says: "I set out alone from the city of Upsal on Friday May 12, 1732, at eleven o'clock, being at that time within half a day of twenty-five years of age." Sixteen days later, when at a place called Genow, the young naturalist had the opportunity, apparently for the first time, of examining a recently killed Beaver. Of it he said, "I inquired concerning the food of this animal, and was told it was the bark of trees, the birch, fir, and mountain ash, but more especially the aspen, and the castor becomes larger in proportion as the Beaver can get more of the aspen bark. This confirmed the truth of what Assessor Rothman formerly asserted, that castor is secreted from the intermediate bark of the poplar, which has the same scent, though not quite so strong: hence it is to be presumed that a decoction of this bark, if the dose were sufficiently large, would have the same medicinal effects. I wonder no naturalist has classed this animal with the Mouse tribe [which term was then applied to all Rodents], as its broad depressed form at first sight suggested to me that it was of that family." † Thus, only a century and a half ago, appeared the germ of the idea that recognized in the structure of the Beaver its affinities with the members of the order Glires, to which order it was assigned by Linnæus in his great work, the *Systema Naturæ*.

Thomas Pennant said: "The skins are a prodigious article of trade ; being the foundation of the hat manufactory. In 1763 were sold, in a single sale of the *Hudson's Bay* Company, 54,670 skins." ‡

---

* Documentary History of New York, Vol. IV, pp. 120–121.

† Lachesis Lapponica, Vol. I, 1811, pp. 88–89.

‡ Synopsis of Quadrupeds, 1771, p. 258.

Family MURIDÆ.

## MUS DECUMANUS Pallas.

### Rat.

This ubiquitous naturalized exotic is found even within the confines of the Adirondacks. But his presence here omens no good. Like the lumberman, whose footsteps he follows, he is the personification of destruction, and desecrates the soil on which he treads.

He is omnivorous, greedy, and fierce, and is totally lacking in qualities of a compensatory character. His long residence in the very stronghold of his enemies has developed hereditary habits of great circumspection, and where much persecuted he is one of the most cunning and crafty of mammals. The means devised for his extermination may be numbered by hundreds, but he is so prolific, and so soon learns to avoid the artifices designed for his capture, that he has spread himself over nearly the whole civilized world.

The Rat ranks among the worst enemies of the farmer. Not only does he force his way into the cellar, the milk-house, and the granary; but he also commits great havoc in the poultry-yard. He wantonly destroys far more than he consumes. The choicest fruits and vegetables are ruined by a single bite; smoked hams suspended from the rafters show the marks of his sharp teeth; pans of rich cream are soiled by his lash-like tail; large holes through the plank-walls of the oat-bin leave no doubt as to the identity of the thief; and the constant loss of eggs and of young chickens and ducks may be regarded as one of the most serious evils his presence occasions. Even the sleeping child and the shrouded corpse have been mutilated by his cruel jaws.

He is not content with deriving his sustenance at our expense, but, to save himself the trouble of a walk between meals, takes up his abode in or under our dwellings and outhouses. In unsettled regions he often makes long journeys from house to house, but I have never known him to make his home at any great distance from buildings.

Rats are good swimmers, and in their migrations from place to place (which are usually performed at night, and thus escape notice) they do not hesitate to swim rivers and ponds that lie in the way. Though chiefly nocturnal, they are often seen in the day-time.

They are excessively prolific, commonly bringing forth from seven to twelve young at a birth, and having several litters each season. Some idea of the number of Rats inhabiting large cities may be had from the fact that, at Paris, in a fortnight's time, more than six hundred thousand were killed in the sewers. Their skins were manufactured into kid gloves.

## MUS MUSCULUS Linnæus.

### *House Mouse.*

The House Mouse is another exotic that has found the climate and productions of America so much to its liking that it has multi-plied and diffused itself over the whole of the inhabited portions of our continent.

Like the rat, it abounds in our largest cities and makes itself a conspicuous, albeit unwelcome, member of the household; but unlike the latter it also inhabits districts as yet unoccupied by civilized man.

Such places, however, do not seem congenial to its urban disposi-tion, and it is probable that none but those who, from long residence in the country, have acquired a taste for adventure, make bold to desert their traditional haunts, together with the cats and traps with which they have been for generations familiar, to seek new homes, amid new surroundings and new enemies.

I have observed the House Mouse in many of the camps scattered through the Adirondacks, and have killed it, though rarely, at a considerable distance from the habitations of man. It is common in the fertile valleys along the outskirts of the Wilderness, living in the fields during the short summer season, and returning to the dwellings, barns, and haystacks at the approach of winter.

It is omnivorous, and, in the main, nocturnal. It usually gives birth to from five to nine young at a time, and has several litters in a season.

### The House Mouse as a Vocalist.

It has long been known that individuals of the common House Mouse occasionally possess very exceptional vocal powers. These "singing mice" have appeared, from time to time, in various parts of the country, and their performances have been eagerly listened to and carefully recorded by the delighted hearers.

My aunt, Mrs. Helen M. Bagg, once had a singing Mouse in her house at Detroit, Michigan, and has kindly favored me with the following account of it : "Early in the spring of 1858 I would occasionally hear faint musical sounds, like the warbling of a young bird, issue from the china closet, which was on one side of the dining room. Several days passed before I could get any clew to the sounds. We had singing birds—a mocking bird and canaries—and every one declared it was the birds I had heard, but I felt equally certain the sounds came from the closet. One afternoon when the house was quiet, the children taking their naps, and the cook having ceased to rattle her dishes, I opened the closet door and sat down where I could have a full view of the inside. After a long and patient waiting a mouse peered out from behind the plates, climbed up a little way on the brackets, and after looking around several times, began to sing! I need not describe my feelings. Its song was not much of a song, ' as songs go,' but still a distinct musical effort. Sometimes it would run up an octave and end with a decided attempt at a trill. Sometimes it would try to trill all the notes. An octave seemed to be about its range. I could distinctly see the expansion and vibration of its throat and chest as one can in a song bird. Its favorite position when singing was an erect one, standing on its hind feet, and holding by its forward ones to the wall or bracket, almost invariably turning its face toward us. It remained with us several weeks, and at length became so familiar as to appear to enjoy company, seemingly putting forth all its strength to amuse us with its little song, which improved daily in tone and volume, but not in compass. Its voice became so clear that we could frequently hear it in the parlor that opened out of the dining room. I frequently invited my visitors to listen to it. My next-door neighbors occasionally heard it in their house, but not very distinctly. It evidently did not feel at home there. Suddenly as it came it disappeared—probably falling a prey to some cat during its rambles from house to house."

In 1804 Dr. Samuel Cramer, of Virginia, communicated to Dr. Barton the following very curious account of the influence of music upon the common House Mouse. He said : " One evening, in the month of December, as a few officers on board of a British man of war, in the harbour of Portsmouth, were seated around the fire, one of them began to play a *plaintive* air on the violin. He had scarcely performed ten minutes, when a mouse, apparently frantic, made its appearance, in the centre of the floor, near the large table which usually stands in the wardroom, the residence of the lieutenants in ships of the line. The strange gestures of the little animal strongly excited the attention of the officers, who, with one consent, resolved to suffer it to continue its singular actions unmolested. Its exertions now appeared to be greater, every moment. It shook its head, leaped about the table, and exhibited signs of the most extatic delight.

" It was observed, that in proportion to the gradation of the tones of the soft point, the extacy of the animal appeared to be increased, and *vice versa*. After performing actions, which an animal so diminutive would, at first sight, seem incapable of, the little creature, to the astonishment of the delighted spectators, suddenly ceased to move; fell down, and expired, without evincing any symptoms of pain." *

Linnæus, in his brief diagnosis of this species, said : " *Delectatur musica.*" †

## HESPEROMYS LEUCOPUS (Raf.) LeConte.

*White-footed Mouse ; Deer Mouse; Field Mouse.*

The White-footed Mouse is common in all parts of the Adirondacks. In the wild state it feeds upon beechnuts and a variety of seeds ; in captivity it is omnivorous.

Its haunts are various. Some take up their abode in dense evergreen forests, others in hardwood groves, and others still in the open fields. Many find the way into the hunter's camp and the log-house of the frontiersman ; while in the more cultivated districts they vie with the common house mouse in the possession of our homes. Dr. Richardson tells us that in the Hudson's Bay Company's Territory, " no sooner is a fur-post established than this little animal becomes an inmate of the dwelling-houses " (Fauna Boreali Americana, 1829, p. 142).

It is an excellent climber and I have often found its nest in holes in living trees, more than seventy feet (21.33 metres) above the ground While on a snow-shoe walk with a friend one bright moonlight evening, several winters ago, one of them was observed skipping lightly over the snow a short distance ahead. We gave chase, but the mouse escaped by running up the trunk of a smooth-barked beech hard by. My friend, who was not aware of its climbing propensities, looked on in amazement while the mouse, with as much ease and nimbleness as a squirrel, ascended the tree and disappeared in a knot-hole high among the branches.

The White-footed Mouse does not hibernate. Except during the

---

* The Philadelphia Medical and Physical Journal, Vol. I, 1804, pp. 37–38.
† Systema Naturæ, Ed. X, Vol. I, 1758, p. 62.

severest weather its tracks may be seen on the snow throughout the winter, its long tail leaving a furrow by which it may always be recognized. In the autumn it lays up an immense store of provision for so small an animal. The beechnut constitutes its favorite food, and in seasons when it is to be had no other article of diet is sought. The hoards are generally established in holes in trees or in hollow logs, and are, therefore, frequently discovered by the wood-chopper. The beechnuts they contain are usually shucked, and I have, on several occasions, removed two or three quarts from a single hoard.

Robert Kennicott tells us that in western New York, Joseph Kennicott found, "within a stump in a clover-field, several quarts of clean seed of red clover, collected by a family of these mice." *

They sometimes select odd sites for their store-houses. In October and November, 1881, Drs. Hoadley, Fisher, and myself occupied the neat log-house that is commonly known as the "Club Camp" at Big Moose Lake. We were here much annoyed by the White-footed Mice, which not only made way with any eatables that happened to be lying about, but also lugged off a quantity of the cotton we had brought for stuffing birds. They even climbed up to our drying-boards and pulled out the cotton which we had carefully tucked under the shoulders and backs of the newly-made bird skins. No place was free from their depredations, and the skins were only made secure by suspending them from the ceiling by means of cleats fastened to the smooth spruce rafters. The loss of the cotton was a matter of no small consequence, since it had to be carried there from a distance of more than forty miles. A careful search was begun, but no trace of it could be found till a small cupboard, supposed to be mouse-proof, was unlocked, when the whole of it fell in view. In this same cupboard we discovered an old shoe well filled with crackers and sugar which had been taken from the kitchen, and beechnut meats which had been brought from some distance outside. The

---

* Quadrupeds of Illinois, 1857, p. 91.

locker was entered from the top, and the path to it was circuitous and difficult.

The White-footed Mouse is fond of flesh and, like the flying squirrel, eagerly devours dead birds placed in its way. Indeed, this is done so naturally, that the suspicion arises as to whether it does not sometimes capture and prey upon the smaller birds while on their roosts at night.

Dr. Samuel Lockwood had a caged *Hesperomys* from Florida. " Sometimes a fly would enter the cage, when she would spring at, and catch it, sometimes with her mouth, and at others with her hands. This she would eat with great relish. . . . A little sod of fresh grass and white clover was occasionally put into the cage. This she enjoyed greatly, eating the greens like a rabbit; only always insisting on sitting up to do it. It was interesting to witness how ready she was for emergencies. Sitting on her hind feet, she would take hold with her hands of a blade of grass, and begin eating at the tip. The spear would rapidly shorten, and seemingly she must now stoop to finish it, or do it in the ordinary quadrupedal style. Now that was just what she did not choose to do. So when the emergency came, she would stoop down, and in a trice cut the blade off close to the sod with just one nip ; then up again on her feet in a sitting posture, she would finish it in a comfortable and becoming way." *

In personal appearance the White-footed Mouse is far more attractive than the other members of the family. Its prominent, bead-like eyes, large ears, and long tail are striking characteristics, while the rich fawn-color of the sides and back, sharply contrasted with the snowy white of the under parts and feet, combine to produce an exterior of much beauty. Add to this the natural agility and grace of its movements and we have an animal that, by any other name than *mouse*, would be regarded as one of the most interesting inhabitants of our forests.

---

* American Naturalist, Vol. V, No. 12, Dec., 1871, p. 763.

Its disposition is in perfect harmony with its attractive appearance, for even the flying squirrel is not more gentle and affectionate. When first captured it rarely offers to bite, and within a few hours will generally eat from the hand. It manifests neither fear nor suspicion while in its box or on one's person, but if let loose in a large room is frightened when approached, and seeks to hide. If given the opportunity, it is pretty sure to select some particular pocket for its home. It is also fond of running up one's sleeves, and when pinched by the movements of the arm will never think of biting.

A few years ago I had a tame White-footed Mouse to which I had become considerably attached. During the day it never left my person, and at night was always placed in a large glass jar with an abundance of cotton. It would eat almost anything offered, sitting on its haunches on my hand or shoulder, and would eagerly lap water or milk from a glass, or from a finger wet in the same. It was scrupulously neat, continually washing its face and cleaning its soft fur. Many times each day it would reach back and grasp its long tail, which, guided and manipulated by the fore-paws, was several times in succession drawn for its entire length through the mouth. When let loose on the snow it invariably burrowed down with great rapidity. One clear cold day in midwinter, the temperature being many degrees below zero, I started on my usual snow-shoe walk with the Mouse asleep in my coat pocket. I had gone some distance and forgotten its presence, when a faint cry of distress warned me that all was not right. It responded to my call only by another cry of pain, fainter even than the first. On taking it from my pocket, it gave me a slight nip, and almost immediately expired. It was *very* cold, and in a few minutes was frozen through.

In the selection of sites for their nests scarcely less individuality is shown than in the choice of their haunts. Those that live in the deep forests commonly build in holes in trees or logs, or in the roots of stumps ; while those that dwell in open fields excavate chambers in the earth several inches below the surface, in which the young are reared. Mr. Kennicott says he has known of " numerous instances in which several have been observed inhabiting the same hole in a tree with a family of flying squirrels."

I have found this species with young at various times from April until November, but do not know how many litters it has in a season. As late as the 8th of November (1883) a nest was ploughed up in one of our fields at Locust Grove. It was lined with feathers and contained half-grown young. On the 29th of the same month I secured in one trap a female and her young, which were two-thirds grown. The mother bore evidence of having recently been nursed, and the stomach of the youngsters contained nothing but milk. From three to six are produced at a birth.

The young are leaden-gray in color and their ears are disproportionately large. Late in June the first litter begins to show pale fawn color—generally commencing on the flanks.

Throughout its southern range, and even so far north as southern New England and portions of New York, the White-footed Mouse, like the red, gray, and flying squirrels, is known to construct " outside nests " for the reception of its young. Such nests are usually more or less cocoa-nut shaped, and sometimes measure a foot in longest diameter. They consist of moss, grasses, leaves, inner bark, and other similar substances. The opening is at or near the bottom. They are commonly placed on a horizontal branch at a varying distance from the ground. Those that I have found have generally been in thickets overrun with *Smilax*, and were rarely more than ten feet high. Nests of birds are sometimes refitted and occupied by these animals. In the Adirondacks I have never known them to build or inhabit outside nests.

Dr. Barton, in 1804, published a note "On a species of North-American Wandering Mouse," which, from the meagre description given, seems to have been the White-footed Mouse. The Doctor says :—

18

"In the year 1796, a particular species of Mouse made its appearance àt Burlington-Bay, on the west end of Lake-Ontario, and at Long-Point, on the north side of Lake-Erie. They came out of the woods, from the northward, in troops of thousands, and committed great havoc among the Indian-corn.

"These animals were so numerous, that, for a good while, they were caught by hundreds, at a time. It is said, that the cats, tired of killing them, came, at length, to play with them, without offering them any injury.

"Even in the winter-time, the corn-cribs were extremely offensive, from the great numbers of these mice, that had perished in them.

"This mouse is described as a small species, smaller than the common House-Mouse ; with a white belly, and a very long tail. The general colour was that of the House-Mouse." *

### Hesperomys as a Vocalist.

Mr. W. O. Hiskey, in a note in the *American Naturalist* for May, 1871 (Vol. V, No. 3, pp. 171–172) states : " I was sitting a few evenings since, not far from a half-open closet door, when I was startled by a sound issuing from the closet, of such marvellous beauty that I at once asked my wife how Bobbie Burns (our canary) had found his way into the closet, and what could start him to singing such a queer and sweet song in the dark. I procured a light and found it to be a *mouse !* He had filled an over-shoe from a basket of pop-corn which had been popped and placed in the closet in the morning. Whether this rare collection of food inspired him with song I know not, but I had not the heart to disturb his corn, hoping to hear from him again. Last night his song was renewed. I approached with a subdued light and with great caution, and had the pleasure of seeing him sitting among his corn and singing his beautiful solo. I observed him without interruption for ten minutes, not over four feet

---

* The Philadelphia Medical and Physical Journal, Vol. I, 1804, pp. 31–32.

from him. His song was not a *chirp*, but a continuous song of musical tone, a kind of *to-wit-to-wee-woo-woo-wee-woo*, quite varied in pitch."

The most extended and interesting account that I have seen of a singing *Hesperomys* is from the pen of the Rev. Samuel Lockwood. The subject of his sketch was caught in Florida by Philip Ryall, Esq., and was presented to Dr. Lockwood, who named it *Hespie*. Its vocal powers were extraordinary, and two of its most frequently repeated performances were termed respectively the *Wheel Song* and the *Grand Role*, and were expressed in musical notation by Mr. Ferris C. Lockwood. After describing her ordinary songs in great detail, Dr. Lockwood observes : " A remarkable fact in the above *role* is the scope of little Hespie's musical powers. Her soft, clear voice falls an octave with all the precision possible ; then at the wind-up, it rises again into a very quick trill on C sharp and D.

" Though it be at the risk of taxing belief, yet I must in duty record one of Hespie's most remarkable performances. She was gamboling in the large compartment of her cage, in a mood indicating intense animal enjoyment, having woke from a long sleep, and partaken of some favorite food. She burst into a fulness of song very rich in its variety. While running and jumping, she rolled off what I have called her Grand Role, then sitting, she went over it again, ringing out the strangest diversity of changes, by an almost whimsical transposition of the bars ; then without for an instant stopping the music, she leapt into the wheel, started it revolving at its highest speed, and went through the Wheel Song in exquisite style, giving several repetitions of it. After this she returned to the large compartment, took up again the Grand Role, and put into it some variations of execution which astonished me. One measure I remember was so silvery and soft, that I said to a lady who was listening, that a canary able to execute that would be worth a hundred dollars. I occasionally detected what I am utterly unable to explain, a literal dual sound, very like a boy whistling as he draws a stick along the pickets of a fence.

So the music went on, as I listened, watch in hand, until actually *nine minutes had elapsed*. Now the wonderful fact is that the rest between the roles was never much more than for a second of time ; and during all this singing the muscles could be seen in vigorous action through the entire length of the abdomen. This feat would be impossible to a professional singer ; and the nearest to it that I have seen was the singing of a wild mocking bird in a grove.

" For several days the wheel grated on its axle. This afforded Hespie great delight ; and her own little warble was completely lost in the harsher sound. It was pretty much as it is with some of the modern methods of praise ; as when the vocal is subordinated to the instrumental, a mere murmur of song, on which the organist comes down as with the sound of many waters. A drop of oil, and the sound of the friction stopped. This quite excited her temper ; and she bit the wires of her wheel most viciously. A little device was hit upon which set her in good humor again. A strip of stout writing paper, a half inch wide, was pinned down in such a way that its clean cut upper edge pressed against the wires of the wheel, making with its revolution a pleasant, purring sound. It was on the principle, exactly, of the old-time watchman's rattle, and the old toy known as a cricket. This for a while greatly delighted the capricious creature, and she made the wheel almost fly ; at the same time, in unison with the whirr of the wheel, was her own soft, cheery warble. It was very low, yet very distinct."

Another noteworthy peculiarity of Hespie's was that she sometimes ate and sang at the same time. On one occasion a slender twig of black alder, about an inch in length, was given her. " She was delighted, and at once began in her usual pretty way, sitting up, to eat the bark, although it was very bitter. Thus she sat ' bolt upright ; ' and the manner in which she held this little black stick in both hands up to her mouth, at the precise angle in which a fife is held, although nibbling away, yet singing at the same time, it looked so like a little fifer playing on an ebony fife that laughter was irresistible." *

## EVOTOMYS RUTILUS GAPPERI (Vigors) Coues.

### Red-backed Mouse ; Long-eared Wood Mouse.

The Red-backed Mouse is abundant in all parts of the Adirondacks. It occurs on the summits of the tree-covered mountains as well as in the deepest valleys. It is essentially a *wood* species in its local distribution, rarely frequenting the beaver meadows or the fields of the farmer. It often enters the woodman's camp, and I have sometimes caught it even in the luxurious log-houses which have, during the past few years, supplanted the old-time shanties in many parts of the Adirondacks.

It feeds upon beechnuts and a variety of seeds, berries, and roots, and also, at certain times in the winter season, upon the bark of shrubs and trees. The beech, maple, ash, and bass suffer most severely from its attacks, and in the order named. The bark is generally removed in irregular areas from the large roots just above the ground ; but sometimes saplings, and even trees a foot (305 mm.) or more in diameter are completely girdled to the height of three or four feet (approximately 915 to 1220 mm.). The damage thus done to our deciduous groves is sometimes great, but does not compare with the ravages committed by the field mouse (*Arvicola riparius*).

The Wood Mouse is terrestrial, like the other members of the *Arvicolinæ* series, and commonly lives in burrows in the ground. It sometimes makes regular runways similar to those of the field mouse, but usually travels freely over the surface, not confining itself to any prescribed course. It is both diurnal and nocturnal. I have shot it at noonday, scampering over the leaves in the deep woods, and dodging in and out between the rocks of a lake shore. I have also seen it after dark in shanties and log-houses ; and have caught many

---

* American Naturalist, Vol. V, No. 12, Dec., 1871, pp. 765–767.

during the night in traps baited with beechnuts and meat.    Its
ordinary gait is a moderately fast trot; I have never seen it proceed in leaps.    Still, it runs swiftly for a short distance and its
quick movements render it difficult of capture.

The nest of the Red-backed Mouse is usually, in this region, placed
in a burrow in the earth, though it is sometimes found in a half-
decayed log, or under the roots of a stump.    I have shot females,
each containing four young, as early as the 3d of April, and as late
as the 4th of October.    I have also taken a female early in June that
was nursing her second brood.    Hence it is clear that several litters
are produced in a season.

The flesh of the Red-backed Mouse is tender and well flavored.


## ARVICOLA RIPARIUS Ord.

### *Meadow Mouse ; Field Mouse.*

The Meadow Mouse is common in the cleared lands within and
around the Adirondack region.    It occurs on many of the beaver
meadows, but is never abundant in the coniferous forests.

It feeds, in the main, upon the roots of grasses, though in winter it
sometimes commits great havoc by gnawing the bark of trees.    Rich
meadows and pasture lands constitute its favorite haunts, and are apt
to be cut up, in all directions, by its deeply-worn runways.    It is
strictly terrestrial, rarely mounting even the log or limb that may lie
in its path, and is both nocturnal and diurnal.

It does not hibernate.    In the beginning of winter, when the
ground is frozen for some distance below the surface, it abandons its
burrows and lives entirely above ground.    Its nests of dry grass then
lie flat upon the surface, without attempt at concealment, and are
soon buried in the snow.    As winter advances and the snow becomes
deeper, the Meadow Mice regularly betake themselves to their nests
for rest.    The heat from their bodies soon melts the snow in contact
with and immediately adjoining the nests, which, from the continued

operation of the same cause, come to be surrounded by slowly-grow-ing dome-shaped chambers. These increase in size until the spring thaws, in March and April, melt away their roofs, thus admitting the light and cold. They are then deserted. During snow-shoe tramps over the fields at this season I have often noticed holes, from a few inches to a foot in diameter, appearing as if sharply cut in the surface. On inspection, they invariably proved to be the summits of these dome-shaped cavities, and a nest was always found at the bottom of each, surrounded by a zone of bare ground. They ranged from one to two feet (approximately 300 to 600 mm.) in diameter, and most of them were two feet in height. From the bottom of each chamber numerous runways and burrows penetrated the snow in all directions. Some followed along directly upon the ground, while others sloped upward at various angles. Many ran horizontally at varying levels, resting upon the dense strata that indicated the surface lines at different times during the winter. Near each nest was one or more burrows that reached the surface and contained considerable accumu-lations of the animal's dejections. These seemed to be watch holes where the Mice came regularly to look at the prospect outside.

Meadow Mice sometimes, but not often, travel upon the snow, and they occasionally stray so far that they are unable to find the holes through which they came up. If this happens when there is a hard crust, through which they cannot burrow, they wander aimlessly about for a while and finally perish from the cold. In March and April I have several times found them frozen to death upon the crust.

They are always present in greater or less numbers, but are not often sufficiently abundant to direct the attention of the farmer to their depredations. Occasionally, however, they multiply to such an alarming extent that the most superficial observer is impressed with the magnitude of their ravages. They devastate the meadows, grain-fields, and orchards of the farmer, and ruin the nurseries of the horticulturist. Whether these periodical invasions are the result of unchecked reproduction, or of migration, has not been positively ascertained. Fortunately, they generally recur at long intervals. Arboreous vegetation suffers most during winters of deep snow, the snow enabling the Mice to reach the bark at a considerable height, and at the same time protecting them from the inclemencies of the weather. I have seen fruit trees, and also saplings of the maple and beech, more or less completely girdled to the height of four and even five feet (1.21 to 1.52 metres). During the winter of 1868 or 1869 thousands of young trees were destroyed in Lewis County alone.

In places where corn or grain is allowed to stand in shocks for any length of time, large losses are occasioned by the Mice. The amount of food consumed by a single individual is of course comparatively insignificant, but that required to sustain the total number inhabiting a given district is not to be ignored. And when it is borne in mind that the food of this species consists almost exclusively of the produce of the agriculturist, the fact becomes evident that the animal is a source of continuous pecuniary loss to the farmer. Omitting reference to the years when the species is present in excessive numbers, it is a low estimate to say that twenty-five Mice live upon every acre of meadow land. Hence the total number present upon an ordinarily productive farm of two hundred acres would not be less than five thousand. Now suppose that the owner of a farm of this size should capture and keep in confinement five thousand Meadow Mice, feeding them upon their natural food, grain and the roots of grass. Would it be strange if, in the course of a few months, he should become so alarmed at the cost in dollars and cents, of keeping such a host of these ravenous creatures that he should have them all put to death? And yet, our farmers not only look on in stolid indifference while their property and the fruits of their labors suffer, from this source, annual losses which they can ill afford to bear, but they even help the Mice to increase in numbers and maintain supremacy over their fields! This they do in several ways, chiefly by neglecting measures for the riddance of the Mice, and, what is of vastly more consequence, by encouraging the destruction of those birds and mammals that habitually prey upon Mice. Pre-eminent among these may be mentioned the marsh and rough-legged hawks, all the smaller hawks and owls, the shrike, the skunk, and the weasels. Thus the farmer in his short-sightedness omits no opportunity to deprive himself of nature's means of holding in check the vermin that ruin his crops.

When a field is overrun by Meadow Mice, immense numbers of them may be captured in narrow trenches, a spade's breadth in width, and a foot and a half (457 mm.) in depth. The trenches should be a trifle wider at the bottom than at the top. Into these the Mice tumble, without being able to escape.

The Meadow Mouse is exceedingly prolific, giving birth to from four to eight young at a time, and having several litters in a season. In early spring its nests are generally made just beneath the surface, but after the grass has attained a little height they are usually placed in slight depressions directly on the ground.

## FIBER ZIBETHICUS (Linn.) Cuvier.

### *Muskrat ; Musquash.*

Colonies of Muskrats may be found at suitable ponds, swamps, and sluggish streams in all parts of the Adirondacks.

These animals are in the main herbivorous, subsisting chiefly upon the roots of marsh grasses and aquatic plants. Still, they occasional-ly prey upon fish, and sometimes manifest evidences of cannibalism, devouring those of their own kind that are found dead or wounded and unable to escape. They are extremely fond of the fresh-water mussels (*Unio* and *Anodon*) and large quantities of empty shells may often be found near their homes.

Although the Muskrat and the beaver are the most strictly aquatic of all our mammals, the former not infrequently, in autumn, visits orchards in the neighborhood of water-courses to feed upon the apples that have fallen to the ground; and I have known it to follow up drains and enter the cellars of inhabited houses, and to attack the potatoes, carrots, turnips, parsnips, and other vegetables stored there. Not many years ago an aged couple lived alone in an old house in the town of Leyden, in Lewis County. They were at one time very much annoyed by curious sounds that were heard every night, and sometimes by day as well, and which seemed to come from beneath the floor near the open fire-place. Having determined at length to investigate the source of these mysterious noises, the aged pair commenced by removing some of the hearth bricks that covered the very spot whence the sound usually came. Imagine their astonishment to find here two full-grown living Muskrats! The luckless beasts were lifted out with the old iron tongs and slain upon the spot.

The Muskrat, though chiefly nocturnal, is frequently seen swimming and feeding about the borders of ponds and streams in the day-time, particularly in cloudy weather. And when resting on the edge of a bog it so resembles a lump of mud as to escape the notice of those unacquainted with its habits. The distance that it can swim under water without coming to the surface to breathe is remarkable.

Its homes are of two principal kinds : huts and burrows. The latter are always present and may be inhabited at all times of the year, while the huts are for winter use and are confined to certain more or less restricted localities.

The burrows are excavated in the shores of the water-courses which the animals inhabit. The entrance is under water, the burrow thence sloping upward into the bank a distance of ten or fifteen feet (3 to 4½ metres) to an air-chamber eighteen inches (about half a metre) or more in diameter, which often contains a nest. There may be several passages leading to this nest, all of which are under water the greater part of the year. The roof of the air-chamber is generally so near the surface of the ground that it frequently falls in, particularly in pastures where cattle abound. Leading away from it, one or more galleries commonly extend back a considerable distance, keeping so near the surface that their occasional " caving in " may result in extensive damage to the fields of the farmer. When the animal takes up its abode near dykes or dams, its perforations are liable to do great mischief.

In moving about on their feeding grounds Muskrats are in the habit of travelling along the same paths till they become deeply worn channels. Steel traps properly concealed in these runways are almost certain to capture the first animal that passes.

In places where the water is from two to six feet deep the Muskrat, in the fall of the year, sometimes collects and heaps together a large quantity of aquatic and marsh plants, the resulting mass taking a shape not unlike that of a " haycock," though commonly far less symmetrical. This accumulation of vegetation, with more or less adhering mud,* is called a Muskrat " hut" or " house." It varies greatly in size, those placed in water occasionally attaining extraordinary dimensions. The summit of the structure is commonly high enough out of water to admit of an air-chamber within, which communicates with the outside world by means of a hole through the centre of the mass, the entrance or entrances being under water. Many of the houses contain no mud or sticks, but consist wholly of balls and knots of roots and swamp grasses. It seems clear that the animals make no attempt to construct a dwelling of any particular shape, but merely heap the materials together without plan or order, the resulting mound naturally assuming, in a general way, the form of a flattened cone. In some cases the summit is quite dome-shaped, but I am convinced that this is purely the result of accident, for their upper parts are usually very irregular. The materials of which the hut is composed, it will be observed, are such as serve as food for the animals during the long winters ; hence the Muskrat's house is, in reality, a store-house, which he devours piecemeal as the winter advances ! The one structure supplies both the food itself, and the

---

* I have never seen a Muskrat house that was built of mud, or that even consisted largely of this material ; but they must occur in certain localities, for no less trustworthy an authority than Sir John Richardson wrote : "In the autumn, before the shallow lakes and swamps freeze over, the Musquash builds its house of mud, giving it a conical form, and a sufficient base to raise the chamber above the level of the water." (Fauna Boreali Americana, Vol. I, 1829, p. 117.)

shelter in which it is eaten.  It is quite a conspicuous object, the summit projecting above the water or ice, and is therefore most commonly found in places that are a little out of the beaten paths of man.  During the fall and winter, Muskrats speedily repair injuries done to their houses.  This habit is put to advantage by the trapper, who, chopping a hole in the side of the hut and placing a trap in the breach, often secures the entire family in the course of a few days. The above remarks apply to the highest type of Muskrat architecture. There are many less perfect, and at the same time less conspicuous forms of these store-houses, that are to be met with in almost every locality where the species exists in any numbers.  Along the borders of ponds and sluggish streams there often stand old hollow stumps whose roots extend out under the water.  Such stumps will frequently be found, as cold weather approaches, stuffed full of the wads of grass that are used in hut building, the angles and crevices between the roots being packed with the same material.  Advantage is also taken of other inconspicuous places in which to deposit food, and sometimes, where there is no current, floating hoards of grass and roots are established—veritable floating islands in miniature—in the vicinity of their huts.  When the ice is not too thick they generally keep open a few breathing holes at certain favorite feeding grounds in very shallow water, frequently covering them over with grass.

My observation that the Muskrat, in the North, habitually lays up provisions for winter's use does not accord with the statements of others, the only allusion to such a habit that I have seen being contained in the following very interesting narrative from Audubon and Bachman (who, by the way, evidently considered it as exceptional):—

"An acquaintance who had a garden in the neighborhood of a meadow which contained a large number of Musk-Rats, sent one day, to enquire whether we could aid in discovering the robbers who carried off almost every night a quantity of turnips.  We were surprised to find on examining the premises, that the garden had been plundered and nearly ruined by these Rats.  There were paths extending from the muddy banks of the stream, winding among the rank weeds and grasses, passing through the old worm fence, and leading to the various beds of vegetables. Many of the turnips had disappeared on the previous night—the duck-like tracks of the Musk-Rat were seen on the beds in every direction. The paths were strewn with turnip leaves, which either had dropped, or were bitten off, to render the transportation more convenient. Their paths after entering the meadow diverged to several burrows, all of which gave evidence that their tenants had been on a foraging expedition on the previous night. The most convenient burrow was opened, and we discovered in the nest so many different articles of food, that we were for some time under an impression, that like the chipping squirrel, chickaree, &c., this species laid up in autumn a store of food for winter use. There were carrots, and parsnips which appeared to have been cut in halves, the lower part of the root having been left in the ground; but what struck us as most singular, was that ears of corn (maize) not yet quite ripe, had been dragged into the burrow, with a considerable portion of the stock attached." *

As has already been remarked, the Muskrat is exceedingly fond of our common fresh-water mussels, and it is usual to find large numbers of their empty but unbroken shells strewn along the shore or in shallow water covering the mud or sand bottoms where it abounds. Instead of devouring the mussels where he finds them, the Muskrat often carries them to particular spots, where large accumulations of their shells may be found.

In the course of their remarks upon the habits of this species, Audubon and Bachman relate an experience that is as interesting and remarkable as it seems to be unique: "It is a well-known fact that many species of quadrupeds and birds, are endowed by Nature with the faculty of foreseeing or foreknowing, the changes of the seasons, and have premonitions of the coming storm. . . . After an unusual drought, succeeded by a warm Indian-summer, as we were one day

---

* Quadrupeds of North America, Vol. I, 1846, pp. 118–119.

passing near a mill-pond, inhabited by some families of Musk-Rats, we observed numbers of them swimming about in every direction, carrying mouthfuls of withered grasses, and building their huts higher on the land than any we had seen before. We had scarcely ever observed them in this locality in the middle of the day, and then only for a moment as they swam from one side of the pond to the other; but now they seemed bent on preparing for some approaching event, and the successive reports of several guns fired by some hunters, only produced a pause in their operations for five or ten minutes. Although the day was bright and fair, on that very night there fell torrents of rain succeeded by an unusual freshet, and intensely cold weather." *

Spearing the Muskrat in their huts, in the early winter, is an exciting and sometimes profitable occupation. The best account of this mode of hunting which I have seen is from the pen of Henry Thacker, who thus graphically describes his excursions to a large marsh in the vicinity of Chicago in the winter of 1844–45 :—

" With feelings of interest and excitement, I marched up to a large house very cautiously (for, with the least jar or crack of the ice, away goes your game), and, with uplifted spear, made ready for a thrust. I hesitated. There was a difficulty I had not taken into account; I knew not where to strike. The chances of missing the game were apparent, but there was no time to be lost; so bang! went the spear into a hard, frozen mass, penetrating it not more than three or four inches, and away went the game in every direction. With feelings of some chagrin I withdrew my spear, and began feeling about for a more vulnerable spot, which I was not long in detecting. It being a cold, freezing day, I discovered an accumulation of white frost on a certain spot of the house, and putting my spear on the place I found it readily entered. The mystery was solved at once; this frost on the outside of the house was caused by the breath and heat of the animals immediately beneath it, and it was generally

---

* Quadrupeds of North America, Vol. I, 1846, pp. 122–123.

on the southeast side of the centre of the house, this being the
warmest side.    Acting on these discoveries, I made another trial, and
was successful ; and now the sport began in good earnest.    Whenever I made a thrust, I would cùt a hole through the wall of the house
with my hatchet, and take out the game, close up the hole, and start
for another house.    The remaining members of the family would
soon return, and immediately set about repairing the breach.    I
sometimes succeeded in pinning two rats at one thrust.    I also became quite expert in taking the game in another way, as follows :
Whenever I made an unsuccessful thrust into a house, the rats would
dive into the water through their paths or run-ways, and disappear in
all directions.    I now found I could easily drive my one tined spear
through the ice two inches thick, and pin a rat with considerable
certainty, which very much increased the sport, and I was not long
in securing a pile of fifteen or twenty rats.

" Here I made a discovery of what, until now, had been a mystery
to me, namely, how a muskrat managed to remain so long a time in
the water under the ice without drowning.    The muskrat, I perceived, on leaving his house inhaled a full breath, and would then stay
under water as long as he could without breathing ; when he would
rise up with his nose against the ice, and breathe out his breath,
which seemed to displace the water, forming a bubble.    I could distinctly see him breathe his bubble in and out several times, and then
dive again.    In this way I have chased them about under the ice for
some time before capturing them.    .   .   .

" As I frequently speared the muskrat on his feeding-bed, and
subsequently found it to be the best and surest place to set a trap for
him, I will, for the benefit of the novice, undertake to describe one
as found in the marshes.    A feeding-bed is a place where the muskrat goes to feed, generally at night, and is frequently many rods from
his house.    Here he selects a place where his food is convenient,
and by the aid of the refuse material of the roots, &c., which he
carries here for food, he elevates himself partly out of water, in a sort

of hut.   Here he sits and eats his food, and at the slightest noise, or least appearance of danger, disappears in an instant under water.   In the winter these feeding-places are readily discovered by a bunch of wadded grass, flag, or some other material, about the size of a man's hat, protruding above the ice.   This little mound is hollow, and is only large enough for a single rat, where he sits and eats his food, with his lower parts in the water.   When the rats were disturbed in their house, I found they generally fled to these feeding-huts, where they were almost a certain mark for the spearman.   .   .   .

"In my next excursion, not many days after, to the same place, I had still better success.   As the ice had now become too thick to be easily penetrated by my spear, I adopted, in part, a different mode of taking the game.   This time I carried with me, in addition to my spear, two dozen steel-traps, and a bundle of willow sticks (cut on the way) about three feet long.   On arriving at the hunting grounds I prepared myself for the day's sport by putting on my mufflers, and with traps and willow sticks slung upon my back, began the work by driving my spear into the first house I came to.   I could not now see the rats as they fled from the house, on account of the thickness of the ice and a slight snow that lay upon it.   Consequently the sport of spearing them through the ice was cut off.   But as often as I had occasion to cut through the walls of the house to take out my game, I set a steel-trap in the nest, slipped a willow stick through the ring of the chain, laid it across the hole, slightly stopped it up, and then passed on to the next house ; and so on, until my traps were all gone. I then started back to the place of beginning, driving my spear into every feeding-hut in my course, and killing many rats.   Finally, I began going over the ground again, first driving my spear into a house, then examining the trap, taking out the game and re-setting the trap.   In this course I was quite successful.   I found by setting the trap in the right place, near the edge, and a little under the water, I was almost certain to take the first rat that returned.   In making two or three rounds in this way, I found the rats became somewhat disturbed, and sought temporary shelter elsewhere ; when I would move to a new place, giving them time to recover from their fright." *

That the Muskrat was at one time a very important article of commerce is evident from the fact that Dr. Richardson, in writing of it in 1829, stated : "Between four and five hundred thousand skins are annually imported into Great Britain from North America." †    And even at the present day several thousand are killed each year in the United States alone.    It is probable that no other North American mammal is so extensively trapped by the rural small boy.    This is due to the great abundance of the species, even in populous districts, and the ease with which it is trapped, rather than to its value, for Muskrat pelts have always ranked among the cheaper furs, a single skin rarely fetching more than fifteen or twenty cents.

The Muskrat is a very prolific animal.    It brings forth from five to nine young at a birth, and is said to raise three litters in a season. The nest is usually placed in a hole in the bank, at some little distance from the water, though it is sometimes built in the hut.    Robert Kennicott, in his very valuable paper upon The Quadrupeds of Illinois, says : "Though the young are generally brought forth in burrows, they were often found in the houses in the sloughs, only one female, however, remaining in a house." ‡    Mr. Thomas S. Roberts thus describes a litter of young that he found near Minneapolis, Minnesota, May 24th, 1880 : " Upon knocking the top off from a Muskrat house on the edge of a slough, nine young Muskrats apparently but a day or two old were disclosed.    They were hairless and showed not the least sign of their eyes opening.    The nest was of dry grass and not more than an inch or two above the level of the water." §

The noise a Muskrat makes in diving is out of all proportion to its

---

* The Trapper's Guide.    By S. Newhouse.    Published by Oneida Community, Wallingford, Conn., 1867, pp. 147–150.

† Fauna Boreali Americana, Vol. I, 1829, p. 118.

‡ Report of the Commissioner of Patents for the year 1856.    Agriculture, 1857, p. 108.

§ Forest and Stream, Vol. XIV, No. 22, July 1, 1880, pp. 428–429.

19

size, and many a drowsy hunter, while floating for deer, has been startled by its sudden plunge. A loud report is made by striking the flat tail against the water.

Dr. Richardson, writing in 1829, said that in the Fur Countries they were "subject at uncertain intervals to a great mortality from some unknown cause. Their great fecundity, however, enables them to recover these losses in a very few years, although the deaths at times are so numerous, that a fur-post, where the Musquash is the principal return, is not unfrequently abandoned until they have re-cruited." * Among the foes of the Muskrat may be mentioned the fox and mink, and the larger hawks and owls; the mink and the great-horned owl being its greatest enemies.

The flesh of the Muskrat is red and rather flabby; still it is fair eating for a time when other meat is unattainable. Thomas Pennant, whose notions of the causes of things were sometimes strangely sophistical, mentions that the Muskrat feeds upon the sweet flag, and then goes on to say: "This perhaps gives them that strong musky smell these animals are so remarkable for; which they lose during winter, probably when this species of plant is not to be got." †

Many distinguished naturalists, whose works are still regarded standard, give meagre and very erroneous accounts of the habits of the animals they describe. It is stated in the third volume of Griffith's Cuvier, published in 1827, that Muskrats "construct in winter, on the ice, a hut of clay, where they inhabit in great numbers, proceeding through a hole, to seek at the bottom the roots *acorus*, on which they subsist. When the ice closes their holes, they are reduced to feed upon each other" (p. 67). It is hardly necessary to add that the above is fallacious in almost every particular.

---

* Fauna Boreali Americana, Vol. I, 1829, p. 117.
† Arctic Zoology, Vol. I, 1792, p. 123.

*The Muskrat as a Fish-eater.*

That the Muskrat is not commonly considered a fish-eater is evident from the absence of reference to such habit in the published accounts of the animal. Robert Kennicott and Gov. DeWitt Clinton are, so far as I have been able to ascertain, the only authors who mention this trait. Kennicott says : " Excepting in eating mollusks, and occasionally a dead fish, I am not aware that this species departs from a vegetable diet." *

Gov. Clinton, writing in 1820 of the then newly built Erie Canal, in New York, said : " In winter, when the water is frozen, muskrats go under the ice and prey on the fish. They are very destructive to trout, which is already in the canal." †

At a meeting of the Biological Society of Washington, held in the National Museum, December 14th, 1883, Mr. Henry W. Elliott spoke of the " *Appetite of the Muskrat.*" He stated that in certain parts of Ohio the Muskrat did great injury to Carp ponds, not only by perforating the banks and dams and thus letting off the water, but also by actually capturing and devouring the Carp, which is a sluggish fish, often remaining motionless, half buried in the mud. In the discussion that followed, Dr. Mason Graham Ellzey said that from boyhood he had been familiar with the fact that the Muskrat sometimes ate fish. In fact, he had seen Muskrats in the act of devouring fish that had recently been caught and left upon the bank. The President, Dr. Charles A. White, narrated a similar experience.

On the 7th of February, 1884, I brought this subject to the notice of the Linnæan Society of New York, and asked if any of the members knew the Muskrat to be a fish-eater. Dr. Edgar A. Mearns said that he had long been familiar with the fact, and that it was no uncommon thing to see a Muskrat munching a dead fish upon the borders of the salt marshes along the Hudson. He had shot them

---

* Quadrupeds of Illinois Injurious and Beneficial to the Farmer, 1857, p. 106.

† Letters on the Natural History and Internal Resources of the State of New York. By Hibernicus, 1822, p. 46.

while so engaged. He further stated that the Muskrat is very destructive to nets, destroying the fishermen's fykes by scores, by
entering them in quest of fishes and then tearing the nets in order
to escape.

Dr. A. K. Fisher said that at Sing Sing, New York, he had often
known Muskrats to enter fykes, sometimes drowning, but oftener
escaping by gnawing the meshes, thus doing considerable injury to
the nets. He supposed they entered the nets because placed in
their line of travel. He further stated that he knew that fykes made
of fine wire were used with success in capturing these animals.

Mr. Wm. H. Dall, the well-known Alaskan explorer, now of the
Coast Survey, in response to inquiry has kindly favored me with the
following : " In 1863, I visited Kankakee, Illinois, on a collecting
tour for river mollusks, in July. You know how the Muskrats throw
up mounds of the shells they dig out  I examined many of these
for *Unios*, etc. On several I saw the skeletons of fish (chiefly suck-
ers I believe) partly or wholly denuded of their flesh, and showing
the marks of Muskrat (or at least rodent) teeth. I also saw the shell
of a common mud turtle, so gnawed and in the same situation. I
did not see the animal in the act of feasting, which I believe is chiefly
done at night, but I have no doubt that the fish and turtle were eaten
by the Muskrat, as well as the mollusks associated with them in the
same pile."

Under date of March 5th, 1884, I have received from Dr. Fisher,
the most valuable record yet obtained concerning the habit in question. Dr. Fisher writes : " A few days since, two young men were
fishing through the ice for pickerel, with live bait, at Croton Lake,
Westchester County, N. Y. Several times they were troubled by
having one of the lines pulled violently off the bush and run out to
its full length. Finally they saw the line start again, and by pulling
it up quickly they landed a large Muskrat on the ice." Here is an
authentic instance where a Muskrat has actually captured a live fish

in the water.    Fortunately, the fish was attached to a hook and line, and the Muskrat was caught and killed.

The above facts, which were published in *Forest and Stream* of March 27th and April 3d, 1884, fell under the eye of Mr. E W. Nelson, late Signal Observer at St. Michæls, Alaska, and elicited from him the following additional testimony : " The Muskrat is the most abundant mammal to be found in all the marshy parts of Alaska, south of the Arctic circle at least, and during my residence in that country I had frequent opportunity to learn of its fondness for fish. Often when skirting the border of a pool or following the edge of some sluggish stream in the evening or during the dim light of the Arctic nights in summer, I frightened the Muskrats from the body of dead fish on the bank at the water's edge.   The fish were usually small sluggish species and such as could have been easily caught by the animal itself, although it feeds upon fish not killed by itself. That the Muskrat will feed upon dead water fowl I have also had frequent occasion to notice." *

Mr. Charles F. Carr writes me that in Wolf River, Wisconsin, twelve or fifteen years ago, Muskrats were in the habit of eating fish from a gill net set there by a man named Rich.

### Ferocious Tendencies of the Muskrat.

Under the above heading Mr. W. H. Ballou, in the *American Naturalist* for July, 1880, narrates the following very unusual expe - rience : " I was sauntering along a prairie road just out of Boone, Iowa, one night during the past winter.   There was no snow on the ground and the moon was just glimmering through the clouds.   Of a sudden I was startled by the appearance of some animal from the long grass by the wayside, which dashed up my leg.   I knocked it off, picked up a frozen piece of mud and broke its leg.   Again it made a rush for me, and another piece of mud sent it rolling over.

---

* Forest and Stream, Vol. XXII, No. 15, May 8, 1884, p. 285.

I took hold of its tail during this little scene, and ended the matter by giving its head a severe bump on the ground. When I had access to more light I found that it was a full-grown Muskrat of enormous size. I can neither account for its attack nor appearance there. The previous summer season had dried up all the sloughs and there was no water in the vicinity. The houses of these animals had been deserted for some time previous, and nowhere on the prairies had I been able to find one with any inhabitants (they build in the sloughs of western prairies extensively). Alone and well away from its most natural element it had attacked me without provocation. The matter led to an inquiry among the farmers. The general statement was to the effect that considerable fun and some trouble was had with this species during each hay time, as they did not hesitate, when out of the water, to ferociously attack man or beast, with seldom any damage. One man related, however, that he received a severe bite in the hand from one of them, which laid him up for some time. It is either very courageous or very luny." *

The most remarkable foray of this kind which has come to my knowledge occurred in the city of Charlotte, North Carolina, during the evening of March 17th, 1884. It is thus recorded in the *Charlotte Observer* of March 18th : " Charlie Fox's adventure with a pack of Muskrats on Trade street one night about a year ago, was brought vividly to mind last night when several runners came into the Observer office bringing tidings of three sanguinary battles fought between citizens who had encountered bodies of the savage *Musquash* in the streets. It appears that all these fights occurred at 8 o'clock. Mr. John Davidson was going home about that hour when he was encountered at the corner of Tyron and Fifth streets, by a large and ferocious rat, which he finally killed with a stick. He sent his fallen foe to the *Observer* office for inspection. It was almost as large as a 'possum. When this fight was going on there was a lively scene on Trade street, opposite the mint, where the Muskrats fairly swarmed.

---

* The American Naturalist, July. 1880, Vol. XIV, No. 7, p. 524.

Mr. Martin McRae, a clerk of T. L. Seigle & Co , was set upon by seven of the 'varmints' and was put to flight, not having any weapons with which to defend himself. Shortly afterwards, Larkin Saddler, the *Observer's* janitor, passed by and about twenty of the rats began biting at his legs. Larkin kicked about for dear life and finally got one rat under his foot and crushed it to death. Their sharp teeth began perforating his hide, and jumping over the fence he fled across the mint yard and got away from them. John Smith, colored, an employee of the Air Line road, came along next, and seeing the curious pack that beset his ankles, uttered a terrific yell and fled at the top of his speed. Wm. Norman, a colored employee of Duls & Co., was the next victim. He had a stick and giving the Muskrats battle killed one of their number and put the others to flight.

"This is the second annual appearance of these savage pests upon our streets. Where do they come from and who can account for their appearance in our city in such numbers? One theory is that they come from Irwin's creek, making their way up the cemetery branch to the flats below the First Presbyterian church and thence to the streets of the city. It is very nearly opposite the mint that Charlie Fox was attacked by the rats last year."

Mr. Ernest E. T. Seton, of Manitoba, writes me that, September 13th, 1883, near Carberry, he found a Muskrat in a field of standing wheat a mile and a half from water. The animal showed fight and was captured alive. Mr. Seton writes further: "While travelling on the Rapid City trail in Manitoba, October 2d, 1883, the oxen suddenly shied and turned off the road. Then I saw just ahead what proved to be a Muskrat! It was in a threatening attitude and sprang toward the nose of one of the cattle. On running to it, it seized my trousers in its teeth and held on. When kicked off it did not attempt to escape, but fought until killed. It was a male.'

## Family ZAPODIDÆ.

### ZAPUS HUDSONIUS (Zimm.) Coues.

*Jumping Mouse; Labrador Mouse.*

The Jumping Mouse is common in many parts of the Adirondacks, as well as in the surrounding country. It feeds upon beechnuts, and various seeds and berries.

Within the Wilderness it is most often observed in the tangled borders of low shrubs that surround the lakes and beaver meadows; while beyond the confines of the region it inhabits both the clearings and woodlands. It delights in grain fields, and in meadows of tall waving grass, where it finds abundant food and can readily escape its most active enemies. But when the time for haying and harvesting arrives, the Mice are suddenly deprived of their accustomed shelter and many seek protection beneath the haycocks and stacks of grain. By quickly overturning these, they are confused and frightened and may be captured with comparative ease.

When stationed to watch for deer, on the borders of our Adirondack lakes, I have often remained in one place during the greater part of the day. Seated, sometimes on a log that crossed a narrow belt of marsh along the shore, sometimes on the mossy slope of a well-wooded knoll hard by, and hidden by the dense frontage of undershrubs, or by the more open shelter of a slender tamarack, I have learned much that fills these pages. Encroaching upon the very water's edge is a net-work of wiry bushes, repelling the canoe that attempts to land. It consists chiefly of the leather leaf (*Cassandra calyculata*) and sweet gale (*Myrica gale*), with smaller quantities of the wild rosemary (*Andromeda polifolia*), meadow sweet (*Spiræa salicifolia*), and swamp laurel (*Kalmia glauca*). Adjoining this is a strip of sphagnous bog which supports a luxuriant growth of the curious pitcher plant, interspersed with straggling cranberries. Careful search may reveal the insect-eating *Drosera*, as well as several rare species of orchids. Where the sloping hill-side meets the marsh, another miniature thicket bars the way. Like the first, it is largely made up of the tough *Cassandra*, which here intertwines with Labrador tea (*Ledum latifolium*), sheep laurel (*Kalmia angustifolia*), and winterberry (*Ilex lævigata*). The beautiful *Azalea* and the woolly steeple bush (*Spiræa tomentosa*) are also usually present, while several species of *Viburnum* and *Cornus* contribute their share to the prominent features of the local flora.

While silently seated in the midst of these surroundings, I have on more than one occasion observed the Jumping Mouse. Sometimes he has crept quietly over the bog, winding his way amongst the pitcher plants and low clumps of matted bushes, presenting much the appearance of the white-footed mouse. At other times he has bounded lightly by, clearing the tops of the bushes with every leap, and disappearing so quickly that his identity was with difficulty determined. Indeed, when he hides after the first or second leap he is not rarely mistaken for the wood frog (*Rana temporaria sylvatica*), which he resembles in color.

The agility of these animals is almost incredible. I have repeatedly known them to clear a distance of more than ten feet (a trifle over 3 metres) at a single bound, and their leaps are made in such rapid succession that their feet seem barely to touch the ground. To attempt to catch one when any covert is near is a hopeless task.

The Jumping Mouse is said, by most writers, to be strictly nocturnal, but this is not the case. It is crepuscular, like the majority of our mammalia, and is also not infrequently seen abroad by day.

It nests in a variety of situations : sometimes in hollow stumps and trees, which it is said to climb from the inside ; more often under logs and rails, and in piles of rubbish ; frequently in crevices of rocky ledges ; and occasionally in open fields, a short distance under the surface.

Since the foregoing was written, Mr. Elisha Slade, of Somerset, Bristol County, Massachusetts, has favored me with a very interesting and detailed account of the habits of this species, portions of which are here reproduced.    Mr. Slade says : " The Long-tailed Jumping Mouse inhabits high land or low land, forest or pasture, cultivated field or swamp, and appears to be equally at home in either, and not numerous in any situation.    It possesses a momentary agility second to no other Rodent, and a muscular strength of enormous power for so small a creature.    When suddenly disturbed it often moves away in a direct line, the first three or four leaps being eight or ten feet in length ; but these distances rapidly decline to about four feet, which are continued until it considers itself out of danger.    This is not always the case, however, for it frequently takes an irregular course and jumps at diverse angles for several successive leaps, keeping the same general direction or changing at will.    It can double, and quickly too, if pursued, and by its manœuvers and instantaneous squattings can, and often does, elude a hawk or an owl ;  and its spontaneous irregularities enable it to escape being brained by a weasel, or swallowed whole by the common black snake.  .  .  .    It feeds upon the buds, leaves, and twigs, of many kinds of plants ;  upon seeds, grain, wild berries, chestnuts, acorns, grass, and to some extent upon the bark of shrubs.  .  .  .    As a rule, three litters are produced in a season, each consisting of from two to four young."

Barton, writing of this species in 1795, says : " Upon showing my drawing of the animal to an intelligent Indian who is settled at Oneida, he assured me that the same animal is very common at that place.    This Indian, who is a Mohegan, moreover said, that in his language this Dipus is called *Wauh peh Sous*, which signifies *the creature that jumps or skips like a deer*."    He also says : " It often gets into the graneries of the Indians settled at Oneida, in the State of New York, and proves very destructive to the Indian-corn.  .  .  .    I have not learned, with certainty, at what time this animal brings forth its young. But it has been seen leaping about with the young ones strongly attached to its teats. Four young ones have been seen thus attached."

Dr. DeKay says that Mr. Jesse Booth, of Orange County, New York, writes him : " In cross-plowing some years since, my attention was taken up by seeing some small thing move off from near my plough, at about the moderate walk of a man. It went over ridges and descended the hollows of the furrows, bearing some resemblance to an old withered oak leaf. I pursued it, when it proved to be one of these *wood-mice*, or *jumping mice ;* a female, with four young ones attached by their mouths to its teats." *

### The Hibernation of the Jumping Mouse.

Dr. Benjamin Smith Barton, of Philadelphia, was the first to make known the fact that the Jumping Mouse hibernates. On the 2d of October, 1795, he read a paper before the American Philosophical Society (which was not published, however, till 1799) in which he states : " In the month of February, one of these animals was found, seemingly in a torpid-state, under a stone, in opening a quarry." He further says, that a farmer, living near Philadelphia, has often discovered them, " at the depth of eighteen inches or two feet under ground, when he has been digging for the roots of horse-radish and parsley, in the winter-time." † In a supplement to this article, published in 1804, the same author observes :—

" In the month of August, 1796, one of these little animals was brought to me from the vicinity of this city. It was put into a large glass jar, where I was so fortunate as to preserve it for near four months. Though it made many efforts to escape from its

---

* Zoology of New York, Part I, 1842, p. 72.

† Some account of an American Species of Dipus, or Jerboa. By Benjamin Smith Barton, M. D. Transactions of the American Philosophical Society, Vol. IV, No. XII, 1799, p. 122. Barton again refers to the hibernation of this species in his Fragments of the Natural History of Pennsylvania, 1799, pp. xii, xiii.

confinement, it seemed, upon the whole, pretty well reconciled to it. It continued active, and both ate and drank abundantly.    I fed it upon bread, the grain of Indian corn (Zea Mays), and the berries of the Prinos verticillatus, sometimes called black-alder.

"On or about the 22d of November, it passed into the torpid state.    It is curious to observe, that at the time it became torpid, the weather was unusually mild for the season of the year, and moreover the animal was kept in a warm room, in which there was a large fire the greater part of the day and night.    I sometimes roused it from its torpid state ; at other times it came spontaneously out of it.    During the intervals of its waking, it both ate and drank.    It was frequently most active, while the weather was extremely cold in December ; but when I placed the jar upon a thick cake of ice, in the open air, its movements or activity seemed wholly directed to the making of a comfortable habitation out of the hay with which I supplied it.    It was sufficiently evident, however, that the cold was not the only cause of its torpid state.    It was finally killed by the application of too great a degree of heat to it, whilst in its torpor.

" During its torpor, it commonly laid with its head between its hind legs, with the claws or feet of these closely applied to the head.    Its respiration could always be perceived, but was very slow.

" The fact of the torpidity of this little animal is known to the gardeners and others near the city.    They call it the 'seven sleepers,' and assert, that it is frequently found in the earth, at the lower extremity of the horse-radish, and other perpendicular roots.    Does it use these as a measure of the distance to which it shall go in the earth, to avoid the influence of the frost ?

" I have said, that the Dipus Americanus becomes torpid in the neighborhood of this city.    But this, I believe, is not always the case.    During the winter-season, this little animal and another species, which I call Dipus mellivorus, take possession of the hives of bees, in which they form for themselves, a warm and comfortable habitation, having ingeniously scooped away some wax. The materials of its nest are fine dry grass, down of feathers, and old rags. It lives upon the honey, and seems to grow very fat upon it. I believe two individuals, a male and a female, commonly inhabit one hive. They sometimes devour the greater part of the honey of a hive.

" The circumstance just mentioned is not altogether uninteresting. It plainly proves what I have, long since, asserted, that the torpid state of animals is altogether 'an accidental circumstance,' and by no means constitutes a specific character. The same species becomes torpid in one country and not in another. Nay, different individuals of the same species become torpid, or continue awake, in the same neighborhood, and even on the same farm." *

On the 6th of June, 1797, Major-General Thomas Davies presented, before the Linnæan Society of London, " An account of the Jumping Mouse of Canada," which he supposed to be an undescribed species. This account was published in the Linnæan Transactions for 1798. Hence, though not read till more than a year and a half after Dr. Barton had presented his paper before the American Philosophical Society, it appeared in print before the publication of the latter.

General Davies gives a figure of the animal in the dormant state, observing that the specimen " was found by some workmen, in digging the foundation for a summer house, in a gentleman's garden about two miles from Quebec, in the latter end of May, 1787. It was discovered enclosed in a ball of clay, about the size of a cricket ball, nearly an inch in thickness, perfectly smooth within, and about twenty inches under ground. The man who first discovered it, not knowing what it was, struck the ball with his spade, by which means it was broken to pieces, or the ball also would have been presented to me. The drawing will perfectly

* Transactions of the American Philosophical Society, Vol. VI, 1804, pp. 143–144.

show, how the animal is laid during its dormant state. How long it had been under ground, it is impossible to say; but as I never could observe these animals in any part of the country after the beginning of September, I conceive they lay themselves up some time in that month, or beginning of October, when the frost becomes sharp; nor did I ever see them again before the last week in May, or beginning of June. From their being enveloped in balls of clay, without any appearance of food, I conceive they sleep during the Winter, and remain for that term without sustenance."

In the third volume of Griffith's Cuvier, published in 1827, it is stated: "One single species, the *Gerbillus* of Canada, has been found in a state of hibernation" (p. 154). And again: "In the winter it retires and falls asleep, rolled up like a ball, in a burrow about twenty inches deep. It places itself then in a sort of little chamber, of an oval form, and never stirs until the middle of spring. No provision is found in this retreat, nor is it exactly known on what substances it feeds" (p. 159).

Godman says: "At the commencement of cool weather, or about the time the frost sets in, the jumping mice go into their winter quarters, where they remain in a torpid state until the last of May or first of June." * Zadock Thompson also tells us that "they pass the winter in a torpid state and are not usually out in the spring before June." †

Is it not surprising, in the face of the evidence above narrated, ‡ that Audubon and Bachman should have given utterance to the following: "It is generally believed, that the Jumping Mouse, like the Hampster of Europe, (*Cricetus vulgaris*), and the Marmots, (*Arctomys*), hibernates, and passes the winter in a profound lethar-

---

* American Natural History, Vol. I, 1842, p. 322.

† Natural and Civil History of Vermont, 1842, p. 44.

‡ The statement in Griffith's Cuvier was unquestionably based upon General Davies' article, and it is probable that both Godman and Thompson derived their information from the same source. But even in this case there remain the two original, independent, and almost simultaneous accounts (those of Barton and Davies), the trustworthiness of which cannot be called in question.

gy. Although we made some efforts many years ago, to place this matter beyond a doubt by personal observation, we regret that our residence, being in a region where this species does not exist, no favorable opportunity has since been afforded us. Naturalists residing in the Northern and Middle States could easily solve the whole matter, by preserving the animal in confinement through the winter." *

If, in Audubon's time, there were grounds for questioning that this species hibernates, there are none at present. Robert Kennicott, in his valuable contribution to economic agriculture, states : " Dr. Hoy informs me that, when he was a boy in digging out a rabbit in winter, he found a pair of this species in a state of profound torpor, exhibiting all the phenomena of perfect hibernation. They were in a large nest of leaves situated two or three feet below the surface." †

In the *American Naturalist* for June, 1872 (Vol. VI, No. 6, pp. 330–332), the late Professor Sanborn Tenney published an article entitled " Hibernation of the Jumping Mouse." Without referring to a single published record or opinion, he narrates a personal experience so full of interest that I take pleasure in presenting it to my readers. Professor Tenney says :—

" On the 18th of January of the present year (1872), I went with Dr. A. Patton of Vincennes, Indiana, to visit a mound situated about a mile or a mile and a half in an easterly direction from Vincennes. While digging in the mound in search of relics that might throw light upon its origin and history, we came to a nest about two feet below the surface of the ground, carefully made of bits of grass, and in this nest was a Jumping Mouse (*Jaculus Hudsonius* Baird) apparently dead. It was coiled up as tightly as it could be, the nose being placed upon the belly, and the long tail coiled around the ball-like form which the animal had assumed. I

---

* Quadrupeds of North America, Vol. II, 1851, p. 355.
† Patent Office Report for 1856, 1857, p. 97.

took the little, mouse into my hand. It exhibited no motion or sign of life. Its eyes and mouth were shut tight, and its little fore feet or hands were shut and placed close together. Everything indicated that the mouse was perfectly dead, excepting the fact that it was not as rigid as perhaps a dead mouse would be in the winter. I tied the mouse and nest in my handkerchief and carried them to Vincennes. Arriving at Dr. Patton's office I untied my treasures, and took out the mouse and held it for some time in my hand; it still exhibited no sign of life; but at length I thought I saw a very slight movement in one of the hind legs. Presently there was a very slight movement of the head, yet so feeble that one could hardly be sure it was real. Then there came to be some evidence of breathing, and a slight pressure of my fingers upon the tail near the body was followed by an immediate but feeble movement of one of the hind legs. At length there was unmis-takable evidence that the animal was breathing, but the breathing was a labored action, and seemingly performed with great diffi-culty. As the mouse became warmer the signs of life became more and more marked; and in the course of the same afternoon on which I brought it into the warm room it became perfectly active, and was as ready to jump about as any other member of its species.

"I put this mouse into a little tin box with holes in the cover, and took him with me in my journeyings, taking care to put in the box a portion of an ear of corn and pieces of paper. It ate the corn by gnawing from the outside of the kernel, and it gnawed the paper into bits with which it made a nest. On the fourth day after its capture I gave it water which it seemed to relish. On the 23d of January, I took it with me to Elgin, Illinois, nearly three hundred miles farther north than the region where I found the specimen. The weather was intensely cold. Taking the mouse from the box, I placed it on a newspaper on a table, and covered it with a large glass bell, lifting the edge of the glass so as to admit a supply of air. Under this glass was placed a good supply of waste cotton. Soon after it was fairly established in its new and more commodious quarters, it began to clean every part of its body in the most thorough manner, washing itself very much in the same manner as a cat washes. On coming to the tail it passed that long member, for its whole length, through the mouth from side to side, beginning near the body and ending at the tip. At night as soon as the lights were put out the mouse began gnawing the paper, and during the night it gnawed all the newspaper it could reach, and made the fragments and the cotton into a large nest perhaps five or six inches in diameter, and established itself in the centre. Here it spent the succeeding day. The next night it was supplied with more paper, and it gnawed all it could reach, and thus spent a large part of the night in work. I could hear the work going on when I was awake. In the morning it appeared to be reposing on the top of its nest ; but after watching it for some time, and seeing no motion, I lifted up the glass and took the mouse in my hand. It showed no signs of life. I now felt that perhaps my pet was indeed really dead ; but remembering what I had previously seen, I resolved to try to restore it again to activity. By holding it in my hand and thus warming it, the mouse soon began to show signs of life, and although it was nearly the whole day in coming back to activity, at last it was as lively as ever, and afterward, on being set free in the room, it moved about so swiftly by means of its long leaps, that it required two of us a long time to capture it uninjured.

"On the evening of February 6th I reached my home in Williamstown, and on my arrival the mouse was in good condition. But the next morning it was again apparently dead ; in the course of the day, however, being placed where it was warm, it gradually came back to activity as before."

The statements of Godman and Thompson, that the Jumping Mouse remains torpid till the last of May or first of June, are

without weight, because it is very evident that these authors derive
their knowledge from Davies, whose observations were limited to
a single specimen taken near Quebec.　Moreover, the fact that a
hibernating animal does not emerge from winter-quarters till June
in the latitude of Quebec, affords no reason for supposing it to
remain dormant till this late date in more southern localities.
Indeed, experience points to a contrary conclusion, as well in the
present as in several other species.　On the 11th of February,
1874, I caught an active male at Easthampton, Massachusetts;
and Mr. Elisha Slade writes me that in the vicinity of his home, at
Somerset, Bristol County, Mass., the animal "retires to hollow
trees, stumps, or fissures of rocks, during cold snaps," and reappears with every return of warm weather.　During the winter of
1881–1882, unprecedented for its mildness, I several times observed it in Lewis County, in Northern New York.

## Family HYSTRICIDÆ.

## ERETHIZON DORSATUS (Linn.) F. Cuvier.

### Canada Porcupine.

The Porcupine is a common and well-known resident of all the
wooded parts of the Adirondacks, and is equally abundant in the
lowlands and on the highest mountains.

Of all the mammalian inhabitants of North America, not one
possesses more striking peculiarities.　To a person beholding him
for the first time he seems a veritable prodigy.　He presents a
combination of positive characters which seem directly contradic-
tory to his known habits of life.　He is about twice the size of a
full-grown woodchuck, well-conditioned adults averaging from fifteen to twenty pounds in weight.　His muzzle is short and blunt,
and his eyes and ears are small—the latter almost concealed in the
bristles of the sides of the head.　His neck is short and thick, and
his body is large and chunked.　He is very compactly built, and

remarkably broad across the back.   His legs are short.   The soles of his plantigrade feet are broad and naked, like those of the bear, and his claws are large, well-curved, and channelled beneath.   His tail is most extraordinary.   It is a large, ponderous, and somewhat four-sided structure, capable of dealing a powerful blow.

The entire upper surface of the animal, from in front of the eyes to the tip of the tail, the cheeks, sides of the neck, body and tail, the shoulders, flanks, and hips, are densely covered with thickly-set stout spines, varying from less than an inch (25.5 mm.) to more than four and one quarter inches (108 mm.) in length.   These spines or quills, which in a state of rest are directed backward, are connected at their bases with a layer of muscle by which they may be erected at will.   The mature quills cling so loosely to the skin that they are easily detached, and their finely barbed tips cause them to adhere to any animal with which they come in forcible contact.   After having penetrated the skin, the tendency is to advance, and the muscular action of their victim causes them to become more and more deeply imbedded.   There is no part of the body to which they may not travel.   I have found them in the hind leg of a fisher, firmly fixed between the tibia and fibula.

The Porcupine, owing to this formidable dermal armature, has but few enemies.   Chief among them, as has already been shown (Vol. I, pp. 30, and 48–50), are the panther and fisher ; and since these powerful Carnivores have become rare in the Adirondacks, the Porcupine has been, and still is, on the increase.   He is occasionally attacked by wolves, eagles,* and the great-horned owl.

He is a pretty strict vegetarian, deriving the greater part of his sustenance from different kinds of browse and bark.   Among the conifers, the hemlock furnishes the most palatable food, for he is found upon it more often than upon any other evergreen.   He

---

* In Forest and Stream of March 20, 1884 (p. 144), Mr. J. L. Davison, of Lockport, N. Y., states that he had recently examined a golden eagle that had been shot at Plessis, Jefferson County, N. Y.   He says : " The feet of the eagle were full of porcupine quills, which was probably the last animal he had dined off, and about as hot a meal as he ever had."

also feeds upon the foliage and twigs of the maple and birch, and not infrequently comes to the water's edge to seek the lily-pads within reach from the bank. He is also partial to the staple commodity of the region—the beechnut—and I have killed several whose stomachs were distended with beechnut-meal.

The Porcupine is more strictly nocturnal than the majority of our mammals; still, he occasionally ventures abroad in the daytime. The greater part of his life is spent high in the trees, though his den is usually concealed in some ledge of rocks. He is not so active during extreme cold as at other times, but is not known to hibernate. I have seen fresh tracks * leading to his hole in a rocky side-hill in January, the thermometer indicating a temperature of −27° C. If ledges are not at hand, he is sometimes found asleep under an old log or brush-heap, or in a hollow tree. When he has selected and settled himself in a tree to his liking he may not leave it, day or night, until he has denuded it of the whole of its foliage. I have seen many hemlocks thus completely stripped, not a green twig remaining, even on the smallest bough. It seems incredible that so large and clumsy an animal should be able to climb out far enough on the branches to reach the terminal leaves ; but he distributes his weight by bringing several branches together, and then, with his powerful paws, bends back their ends and passes them through his mouth. When high in the tree-tops he is often passed unnoticed, mistaken, if seen at all, for the nest of a crow or hawk.

He is very fond of salt and frequently comes around camp during the night for the purpose of obtaining it. He will eagerly lick a bag that has contained salt meat, or the dirt where brine has been spilt. He takes pains to devour all pork and ham rinds that fall in his way, and, if occasion offers, will gnaw a buttertub or other wooden receptacle that has contained any saline substance.

---

* His short legs allow his heavy body to drag in the snow, making even a deeper and broader rut than the otter. His footprints are nearer together than those of the otter, and are of a different pattern.

His familiarity at such times is surprising, for, while not aggressive, he is by no means timorous, and explores the camp with coolness and determination.

Porcupines have a curious habit of girdling trees, at a height of from six to thirty feet. The zone from which the bark is removed varies from a few inches to a foot or more in breadth. The spruce is more frequently girdled than any other tree, and those of small diameter more commonly than those of large size.

When feeding on lily-pads along the borders of water-courses they sometimes utter extraordinary noises, and occasionally quarrels arise for the possession of some log which affords them easy access to the coveted plants. At Beaver Lake, in Lewis County, Mr. John Constable once witnessed an encounter during which one of the combatants was tumbled into the water. The animals did not attempt to bite, but growled and snarled and pushed.

Mr. Eugene P. Bicknell, while encamped on the summit of Slide Mountain in the Catskills, in June, 1882, was favored by a visit from a number of these curious animals, and his account of their actions well illustrates some of their prominent characteristics. Mr. Bicknell says: "From evening till morning dusk our cabin on the extreme summit of the mountain was virtually besieged by them, and through the chinks their dark forms could be seen moving about among the shadows in the moonlight, while their sharp cries, and often low conversational chatter, singularly like the voices of infants, were weird interruptions of the midnight silence, or later, of the moaning wind.

"The seeming nocturnal temerity of these creatures appeared to be simply an exhibition of excessive stupidity. It was found impossible to drive them from the camp for any length of time; they seemed to be destitute of the faculty of memory, and even a light charge of shot sent among them was only for the moment effectual. Even when one particularly stupid individual had been shot dead in the doorway trying to effect an entrance by gnawing

its way through a gap, another, shortly after, continued the operation beside the lifeless body of its companion.

"It seems probable that these singular rodents cannot long sur-
vive human settlement.   Incapable of rapid motion they are easily
approached, and their spiny armature, so potent a protection from
their natural enemies, fails before the merciless power of man.   In
the isolation of the mountain top where we have just seen them,
they appeared to be at a loss to understand the nature of their
disturbers, and when met with showed little excitement, or anxiety
to escape.   Their greatest effort in this direction appeared to be
leisurely shuffling out of the immediate way, often climbing with
sluggish effort into a small balsam and composing themselves
among the branches just out of easy reach." *

Among certain Indian tribes the flesh of the Porcupine is a
staple article of diet, and I have been informed by hunters and
trappers that it is by no means bad eating.

In the copper districts of Lake Superior, Porcupines are put to
a novel use.   The following clipping is from the *Ontonagon*
[Michigan] *Miner* of July 28th, 1883 : " Porcupines as Fuel.—Mr.
Stratton who has charge of the work at the Wilmot mine has
found a new article of fuel which is more effective than green
wood, Porcupines !  Yes, Porcupines.   These pests had become so
numerous, that one day he threw a couple of them into the fire
place of the steam-drill, and to his surprise his steam ran up to 80
pounds in a short time.   Having made this discovery he concluded
to follow it up, and the boys are ordered to kill and bring in every
porcupine they can catch, which are thrown in to help make fuel.
They have now killed and burned 126 of them."

By persons ignorant of natural history, the Porcupine is sometimes called "Hedgehog."   The hedgehog is a small animal, related to the mole, and is not found in America.

The Porcupine makes its nest in a ledge of rocks, or in the hol-

---

* Transactions of the Linnæan Society of New York, Vol. I, 1882, pp. 121–122.

low of a tree or log. Its young, generally one or two in number, are born about the first of May, and are monstrous for the size of the species. They are actually larger, and relatively more than thirty times larger, than the young of the black bear at birth.*

Josselyn, in his account of *Two Voyages to New England*, says : " The *Porcupine* likewise I have treated of, only this I forgot to acquaint you with, that they lay Eggs, and are good meat" (p. 75).

The intestines of these animals usually contain large numbers of tape-worms.

## Family LEPORIDÆ.

## LEPUS AMERICANUS Erxleben.

*Great Northern Hare ; Northern Varying Hare.*

The Northern Hare is found in greater or less abundance in most parts of the Adirondacks above the altitude of fifteen hundred feet (477 metres). Below this altitude, particularly on the eastern or Champlain side of the Wilderness, it grades insensibly into the southern variety, *Lepus Americanus Virginianus.*

In summer the Northern Hare feeds upon a variety of tender shoots, grasses, leaves, buds, and berries ; in winter its diet is limited to the twigs and bark of shrubs and small trees, particularly of the poplar, birch, and willow.

The haunts of this species vary somewhat with the season. In summer it is found in the dark evergreen forests, while in winter, when the ground is frozen and covered with snow, it retires to the swamps, and to the dense thickets, chiefly of alder and black spruce,

---

* May 1st, 1882, I shot, at Big Moose Lake, a female Porcupine which contained a fœtus that would certainly have been born within two or three days. It weighed one and one-quarter pound avoirdupois (567 grammes), and measured in total length eleven and one-fourth inches (285 mm.), the head and body measuring about seven and three-fourth inches (just 195 mm.). It was densely covered with long black hair, and the quills on its back measured a little over half an inch (13 mm.) in length. The discoid placenta measured two and one-quarter inches (57 mm.) in diameter.

bordering many of the lakes and beaver meadows.*    At all times
of the year it inhabits the burnt districts that are strewn with
charred logs and grown over with blackberry bushes, studded here
and there with saplings of the poplar, birch, cherry, and shad-bush.

It does not inhabit burrows, nor take refuge in hollow trees, like
the gray rabbit, but seeks temporary shelter under a log, tree-top,
young evergreen, or other covert where it is not likely to be disturbed.    Here it spends the greater part of the day, feeding chiefly
by night.    It follows certain definite routes with such frequency
that regular runways are formed.    In these it is often snared.

About the borders of the Wilderness the Varying Hare is a
favorite object of the chase.    It is hunted with hounds, during the
early winter months, and is shot while circling through the swamps,
or crossing from hill to hill in the burnt districts.    Audubon and
Bachman state that its flesh is not good eating, to which opinion
I take exception, for, having eaten several dozens of them, I am
prepared to pronounce them tender and well-flavored.    When
properly cooked they certainly constitute an excellent article of diet.
The above-mentioned authors observe :  " This species in the
beginning of winter varies from three to six and a half pounds, but
we consider five and a half pounds to be an average weight of a
full-grown animal in good condition." †    In the Adirondack region
a five-pound Hare is exceptionally large, the adults averaging not
more than four and a half pounds (2,041 grammes) in weight.

I have never found the nest, but it is doubtless placed under a
brush heap, or in some other equally secure covert.    From four to
six young are produced at a birth, four being the usual number.
They are born late in May.    There may be two litters in a season,
but I have no proof of it.    This species has many enemies, among

---

* In my journal of a snow-shoe tramp in the Adirondacks, in January, 1883, I find the following
entry concerning this species : "Scarcely a track seen except about the borders of lakes and beaver
meadows.  Very common near Big Otter Lake, and tolerably so at Little Safford Lake and in a
swamp west of Independence Lake ; also between Big Moose and Second Lake of North Branch,
and near the Forge."

† Quadrupeds of North America, Vol. I, 1846, p. 96.

the most formidable of which are the lynx, fox, ermine, mink, marten, fisher, eagle, the snowy and great-horned owls, and the larger hawks.

The Varying Hare derives its name from the well-known circumstance that it changes color in spring and fall—being dark reddish-brown in summer and snowy white in winter. Concerning the method of the change much difference of opinion exists, and some of the ablest of recent writers pass the point in silence.

Pennant says : " These animals, at approach of winter, receive a new coat, which consists of a multitude of long white hairs, twice as long as the summer fur, which still remains beneath." * Dr. Richardson stated that, in his opinion, " the change to the winter dress takes place by a lengthening and blanching of the summer fur ; whilst the change in the beginning of summer consists in the winter coat falling off during the growth of the new and coloured fur." † This opinion comes very near the truth, but does not express the whole truth. The first clause is absolutely correct ; for in the fall the change certainly does occur " by a lengthening and blanching of the summer fur," the individual hairs changing color after the first fall of snow. This species, like the great majority of mammals, is clothed with two kinds of hair—a fine soft fur which densely covers all parts of the body, and longer, stiffer hairs, scattered through, and projecting beyond, the former. These long hairs are black in summer and white in winter. In the fall of the year, when the change begins, they become white at the tips first, the black gradually fading from above downwards until the entire hair is white. In spring the process is reversed, the exposed portion of the long hairs becoming black (though the extreme tip sometimes remains white until the change is far advanced), which color gradually extends downward, at the expense of the white, until the entire hair is black. Sometimes the displacement of the white is

---

* Arctic Zoology, Vol. I, 1792, p. 110.
† Fauna Boreali-Americana, Vol. I, 1829, p. 218.

temporarily interrupted, the two colors appearing in alternate zones. And during the latter part of March, when the body of the animal is still white, it is not uncommon to find hundreds of black hairs scattered over the back, many of them with the extreme apices, and a narrow zone between the middle and base, white. In fall or early winter the soft fur becomes tipped with white, the white portion increasing somewhat in length and diameter. In spring a curious phenomenon takes place. The white portion of the fur loses its vitality, becomes brittle, and breaks off on slight friction, so that the animal, in brushing through the undergrowth, soon rids himself of it. As a rule the long hairs change first.* Both in spring and fall the time of the change seems to be governed by the presence or absence of snow, and is not affected by the temperature. It occurs independently of the moult, and the new hairs assume the prevailing color of the animal, or the color toward which it is tending at the time of their appearance.

Mr. J. A. Allen, in his elaborate monograph of North American Hares, states that instances of melanism " are very rare among the American *Leporidæ*." He further says : " Among the specimens of var. *Americanus* is a single example of melanism, a mutilated skin (No. 6268) labeled as follows : ' *Lepus Americanus*, Rainy Lake, H. B. T.' It is apparently a winter skin, the pelage being very long and full. The color is dull plumbeous-black throughout, there being a slight grayish cast to the surface of the pelage, particularly on the head, breast, and back." † I have had the good fortune to examine two excellent melanistic specimens of this species, both in the collection of Mr. Romeyn B. Hough, of Lowville, New York. The animals were shot in winter (one in March),

---

* Specimens in my museum, killed in Lewis County, December 1st, March 21st, and April 3d, well illustrate the above described conditions of pelage. In spring, while the change is in progress, the attachment of the white tips is so feeble that hundreds may be blown off at a single puff. The change occurs more or less irregularly over the greater part of the body, but is usually symmetrical on the head, giving rise to a very pretty pattern.

† Monographs of North American Rodentia, 1877, p. 305.

in the town of Lyonsdale, in Lewis County. In color they are a uniform dark sooty-brown, lighter on the soles of the feet.

## LEPUS AMERICANUS VIRGINIANUS (Harlan) Allen.

### Southern Varying Hare.

This variety or subspecies of the Varying Hare occurs in the low border-lands of the Adirondacks, particularly in the valleys of Lakes George and Champlain, but is not met with at any great elevation, a few hundred feet constituting, in this latitude, its altitudinal limit.

Its food and habits are not known to differ from those of its nearest relative, the great northern hare, from which it may be distinguished, in winter, by the circumstance that the change to white is not complete, more or less light reddish-brown remaining about the head and ears, and on the upper surfaces of the fore-feet.

Rabbits are not commonly supposed to swim, but Mr. William Brewster has kindly written me of a case that fell under his personal observation. He says: " While at Lake Umbagog, Maine, in the summer of 1873, I saw something which may interest you. I was paddling up Cambridge River one warm July morning when, upon rounding a bend, my attention was attracted by a slight splashing sound ahead, and looking closely I discovered a Rabbit (*Lepus Americanus*) evidently about to attempt the passage of the stream which at that place was perhaps one hundred feet wide, and at least eight or ten deep. He entered the water deliberately, but without apparent fear or hesitation, and was soon beyond his depth and striking out boldly for the opposite shore. A more ridiculous (albeit successful) attempt at swimming can scarcely be imagined. He literally *hopped* through the water, using only his hind legs and kicking with such vigor that the whole forward part of his body was raised above the surface at each stroke. Between the strokes he would sink back until, sometimes, only the tip of the nose was exposed. I fancy that an immense bull-frog, weighted after the manner of 'Mark Twain's' 'Dan'l Webster,' would cut a somewhat similar figure.

"This method of progression was naturally fatiguing, and before the animal reached the opposite bank the strokes became feebler and the intervals between them longer until I began to fear that the tired creature would be drowned. At length, however, he struck bottom, and, loping across a stretch of bare mud, disappeared in the woods. *Such* an appearance as he presented upon emerging from the water !—the lankness of his form revealed by the clinging and bedraggled fur, the ears drooping and the whole expression one of dejection and shame.

"None of the guides or trappers of my acquaintance have ever seen a Rabbit swim, although I have been told of an instance where one was observed to take to the shallow water on the margin of a pond and run through it for several hundred yards before leaping again into the woods. The purpose of this manœuvre was apparent a moment later when a Sable appeared on the Rabbit's track and following it to the water's edge lost it there.

"On the occasion just described, however, no pursuer appeared, nor do I think that *this* Rabbit entered the water under compulsion, or for the purpose of obliterating the scent of his tracks. On the contrary, the action was undertaken so deliberately, that I believe the animal to have been impelled by some idle whim, merely—such as a desire to try fresh pasturage or, perhaps, to see what the world was like on the other side of the stream. However this may be, the case is doubtless exceptional, for *Lepus Americanus* ordinarily has as great an aversion to the water as any house cat."

Mr. Nelson Harris, a well-known Adirondack hunter, tells me that while still-hunting in Northern Michigan, a few winters ago, he saw a white Rabbit, that had stumbled into camp and was 'cornered," plunge fearlessly into a swiftly flowing river and swim to the other side.

## LEPUS SYLVATICUS Bachman.

### Gray Rabbit.

The Gray Rabbit is a more southern animal than either of the species heretofore considered, and only enters the Adirondack region along its southern border, in Fulton, Saratoga, and Warren Counties.

In addition to the food which constitutes the diet of the varying hare, the Gray Rabbit enters the garden and orchard, sometimes committing great havoc. Robert Kennicott says: " In hunting these quadrupeds, every winter, and working every summer, for ten years, in a very large nursery of fruit-trees, where they were numerous, I have never seen a tree from which bark had been gnawed by them, though thousands were severely 'pruned,' the rabbits, in deep snows, appearing to feed entirely upon the twigs and buds of the young apple trees. From the larger limbs they cut off the buds, of which they are fond ; and in the woods, in winter, they can be tracked to living forest trees, recently felled, to which they repair to feed upon the buds. They also feed in winter upon the buds and young shoots of briars, sumach, hazel, thorn, oak, hickory, basswood, poplar, and other shrubs and trees." *

Its favorite haunts, according to my observation,† are pine barrens, and thickets of laurel (*Kalmia latifolia*) and other undergrowth. Like the northern hare, it has regular runways which it uses at all times of the year ; but unlike that species it habitually takes refuge in burrows in the earth and in hollow trees.

---

* Quadrupeds of Illinois Injurious and Beneficial to the Farmer. By Robert Kennicott, 1858, pp. 80–81.

† I have found it in greater or less abundance in the Connecticut Valley in central Massachusetts ; in southern Connecticut ; in southern New York (Westchester County); in the vicinity of Elizabeth, New Jersey; about Aiken, South Carolina ; and in Florida.

Audubon and Bachman state: "In the Northern and Middle States, where the burrows of the Maryland marmot (*Arctomys monax*) and the holes resorted to by the common skunk, (*Mephitis chinga*,) are numerous, the Gray Rabbit, in order to effect its escape when pursued, betakes itself to them, and as they are generally deep, or placed among rocks or roots, it would require more labour to unearth it when it has taken possession of either of these animal's retreats than it is worth, and it is generally left unmolested. It is not always safe in these cases, however, for the skunk occasionally is 'at home' when the Rabbit runs into his hole, and often catches and devours the astonished fugitive before it can retrace its steps and reach the mouth of the burrow." *

Kennicott says: "The grey rabbit is very prolific, producing young three or four times a year, and usually from four to six at a birth.   In open ground the female scratches a shallow hollow, in which to bring forth her young.   In this she forms a nest of soft leaves and grasses, well-lined with fur from her own body; and when she is absent, the young are always completely covered and concealed in the nest, which they leave at an early age, and separate from the mother as soon as able to take care of themselves." †

---

* Quadrupeds of North America, Vol. I, 1846, p. 177.

† Quadrupeds of Illinois Injurious and Beneficial to the Farmer.   By Robert Kennicott, 1858, p. 81.

# INDEX.

# NATURAL SCIENCES IN AMERICA

*An Arno Press Collection*

Allen, J[oel] A[saph]. **The American Bisons,** Living and Extinct. 1876

Allen, Joel Asaph. **History of the North American Pinnipeds:** A Monograph of the Walruses, Sea-Lions, Sea-Bears and Seals of North America. 1880

**American Natural History Studies:** The Bairdian Period. 1974

**American Ornithological Bibliography.** 1974

Anker, Jean. **Bird Books and Bird Art.** 1938

Audubon, John James and John Bachman. **The Quadrupeds of North America.** Three vols. 1854

Baird, Spencer F[ullerton]. **Mammals of North America.** 1859

Baird, S[pencer] F[ullerton], T[homas] M. Brewer and R[obert] Ridgway. **A History of North American Birds:** Land Birds. Three vols., 1874

Baird, Spencer F[ullerton], John Cassin and George N. Lawrence. **The Birds of North America.** 1860. Two vols. in one.

Baird, S[pencer] F[ullerton], T[homas] M. Brewer, and R[obert] Ridgway. **The Water Birds of North America.** 1884. Two vols. in one.

Barton, Benjamin Smith. **Notes on the Animals of North America.** Edited, with an Introduction by Keir B. Sterling. 1792

Bendire, Charles [Emil]. **Life Histories of North American Birds** With Special Reference to Their Breeding Habits and Eggs. 1892/1895. Two vols. in one.

Bonaparte, Charles Lucian [Jules Laurent]. **American Ornithology:** Or The Natural History of Birds Inhabiting the United States, Not Given by Wilson. 1825/1828/1833. Four vols. in one.

Cameron, Jenks. **The Bureau of Biological Survey:** Its History, Activities, and Organization. 1929

Caton, John Dean. **The Antelope and Deer of America:** A Comprehensive Scientific Treatise Upon the Natural History, Including the Characteristics, Habits, Affinities, and Capacity for Domestication of the Antilocapra and Cervidae of North America. 1877

Contributions to American Systematics. 1974

Contributions to the Bibliographical Literature of American Mammals. 1974

Contributions to the History of American Natural History. 1974

Contributions to the History of American Ornithology. 1974

Cooper, J[ames] G[raham]. **Ornithology.** Volume I, Land Birds. 1870

Cope, E[dward] D[rinker]. **The Origin of the Fittest:** Essays on Evolution and **The Primary Factors of Organic Evolution.** 1887/1896. Two vols. in one.

Coues, Elliott. **Birds of the Colorado Valley.** 1878

Coues, Elliott. **Birds of the Northwest.** 1874

Coues, Elliott. **Key To North American Birds.** Two vols. 1903

**Early Nineteenth-Century Studies and Surveys.** 1974

Emmons, Ebenezer. **American Geology:** Containing a Statement of the Principles of the Science. 1855. Two vols. in one.

**Fauna Americana.** 1825-1826

Fisher, A[lbert] K[enrick]. **The Hawks and Owls of the United States in Their Relation to Agriculture.** 1893

Godman, John D. **American Natural History:** Part I — Mastology and **Rambles of a Naturalist.** 1826-28/1833. Three vols. in one.

Gregory, William King. **Evolution Emerging:** A Survey of Changing Patterns from Primeval Life to Man. Two vols. 1951

Hay, Oliver Perry. **Bibliography and Catalogue of the Fossil Vertebrata of North America.** 1902

Heilprin, Angelo. **The Geographical and Geological Distribution of Animals.** 1887

Hitchcock, Edward. **A Report on the Sandstone of the Connecticut Valley,** Especially Its Fossil Footmarks. 1858

Hubbs, Carl L., editor. **Zoogeography.** 1958

[Kessel, Edward L., editor]. **A Century of Progress in the Natural Sciences: 1853-1953.** 1955

Leidy, Joseph. **The Extinct Mammalian Fauna of Dakota and Nebraska,** Including an Account of Some Allied Forms from Other Localities, Together with a Synopsis of the Mammalian Remains of North America. 1869

Lyon, Marcus Ward, Jr. **Mammals of Indiana.** 1936

Matthew, W[illiam] D[iller]. **Climate and Evolution.** 1915

Mayr, Ernst, editor. **The Species Problem.** 1957

Mearns, Edgar Alexander. **Mammals of the Mexican Boundary of the United States.** Part I: Families Didelphiidae to Muridae. 1907

Merriam, Clinton Hart. **The Mammals of the Adirondack Region,** Northeastern New York. 1884

Nuttall, Thomas. **A Manual of the Ornithology of the United States and of Canada.** Two vols. 1832-1834

Nuttall Ornithological Club. **Bulletin of the Nuttall Ornithological Club:** A Quarterly Journal of Ornithology. 1876-1883. Eight vols. in three.

[Pennant, Thomas]. **Arctic Zoology.** 1784-1787. Two vols. in one.

Richardson, John. **Fauna Boreali-Americana;** Or the Zoology of the Northern Parts of British America, Containing Descriptions of the Objects of Natural History Collected on the Late Northern Land Expeditions Under Command of Captain Sir John Franklin, R. N. Part I: Quadrupeds. 1829

Richardson, John and William Swainson. **Fauna Boreali-Americana:** Or the Zoology of the Northern Parts of British America, Containing Descriptions of the Objects of Natural History Collected by the Late Northern Land Expeditions Under Command of Captain Sir John Franklin, R. N. Part II: The Birds. 1831

Ridgway, Robert. **Ornithology.** 1877

**Selected Works By Eighteenth-Century Naturalists and Travellers.** 1974

**Selected Works in Nineteenth-Century North American Paleontology.** 1974

**Selected Works of Clinton Hart Merriam.** 1974

**Selected Works of Joel Asaph Allen.** 1974

**Selections From the Literature of American Biogeography.** 1974

Seton, Ernest Thompson. **Life-Histories of Northern Animals: An Account of the Mammals of Manitoba.** Two vols. 1909

Sterling, Keir Brooks. **Last of the Naturalists:** The Career of C. Hart Merriam. 1974

Vieillot, L. P. **Histoire Naturelle Des Oiseaux de L'Amerique Septentrionale,** Contenant Un Grand Nombre D'Especes Decrites ou Figurees Pour La Premiere Fois. 1807. Two vols. in one.

Wilson, Scott B., assisted by A. H. Evans. **Aves Hawaiienses:** The Birds of the Sandwich Islands. 1890-99

Wood, Casey A., editor. **An Introduction to the Literature of Vertebrate Zoology.** 1931

Zimmer, John Todd. **Catalogue of the Edward E. Ayer Ornithological Library.** 1926